POLITICAL THEORY & SOCIAL CHANGE

THE EDITOR

DAVID SPITZ is Professor of Political Science at Ohio State University, where he has been a member of the faculty since 1947. He received his B.S.S. from the City College of New York and was awarded his A.M. and Ph.D. by Columbia University. He has held fellowships from the Fund for the Advancement of Education, the Fund for the Republic, and the Rockefeller Foundation, and has been Visiting Professor at, among others, Hunter College, Cornell University, Kenyon College, and the University of California at Berkeley. Professor Spitz's books include *Patterns of Anti-Democratic Thought, Democracy and the Challenge of Power,* and *The Liberal Idea of Freedom.*

POLITICAL THEORY

& SOCIAL CHANGE

EDITED WITH AN INTRODUCTION BY

DAVID SPITZ THE OHIO STATE UNIVERSITY

 ATHERTON PRESS · NEW YORK · 1967

CONTRIBUTORS

HANNAH ARENDT   *The University of Chicago*

PETER BACHRACH   *Bryn Mawr College*

CHRISTIAN BAY   *University of Alberta*

JULIAN H. FRANKLIN   *Columbia University*

PAUL KECSKEMETI   *Brandeis University*

DAVID KETTLER   *The Ohio State University*

GUENTER LEWY   *University of Massachusetts*

C. B. MACPHERSON   *University of Toronto*

JUDITH N. SHKLAR   *Harvard University*

MULFORD Q. SIBLEY   *University of Minnesota*

DAVID SPITZ   *The Ohio State University*

E. V. WALTER   *Boston University*

MICHAEL WALZER   *Harvard University*

INTRODUCTION

If a political system were like a timepiece, political actors would be little more than practitioners of a special craft and the political theorist an observer, analyst, and perhaps adviser in an intricate yet finite world. Within this autonomous and comprehensible whole, each of the myriad parts would mesh with another, so that a movement in one place would be registered in every other place; and the reactions to those movements would be so controlled as never to jar or distort the equilibrium. Since machines, like the men who conceive and operate them, are never perfect, a major task of the theorist would be to anticipate and show how to prevent, or to correct, their infrequent dislocations or breakdowns. Given both competence and sensitivity, this task, however difficult it may prove to be in a particular situation, is in principle readily manageable; for the political theorist will always be dealing with a mechanism that stands in a unilateral, one-to-one relationship to its object; the means are always suited to the end—in the one case, the telling of time; in the other, the maintenance of order.

But a political system is not at all like a timepiece. It has neither its delicacy nor its symmetry, for it deals with coarse and disharmonious elements. It is never totally seen; nor do men agree on all of its constituent parts. It is never autonomous but always beleaguered by a multiplicity of economic and social pressures and by the impact of other political systems. It is consequently rarely, if ever, in a state of equilibrium—in such a context what, indeed, does the word "equilibrium" mean?—and always in process of change. Hence it defies description, except in gross and ideal terms. Above all, the purposes a political system is designed to serve are open rather than settled; at the very least, they are many and controversial—ranging through such ambiguous ends as order, liberty, equality, welfare, justice, and the like. It follows that ends and means are forever out of kilter and forever in flux.

This is not to deny that societies can achieve a measure of political stability, or that political systems (however defined) are able to contain or to accommodate to social change. It is only to say that the business of the political theorist, like that of the political actor, is then vast and unending. He must endeavor to understand and to describe the political system—its structure and processes and the ways in which these interact and facilitate or limit social action. He must attend, and teach others to attend, to the maintenance and perpetuation of the arrangements that constitute that system— but only, of course, if the system is worth preserving. If the system is not worth preserving, he must suggest a more desirable and feasible alternative, and the course to follow in order to realize that alternative; he must deal also with ways of resisting injustices under the existing system. Throughout, since we have been talking of just and unjust acts and systems, he must make clear what he means by those terms—whether, for example, he means by justice what is socially accepted, or what is said by certain philosophers to be objectively true, or what is merely his subjective preference. And in all these matters he must recognize that the system he treats is not a static but a changing system, that he deals not simply with stability but also, and always, with the dynamics of political and social change.

In thus dwelling upon the importance of social change, I do not mean to imply that this is or ought to be the sole or primary focus of political theory; it is but one of its many problems or concerns, but an important one. Nor do I wish to suggest that social change is an end in itself and always warranted. It is not. It is always a means to the attainment of desired ends and is thus to be supported or opposed in terms of the merits of those ends. Even if social change is approved, we must consider the pace and the instruments of that change: too rapid or abrupt a change may produce severe social and personal dislocation; inappropriate means may entail disastrous social or personal costs, or even defeat the purpose for which those means were invoked. When to all this we add the obvious facts that there are systems within systems, limited or partial changes as well as general changes, and that a modification in one system or arrangement inevitably produces modifications in other systems or arrangements, we can appreciate even more the immense complexity of the problems with which the political theorist is confronted.

The essays brought together in this volume deal with some of these and related problems. They were initially read at a series of panels on political theory and social change at the annual meeting of the American Political Science Association in 1966. As chairman of that program and editor of this volume, I should perhaps add a word as to the selection of writers and topics.

An initial consideration was to avoid, and by implication to deny the relevance of, one of the more arid controversies now besetting the discipline of political science. This is the alleged cleavage between those who view the discipline as a science and seek only to describe political behavior or to construct political models, and those who see it as an historical or normative enterprise and limit themselves to the writing of intellectual history or biography, or to textual exegesis, or to something called normative theory. (Oddly enough, these things are more often said by each group about the other than they are about themselves.) But few if any empirical theories can avoid nonempirical assumptions and value judgments, and few if any normative theories are devoid of empirical statements and historical assessments. And just as it is much too late in the day to deny the importance and utility of so-called useless history, so it is beyond dispute that to comprehend the teaching of a political thinker one must read his text carefully and sympathetically. What is crucial in all these endeavors is not the approach they take but the enlightenment they yield. Consequently, it seemed best to include here only those political theorists who reject the simplistic confrontation that allegedly divides the two camps and address themselves instead to the serious pursuit of such enlightenment.

To select but a small panel from the many serious and distinguished scholars who occupy this vast middle ground clearly involved arbitrary choices. An effort was made to secure a "representative" group. Setting aside those who were kind enough to serve as discussants or as chairmen of the several panels, or who proved to be unavailable, the persons assembled here are somewhat diverse in age, method, and orientation, but united by the conviction that what lies at the heart of political theory is a concern for the eluci-dation and (if possible) resolution of crucial problems—problems that plague us today precisely because they are problems of more than immediate relevance. They are problems associated with the human condition; consequently, they are universal problems, or at the very least, the problems of an age.

Not all these problems are, of course, treated here; short of a systematic treatise, this is impossible. Moreover, when dealing with productive and independent scholars, it is generally best for a chair-man and editor to be more than a trifle self-effacing. One can but ask such contributors to reflect on the relationship between political systems, principles, or institutions and social change, or on certain contemporary yet persistent issues involved in, making for, or ob-structing social change. That the results will be diverse and even, at times, somewhat marginal, can be discomforting only to those tidy minds who think politics is a mathematical science.

It is a matter of deep personal regret that considerations of space preclude the inclusion of the several commentaries, some brilliantly incisive and penetrating, that were presented by the able discuss-ants. I hope they will accept this note of apology and my heartfelt thanks for their contributions to what was, to those of us who had the good fortune to attend the panels, a most stimulating experience.

DAVID SPITZ

CONTENTS

II ISSUES

I

PRINCIPLES

[1] TRUTH AND POLITICS

I

The subject of these reflections, the antithesis of truth and politics, is a commonplace. No one has ever doubted that truth and politics are on rather bad terms with each other, and no one, as far as I know, has ever counted truthfulness among the political virtues. Lies have always been regarded as necessary and justifiable tools not only of the politician's or the demagogue's but also of the statesman's trade. Why is that so? And what does it mean for the nature and the dignity of the political realm, on one side, and for the nature and the dignity of truth and truthfulness, on the other? Is it of the very essence of truth to be impotent and of the very essence of power to be deceitful? And what kind of reality does truth possess if it is powerless in the public realm, which more than any other sphere of human life guarantees reality of existence to natal and mortal man—that is, to beings who know they have appeared out of non-being and will, after a short while, again disappear into it? Finally, is not impotent truth just as despicable as power that gives no heed to truth? These are uncomfortable questions, but they arise necessarily out of our current convictions in this matter.

What lends this commonplace its high plausibility can still be summed up in the old Latin adage "*Fiat iustitia, et pereat mundus*" ("Let justice be done though the world may perish"). Apart from its probable author in the sixteenth century (Ferdinand I, successor to

Charles V), no one has used it except as a rhetorical question: Should justice be done if the world's survival is at stake? And the only great thinker who dared to go against the grain of the question was Immanuel Kant, who boldly explained that the "proverbial saying . . . means in simple language: 'Justice shall prevail, even though all the rascals in the world should perish as a result.'" Since men would not find it worthwhile to live in a world utterly deprived of justice, this "human right must be held sacred, regardless of how much sacrifice is required of the powers that be . . . regardless of what might be the physical consequences thereof."[1] But isn't this answer absurd? Doesn't the care for existence clearly precede everything else—every virtue and every principle? Is it not obvious that they become mere chimeras if the world, where alone they can be manifested, is in jeopardy? Wasn't the seventeenth century right when it almost unanimously declared that every commonwealth was duty bound to recognize, in Spinoza's words, "no higher law than the safety of [its] own realm?"[2] For surely every principle that transcends sheer existence can be put in the place of justice, and if we put truth in its place—*"Fiat veritas, et pereat mundus"*—the old saying sounds even more plausible. If we understand political action in terms of the means-end category, we may even come to the only seemingly paradoxical conclusion that lying can very well serve to establish or safeguard the conditions for the search after truth—as Hobbes, whose relentless logic never fails to carry arguments to those extremes where their absurdity becomes obvious, pointed out long ago.[3] And lies, since they are often used as substitutes for more violent means, are apt to be considered relatively harmless tools in the arsenal of political action.

To anyone reconsidering the old Latin saying, it will therefore come as something of a surprise that the sacrifice of truth for the survival of the world would be more futile than the sacrifice of any other principle or virtue. For while we may refuse even to ask ourselves whether life would still be worth living in a world deprived of such notions as justice and freedom, the same, curiously, is not possible with respect to the seemingly so much less political idea of truth. What is at stake is survival, the perseverance in existence (*in suo esse perseverare*), and no human world, destined to outlast the short life span of mortals within it, will ever be able to survive without men willing to do what Herodotus was the first to undertake consciously—namely, *legein ta eonta*, to say what is. No permanence, no perseverance in existence, can even be conceived of without men willing to testify to what is and appears to them because it is.

The story of the conflict between truth and politics is an old and complicated one, and nothing would be gained by simplification or moral denunciation. Throughout history, the truth-seekers and truthtellers have been aware of the risks of their business; as long as they did not interfere with the course of the world, they were covered with ridicule, but he who forced his fellow-citizens to take him seriously by trying to set them free from falsehood and illusion was in danger of his life: "If they could lay hands on [such a] man . . . they would kill him," Plato says in the last sentence of the cave allegory. The Platonic conflict between truthteller and citizens cannot be explained by the Latin adage, or any of the later theories that, implicitly or explicitly, justify lying, among other transgressions, if the survival of the world is at stake. No enemy is mentioned in Plato's story; the many live peacefully in their cave among themselves, mere spectators of images, involved in no action and hence threatened by nobody. The members of this community have no reason whatever to regard truth and truthtellers as their worst enemies, and Plato offers no explanation of their perverse love of deception and falsehood. If we could confront him with one of his later colleagues in political philosophy—namely, with Hobbes, who held that only "such truth, as opposeth no man's profit, nor pleasure, is to all men welcome" (an obvious statement, which, however, he thought important enough to end his *Leviathan* with)—he might agree about profit and pleasure but not with the assertion that there existed any kind of truth welcome to all men. Hobbes, but not Plato, consoled himself with the existence of indifferent truth, with "subjects" about which "men care not"—e.g., with mathematical truth, "the doctrine of lines and figures" that "crosses no man's ambition, profit or lust." For, Hobbes wrote, "I doubt not, but if it had been a thing contrary to any man's right of dominion, or to the interest of men that have dominion, that the three angles of a triangle should be equal to two angles of a square; that doctrine should have been, if not disputed, yet by the burning of all books of geometry, suppressed, as far as he whom it concerned was able."[4]

No doubt, there is a decisive difference between Hobbes' mathematical axiom and the true standard for human conduct that Plato's philosopher is supposed to bring back from his journey into the sky of ideas, although Plato, who believed that mathematical truth opened the eyes of the mind to all truths, was not aware of it. Hobbes' example strikes us as relatively harmless; we are inclined to assume that the human mind will always be able to reproduce such axiomatic statements as "the three angles of a triangle should be equal to two angles of a square," and we conclude that "the burning of all books of geometry" would not be radically effective. The danger would be considerably greater with respect to scientific statements; had history taken a different turn, the whole modern scientific development from Galileo to Einstein might not have come to pass. And certainly the most vulnerable truth of this kind would be those highly differentiated and always unique thought trains—of which Plato's doctrine of ideas is an eminent example—whereby men, since time immemorial, have tried to think rationally beyond the limits of human knowledge.

In the modern age, which believes that truth is neither given to nor disclosed to but produced by the human mind, Leibniz assigned mathematical, scientific, and philosophical truths to the common species of rational truth as distinguished from factual truth. I shall use this distinction for convenience sake without discussing its intrinsic legitimacy. Wanting to find out what injury political power is capable of inflicting upon truth, we look into these matters for political rather than philosophical reasons, and hence can afford to disregard the question of what truth is, and be content to take the word in the sense in which men commonly understand it. And if we now think of factual truths—of such modest verities as the role during the Russian Revolution of a man by the name of Trotsky, who appears in none of the Soviet Russian history books—we at once become aware of how much more vulnerable they are than all the kinds of rational truth taken together. Moreover, since facts and events—the invariable outcome of men living and acting together—constitute the very texture of the political realm, it is, of course, factual truth that we are most concerned with here. Dominion (to speak Hobbes' language) when it attacks rational truth oversteps, as it were, its domain, while it gives battle on its own ground when it falsifies or lies away facts. The chances of factual truth's surviving the onslaught of power are very slim indeed; it is always in danger of being maneuvered out of the world not only for a time but, potentially, forever. Facts and events are infinitely more fragile things than axioms, discoveries, theories—even the most wildly speculative ones—produced by the human mind; they occur in the field of the ever-changing affairs of men, in whose flux there is nothing more permanent than the admittedly relative permanence of the human mind's structure. Once they are lost, no rational effort will ever bring them back. Perhaps the chances that Euclidean mathematics or Einstein's theory of relativity—let alone Plato's philosophy—would have been reproduced in time if their authors had been prevented from handing them down to posterity are not very good either, yet they are infinitely better than the chances that a fact of importance, forgotten or, more likely, lied away, will one day be rediscovered.

I I

Although the politically most relevant truths are factual, the conflict between truth and politics was first discovered and articulated with respect to rational truth. The opposite of a rationally true statement is either error and ignorance, as in the sciences, or illusion and opinion, as in philosophy. Deliberate falsehood, the plain lie, plays its role only in the domain of factual statements, and it seems significant, and rather odd, that in the long debate about this antagonism of truth and politics, from Plato to Hobbes, no one, apparently, ever believed that organized lying, as we know it today, could be an adequate weapon against truth. In Plato, the truthteller is in danger of his life, and in Hobbes, where he has become an author, he is threatened with the burning of his books; mere mendacity is not an issue. It is the sophist and the ignoramus rather than the liar who occupy Plato's thought, and where he distinguishes between error and lie—that is, between "involuntary and voluntary *pseudos*"—he is, characteristically, much harsher on people "wallowing in swinish ignorance" than on liars.[5] Is this because organized lying, dominating the public realm, as distinguished from the private liar who tries his luck on his own hook, was still unknown? Or has this something to do with the striking fact that, except for Zoroastrianism, none of the major religions included lying as such, as distinguished from "bearing false witness," in their catalogues of grave sins? Only with the rise of Puritan morality, coinciding with the rise of organized science, whose progress had to be assured on the firm ground of the absolute veracity and reliability of every scientist, were lies considered serious offenses.

However that may be, historically the conflict between truth and politics arose out of two diametrically opposed ways of life—the life of the philosopher, as interpreted first by Parmenides and then by Plato, and the way of life of the citizen. To the citizens' ever-changing opinions about human affairs, which themselves were in a state of constant flux, the philosopher opposed the truth about those things which in their very nature were everlasting and from which, therefore, principles could be derived to stabilize human affairs. Hence the opposite to truth was mere opinion, which was equated with illusion, and it was this degrading of opinion that gave the conflict its political poignancy; for opinion, and not truth, belongs among the indispensable prerequisites of all power. "All governments rest on opinion," James Madison said, and not even the most autocratic ruler or tyrant could ever rise to power, let alone keep it, without the support of those who are like-minded. By the same token, every claim in the sphere of human affairs to an abso-lute truth, whose validity needs no support from the side of opinion, strikes at the very roots of all politics and all governments. This antagonism between truth and opinion was further elaborated by Plato (especially in the *Gorgias*) as the antagonism between com-municating in the form of "dialogue," which is the adequate speech for philosophical truth, and in the form of "rhetoric," by which the demagogue, as we would say today, persuades the multitude.

Traces of this original conflict can still be found in the earlier stages of the modern age, though hardly in the world we live in. In Hobbes, for instance, we still read of an opposition of two "con-trary faculties": "solid reasoning" and "powerful eloquence," the former being "grounded upon principles of truth, the other upon opinions . . . and the passions and interests of men, which are different and mutable."[6] More than a century later, in the Age of Enlightenment, these traces have almost but not quite disappeared, and where the ancient antagonism still survives, the emphasis has shifted. In terms of pre-modern philosophy, Lessing's magnificent *"Sage jeder, was ihm Wahrheit dünkt, und die Wahrheit selbst sei Gott empfohlen"* ("Let each man say what seems to him true, and let's leave truth itself safely in God's hands") would have plainly signified, Man is not capable of truth, all his truths, alas, being *doxai*, mere opinions, whereas for Lessing it meant, on the contrary, Let us thank God that we don't know *the* truth. Even where the note of jubilation—the insight that for men, living in company, the inexhaustible richness of human discourse is infinitely more significant and meaningful than any One Truth could ever be—is absent, the awareness of the frailty of human reason has prevailed since the eighteenth century without giving rise to complaint or lamentation. We can find it in Kant's grandiose *Critique of Pure Reason,* in which reason is led to recognize its own limitations, as we hear it in the words of Madison, who more than once stressed that "the reason of man, like man himself, is timid and cautious when left alone, and acquires firmness and confidence in proportion to the number with which it is associated."[7] Considerations of this kind, much more than notions about the individual's right to self-expression, played a decisive part in the finally more or less successful struggle to obtain freedom of thought for the spoken and the printed word. Thus Spinoza, who still believed in the infallibility of human reason and is often wrongly praised as a champion of free thought and speech, held that "every man is by indefeasible natural right the master of his own thoughts," that "every man's understanding is his own, and that brains are as diverse as palates," from which he concluded that "it is best to grant what cannot be abolished" and that laws prohibiting free thought can only result in "men thinking one thing and saying another," hence in "the corruption of good faith" and "the fostering of . . . perfidy." However, Spinoza nowhere demands freedom of speech, and the argument that human reason needs communication with others and therefore publicity for its own sake is conspicuous by its absence. He even counts man's need for communication, his inability to hide his thoughts and keep silent, among the "common failings" that the philosopher does not share.[8] Kant, on the contrary, stated that "the external power that deprives man of the freedom to communicate his thoughts publicly, *deprives him at the same time of his freedom to think*" (italics added), and that the only guarantee for "the correctness" of our thinking lies in that "we think, as it were, in community with others to whom we communicate our thoughts as they communicate theirs to us." Man's reason, being fallible, can function only if he can make "public use" of it, and this is equally true for those who, still in a state of "tutelage," are unable to use their mind "without the guidance of somebody else" and for the "scholar," who needs "the entire reading public" to examine and control his results.[9]

In this context, the question of numbers, mentioned by Madison, is of special importance. The shift from rational truth to opinion implies a shift from man in the singular to men in the plural, and this means a shift from a domain where, Madison says, nothing counts except the "solid reasoning" of one mind to a realm where "strength of opinion" is determined by the individual's reliance upon "the number which he supposes to have entertained the same opinions"—a number, incidentally, that is not necessarily limited to one's contemporaries. Madison still distinguishes this life in the plural, which is the life of the citizen, from the life of the philosopher, by whom such considerations "ought to be disregarded," but this distinction has no practical consequence, for "a nation of philosophers is as little to be expected as the philosophical race of kings wished for by Plato."[10] We may note in passing that the very notion of "a nation of philosophers" would have been a contradiction in terms for Plato, whose whole political philosophy, including its outspoken tyrannical traits, rests on the conviction that truth can be neither gained nor communicated among the many.

In the world we live in, the last traces of this ancient antagonism between the philosopher's truth and the opinions in the market place have disappeared. Neither the truth of revealed religion, which the political thinkers of the seventeenth century still treated as a major nuisance, nor the truth of the philosopher, disclosed to man in solitude, interferes any longer with the affairs of the world. In respect to the former, the separation of Church and State has given us peace, and as to the latter, it ceased long ago to claim dominion—unless one takes the modern ideologies seriously as philosophies, which is difficult indeed, since their adherents openly proclaim them to be political weapons and consider the whole question of truth and truthfulness irrelevant. Thinking in terms of the tradition, one may feel entitled to conclude from this state of affairs that the old conflict has finally been settled, and especially that its original cause, the clash of rational truth and opinion, has disappeared.

Strangely, however, this is not the case, for the clash of factual truth and politics, which we witness today on such a large scale, has—in some respects, at least—very similar traits. While probably no former time tolerated so many diverse opinions on religious or philosophical matters, factual truth, if it happens to oppose a given group's profit or pleasure, is greeted today with greater hostility than ever before. To be sure, state secrets have always existed;

every government must classify certain information, withhold it from public notice, and he who reveals authentic secrets has always been treated as a traitor. With this I am not concerned here. The facts I have in mind are publicly known, and yet the same public that knows them can successfully, and often spontaneously, taboo their public discussion and treat them as though they were what they are not—namely, secrets. That their assertion then should prove as dangerous as, for instance, preaching atheism or some other heresy proved in former times seems a curious phenomenon, and its significance is enhanced when we find it also in countries that are ruled tyrannically by an ideological government. (Even in Hitler's Germany and Stalin's Russia it was more dangerous to talk about concentration and extermination camps, whose existence was no secret, than to hold and to utter "heretical" views on anti-Semitism, racism, and Communism.) What seems even more disturbing is that to the extent to which unwelcome factual truths are tolerated in free countries they are often, consciously or unconsciously, transformed into opinions—as though the fact of Germany's support of Hitler or of France's collapse before the German armies in 1940 or of Vatican policies during the Second World War were not a matter of historical record but a matter of opinion. Since such factual truths concern issues of immediate political relevance, there is more at stake here than the perhaps inevitable tension between two ways of life within the framework of a common and commonly recognized reality. What is at stake here is this common and factual reality itself, and this is indeed a political problem of the first order. And since factual truth, though it is so much less open to argument than philosophical truth, and so obviously within the grasp of everybody, seems often to suffer a similar fate when it is exposed in the market place—namely, to be countered not by lies and deliberate falsehoods but by opinion—it may be worthwhile to reopen the old and apparently obsolete question of truth versus opinion.

For, seen from the viewpoint of the truthteller, the tendency to transform fact into opinion, to blur the dividing line between them, is no less perplexing than the truthteller's older predicament, so vividly expressed in the cave allegory, in which the philosopher, upon his return from his solitary journey to the sky of everlasting ideas, tries to communicate his truth to the multitude, with the result that it disappears in the diversity of views, which to him are illusions, and is brought down to the uncertain level of opinion, so that now, back in the cave, truth itself appears in the guise of the *dokei moi* ("it seems to me")—the very *doxai* he had hoped to leave behind once and for all. However, the reporter of factual truth is even worse off. He does not return from any journey into regions beyond the realm of human affairs, and he cannot console himself with the thought that he has become a stranger in this world. Similarly, we have no right to console ourselves with the notion that his truth, if truth it should be, is not of this world. If his simple factual statements are not accepted—truths seen and witnessed with the eyes of the body, and not the eyes of the mind—the suspicion arises that it may be in the nature of the political realm to deny or pervert truth of every kind, as though men were unable to come to terms with its unyielding, blatant, unpersuasive stubbornness. If this should be the case, things would look even more desperate than Plato assumed, for Plato's truth, found and actualized in solitude, transcends, by definition, the realm of the many, the world of human affairs. (One can understand that the philosopher, in his isolation, yields to the temptation to use his truth as a standard to be imposed upon human affairs; that is, to equate the transcendence inherent in philosophical truth with the altogether different kind of "transcendence" by which yardsticks and other standards of measurement are separated from the multitude of objects they are to measure, and one can equally well understand that the multitude will resist this standard, since it is actually derived from a sphere that is foreign to the realm of human affairs and whose connection with it can be justified only by a confusion.) Philosophical truth, when it enters the market place, changes its nature and becomes opinion, because a veritable *metabasis eis allo genos*, a shifting not merely from one kind of reasoning to another but from one way of human existence to another, has taken place.

Factual truth, on the contrary, is always related to other people: it concerns events and circumstances in which many are involved; it is established by witnesses and depends upon testimony; it exists only to the extent that it is spoken about, even if it occurs in the domain of privacy. It is political by nature. Facts and opinions, though they must be kept apart, are not antagonistic to each other; they belong to the same realm. Facts inform opinions, and opinions, inspired by different interests and passions, can differ widely and still be legitimate as long as they respect factual truth.

Freedom of opinion is a farce unless factual information is guaranteed and the facts themselves are not in dispute. In other words, factual truth informs political thought just as rational truth informs philosophical speculation.

But do facts, independent of opinion and interpretation, exist at all? Have not generations of historians and philosophers of history demonstrated the impossibility of ascertaining facts without interpretation, since they must first be picked out of a chaos of sheer happenings (and the principles of choice are surely not factual data) and then be fitted into a story that can be told only in a certain perspective, which has nothing to do with the original occurrence? No doubt these and a great many more perplexities inherent in the historical sciences are real, but they are no argument against the existence of factual matter, nor can they serve as a justification for blurring the dividing lines between fact, opinion, and interpretation, or as an excuse for the historian to manipulate facts as he pleases. Even if we admit that every generation has the right to write its own history, we admit no more than that it has the right to rearrange the facts in accordance with its own perspective; we don't admit the right to touch the factual matter itself. To illustrate this point, and as an excuse for not pursuing this issue any further: During the twenties, so a story goes, Clemenceau, shortly before his death, found himself engaged in a debate with a representative of the Weimar Republic on the question of guilt for the outbreak of the First World War. "What, in your opinion," Clemenceau was asked, "will future historians think of this troublesome and controversial issue?" He replied, "This I don't know. But I know for certain that they will not say Belgium invaded Germany." We are concerned here with brutally elementary data of this kind, whose indestructibility has been taken for granted even by the most extreme and most sophisticated believers in historicism.

It is true, considerably more than the whims of historians would be needed to eliminate from the record the fact that on the night of August 4, 1914, German troops crossed the frontier of Belgium; it would require no less than a power monopoly over the entire civilized world. But such a power monopoly is far from being inconceivable, and it is not difficult to imagine what the fate of factual truth would be if power interests, national or social, had the last say in these matters. Which brings us back to our suspicion that it may be in the nature of the political realm to be at war with truth in all its forms, and hence to the question of why a commitment even to factual truth is felt to be an anti-political attitude.

III

When I said that factual, as opposed to rational, truth is not antagonistic to opinion, I stated a half-truth. All truths—not only the various kinds of rational truth but also factual truth—are opposed to opinion in their *mode* of asserting validity. Truth carries within itself an element of coercion, and the frequently tyrannical tendencies so deplorably obvious among professional truthtellers may be caused less by a failing of character than by the strain of habitually living under a kind of compulsion. Statements such as "The three angles of a triangle are equal to two angles of a square," "The earth moves around the sun," "It is better to suffer wrong than to do wrong," "In August, 1914, Germany invaded Belgium" are very different in the way they are arrived at, but, once perceived as true and pronounced to be so, they have in common that they are beyond agreement, dispute, opinion, or consent. For those who accept them, they are not changed by the numbers or lack of numbers who entertain the same proposition; persuasion or dissuasion is useless, for the content of the statement is not of a persuasive nature but of a coercive one. (Thus Plato, in the *Timaeus*, draws a line between men capable of perceiving the truth and those who happen to hold right opinions. In the former, the organ for the perception of truth [*nous*] is awakened through instruction, which of course implies inequality and can be said to be a mild form of coercion, whereas the latter had merely been persuaded. The views of the former, says Plato, are unmovable, while the latter can always be persuaded to change their minds.[11]) What Le Mercier de la Rivière once remarked about mathematical truth applies to all kinds of truth: "*Euclide est un véritable despote; et les vérités géométriques qu'il nous a transmises, sont des lois véritablement despotiques.*" In much the same vein, Grotius, about a hundred years earlier, had insisted—when he wished to limit the power of the absolute prince—that "even God cannot cause two times two not to make four." He was invoking the compelling force of truth against political power; he was not interested in the implied limitation of divine omnipotence. These two remarks illustrate how truth looks in the purely political perspective, from the viewpoint of power, and the question is whether power could and should be checked not only by a constitution, a bill of rights, and by a multiplicity of powers, as in the system of checks and balances, in which, in Montesquieu's words, *"le pouvoir arrête le pouvoir"*—that is, by factors that arise out of and belong to the political realm proper—but by something that arises from without, has its source outside the political realm, and is as independent of the wishes and desires of the citizens as is the will of the worst tyrant.

Seen from the viewpoint of politics, truth has a despotic character. It is therefore hated by tyrants, who rightly fear the competition of a coercive force they cannot monopolize, and it enjoys a rather precarious status in the eyes of governments that rest on consent and abhor coercion. Facts are beyond agreement and consent, and all talk about them—all exchanges of opinion based on correct information—will contribute nothing to their establishment. Unwelcome opinion can be argued with, rejected, or compromised upon, but unwelcome facts possess an infuriating stubbornness that nothing can move except plain lies. The trouble is that factual truth, like all other truth, peremptorily claims to be acknowledged and precludes debate, and debate constitutes the very essence of political life. The modes of thought and communication that deal with truth, if seen from the political perspective, are necessarily domineering; they don't take into account other people's opinions, and taking these into account is the hallmark of all strictly political thinking.

Political thought is representative. I form an opinion by considering a given issue from different viewpoints, by making present to my mind the standpoints of those who are absent; that is, I represent them. This process of representation does not blindly adopt the actual views of those who stand somewhere else, and hence look upon the world from a different perspective; this is a question neither of empathy, as though I tried to be or to feel like somebody else, nor of counting noses and joining a majority but of being and thinking in my own identity where actually I am not. The more people's standpoints I have present in my mind while I am pondering a given issue, and the better I can imagine how I would feel and think if I were in their place, the stronger will be my capacity for representative thinking and the more valid my final conclusions, my opinion. (It is this capacity for an "enlarged mentality" that enables men to judge; as such, it was discovered by Kant, in the first part of his *Critique of Judgment*, though he did not recognize the political and moral implications of his discovery.) The very process of opinion formation is determined by those in whose places somebody thinks and uses his own mind, and the only condition for this exertion of the imagination is disinterestedness, the liberation from one's own private interests. Hence, even if I shun all company or am completely isolated while forming an opinion, I am not simply together only with myself in the solitude of philosophical thought; I remain in this world of universal interdependence, where I can make myself the representative of everybody else. Of course, I can refuse to do this and form an opinion that takes only my own interests, or the interests of the group to which I belong, into account; nothing, indeed, is more common, even among highly sophisticated people, than the blind obstinacy that becomes manifest in lack of imagination and failure to judge. But the very quality of an opinion, as of a judgment, depends upon the degree of its impartiality.

No opinion is self-evident. In matters of opinion, but not in matters of truth, our thinking is truly discursive, running, as it were, from place to place, from one part of the world to another, through all kinds of conflicting views, until it finally ascends from these particularities to some impartial generality. Compared to this process, in which a particular issue is forced into the open that it may show itself from all sides, in every possible perspective, until it is flooded and made transparent by the full light of human comprehension, a statement of truth possesses a peculiar opaqueness. Rational truth enlightens human understanding, and factual truth must inform opinions, but these truths, though they are never obscure, are not transparent, either, and it is in their very nature to withstand further elucidation, as it is in the nature of light to withstand enlightenment. Nowhere, moreover, is this opacity more patent and more irritating than where we are confronted with facts and factual truth, for facts have no conclusive reason whatever for being what they are; they could always have been otherwise, and this annoying contingency is literally unlimited. It is because of the haphazardness of facts that pre-modern philosophy refused to take seriously the realm of human affairs, which is permeated by factuality, or to believe that any meaningful truth could ever be discovered in the "melancholy haphazardness" of a sequence of events (as Kant called it) which constitutes the course of this world. Nor has any modern philosophy of history been able to make its peace with the intractable, unreasonable stubbornness of sheer factuality; modern philosophers have conjured up all kinds of necessity, from the dialectical necessity of a world spirit or of material conditions to the necessities of an allegedly unchangeable and known human nature, in order to cleanse the last vestiges of that apparently arbitrary "it might have been otherwise" (which is the price of freedom) from the only realm where men are truly free. It is true that in retrospect—that is, in historical perspective— every sequence of events looks as though it could not have happened otherwise, but this is an optical, or, rather, an existential, illusion: nothing could ever happen if reality did not kill, by definition, all the other potentialities originally inherent in any given situation.

In other words, factual truth is no more self-evident than opinion, and this may be among the reasons that opinion-holders find it relatively easy to discredit factual truth as just another opinion. Factual evidence, moreover, is established through testimony by eyewitnesses—notoriously unreliable—and by records, documents, and monuments, all of which can be suspected as forgeries. In the event of a dispute, only other witnesses but no third and higher instance can be invoked, and settlement is usually arrived at by way of a majority; that is, in the same way as the settlement of opinion disputes—a wholly unsatisfactory procedure, since there is nothing to prevent a majority of witnesses from being false witnesses. On the contrary, under certain circumstances the feeling of belonging to a majority may even encourage false testimony. In other words, to the extent that factual truth is exposed to the hostility of opinion-holders, it is at least as vulnerable as rational philosophical truth.

I observed before that in some respects the teller of factual truth is worse off than Plato's philosopher—that his truth has no transcendent origin and possesses not even the relatively transcendent qualities of such political principles as freedom, justice, honor, and courage, all of which may inspire, and then become manifest in, human action. We shall now see that this disadvantage has more serious consequences than we had thought; namely, consequences that concern not only the person of the truthteller but—more important—the chances for his truth to survive. Inspiration of and manifestation in human action may not be able to compete with the compelling evidence of truth, but they can compete, as we shall see, with the persuasiveness inherent in opinion. I took the Socratic proposition "It is better to suffer wrong than to do wrong" as an example of a philosophical statement that concerns human conduct, and hence has political implications. My reason was partly that this sentence has become the beginning of Western ethical thought, and partly that, as far as I know, it has remained the only ethical proposition that can be derived directly from the specifically philosophical experience. (Kant's categorical imperative, the only competitor in the field, could be stripped of its Judaeo-Christian ingredients, which account for its formulation as an imperative instead of a simple proposition. Its underlying principle is the axiom of non-contradiction—the thief contradicts himself because he wants to keep the stolen goods as his property—and this axiom owes its validity to the conditions of thought that Socrates was the first to discover.) The Platonic dialogues tell us time and again how paradoxical the Socratic statement (a proposition, and not an imperative) sounded, how easily it stood refuted in the market place where opinion stands against opinion, and how incapable Socrates was of proving and demonstrating it to the satisfaction not of his adversaries alone but also of his friends and disciples. (The most dramatic of these passages can be found in the beginning of the *Republic*.[12] Socrates, having tried in vain to convince his adversary Thrasymachus that justice is better than injustice, is told by his disciples, Glaucon and Adeimantus, that his proof was far from convincing. Socrates admires their speeches: "There must indeed be some divine quality in your nature, if you can plead the cause of injustice so eloquently and still not be convinced yourselves that it is better than justice." In other words, they were convinced before the argument started, and all that was said to uphold the truth of the proposition not only failed to persuade the non-convinced but had not even the force to confirm their convictions.) Everything that can be said in its defense we find in the various Platonic dialogues. The chief argument states that for man, *being one,* it is better to be at odds with the whole world than to be at odds with and contradicted by himself[13]—an argument that is compelling indeed for the philosopher, whose thinking is characterized by Plato as a silent dialogue with himself, and whose existence therefore depends upon a constantly articulated intercourse with himself, a splitting-into-two of the one he nevertheless *is,* for a basic contradiction between the two partners who carry on the thinking dialogue would destroy the very conditions of philosophizing.[14] In other words, since man contains within himself a partner from whom he can never win release, he will be better off not to live in company with a murderer or a liar. Or, since thought is the silent dialogue carried on between me and myself, I must be careful to keep the integrity of this partner intact, for otherwise I shall surely lose the capacity for thought altogether.

To the philosopher—or, rather, to man insofar as he is a thinking being—this ethical proposition about doing and suffering wrong is no less compelling than mathematical truth. But to man insofar as he is a citizen, an acting being concerned with the world and the public welfare rather than with his own well-being—including, for instance, his "immortal soul" whose "health" should have precedence over the needs of a perishable body—the Socratic statement is not true at all. The disastrous consequences for any community that began in all earnest to follow ethical precepts derived from man in the singular—be they Socratic or Platonic or Christian—have been frequently pointed out. Long before Machiavelli recommended protecting the political realm against the undiluted principles of the Christian faith (those who refuse to resist evil permit the wicked "to do as much evil as they please"), Aristotle warned against giving philosophers any say in political matters. (Men who for professional reasons must be so unconcerned with "what is good for themselves" cannot very well be trusted with what is good for others, and least of all with the "common good," the down-to-earth interests of the community.)[15]

Since philosophical truth concerns man in his singularity, it is unpolitical by nature. If the philosopher nevertheless wishes his truth to prevail over the opinions of the multitude, he will suffer defeat, and he is likely to conclude from this defeat that truth is impotent—a truism that is just as meaningful as if the mathematician, unable to square the circle, should deplore the fact that a circle is not a square. He may then be tempted, like Plato, to win the ear of some philosophically inclined tyrant, and in the fortunately highly unlikely case of success he might erect one of those tyrannies of "truth" which we know chiefly from the various political utopias, and which, of course, politically speaking, are as tyrannical as other forms of despotism. In the slightly less unlikely event that his truth should prevail without the help of violence, simply because men happen to concur in it, he would have won a Pyrrhic victory. For truth would then owe its prevalence not to its own compelling quality but to the agreement of the many, who might change their minds tomorrow and agree on something else; what had been philosophical truth would have become mere opinion.

Since, however, philosophical truth carries within itself an element of coercion, it may tempt the statesman under certain conditions, no less than the power of opinion may tempt the philosopher. Thus, in the Declaration of Independence, Jefferson declared certain "truths to be self-evident," because he wished to put the basic consent among the men of the Revolution beyond dispute and argument; like mathematical axioms, they should express "beliefs of men" that "depend not on their own will, but follow involuntarily the evidence proposed to their minds."[16] Yet by saying *We hold* these truths to be self-evident" he conceded, albeit without becoming aware of it, that the statement "All men are created equal" is not self-evident but stands in need of agreement and consent— that equality, if it is to be politically relevant, is a matter of opinion, and not "the truth." There exist, on the other hand, philosophical or religious statements that correspond to this opinion— such as that all men are equal before God, or before death, or insofar as they all belong to the same species of *animal rationale*— but none of them was ever of any political or practical consequence, because the equalizer, whether God, or death, or nature, transcended and remained outside the realm in which human intercourse takes place. Such "truths" are not between men but above them, and nothing of the sort lies behind the modern or the ancient —especially the Greek—consent to equality. That all men are created equal is not self-evident nor can it be proved. We hold this opinion because freedom is possible only among equals, and we believe that the joys and gratifications of free company are to be preferred to the doubtful pleasures of holding dominion. Such preferences are politically of the greatest importance, and there are few things by which men are so profoundly distinguished from each other as by these. Their human quality, one is tempted to say, and certainly the quality of every kind of intercourse with them, depends upon such choices. Still, these are matters of opinion and not of truth— as Jefferson, much against his will, admitted. Their validity depends upon free agreement and consent, they are arrived at by discursive, representative thinking, and they are communicated by means of persuasion and dissuasion.

The Socratic proposition "It is better to suffer wrong than to do wrong" is not an opinion but claims to be truth, and though one may doubt whether it ever had a direct political consequence, its impact upon practical conduct as an ethical precept is undeniable; only religious commandments, which are absolutely binding for the community of believers, can claim greater recognition. Does this fact not stand in clear contradiction to the generally accepted impotence of philosophical truth? And since we know from the Platonic dialogues how unpersuasive Socrates' statement remained for friend and foe alike whenever he tried to prove it, we must ask ourselves how it could ever have obtained its high degree of validation. Obviously, this has been due to a rather unusual kind of persuasion; Socrates decided to stake his life on this truth—to set an example, not when he appeared before the Athenian tribunal but when he refused to escape the death sentence. And this teaching by example is, indeed, the only form of "persuasion" that philosophical truth is capable of without perversion or distortion;[17] by the same token, philosophical truth can become "practical" and inspire action without violating the rules of the political realm only when it manages to become manifest in the guise of an example. This is the only chance for an ethical principle to be verified. Thus, to verify, for instance, the notion of courage we may recall the example of Achilles, and to verify the notion of goodness we are inclined to think of Jesus of Nazareth or of St. Francis; these examples teach or persuade by inspiration, so that whenever we try to perform a deed of courage or of goodness it is as though we imitated someone else—the *imitatio Christi,* or whatever the case may be. It has often been remarked that, as Jefferson said, "a lively and lasting sense of filial duty is more effectually impressed on the mind of a son or daughter by reading 'King Lear' than by all the dry volumes of ethics and divinity that ever were written,"[18] and that, as Kant said, "general precepts learned at the feet either of priests or philosophers, or even drawn from one's own resources, are never so efficacious as an example of virtue or holiness."[19] The reason, as Kant explains, is that we always need "intuitions . . . to verify the reality of our concepts." "If they are pure concepts of the understanding," such as the concept of the triangle, "the intuitions go by the name of schemata," such as the ideal triangle, perceived only by the eyes of the mind and yet indispensable to the recognition of all real triangles; if, however, the concepts are practical, relating to conduct, "the intuitions are called *examples*."[20] And, unlike the schemata, which our mind produces out of its own accord by means of the imagination, these examples derive from history and poetry, through which, as Jefferson pointed out, an altogether different "field of imagination is laid open to our use."

This transformation of a theoretical or speculative statement into exemplary truth—a transformation of which only moral philosophy is capable—is a borderline experience for the philosopher: by setting an example and "persuading" the multitude in the only way open to him, he has begun to act. Today, when hardly any philosophical statement, no matter how daring, will be taken seriously enough to endanger the philosopher's life, even this rare chance of having a philosophical truth politically validated has disappeared. In our context, however, it is important to notice that such a possibility does exist for the teller of rational truth, for it does not exist under any circumstances for the teller of factual truth, who in this respect, as in other respects, is worse off. Not only do factual statements contain no principles upon which men might act and which thus could become manifest in the world; their very content defies this kind of verification. A teller of factual truth, in the unlikely event that he wished to stake his life on a particular fact, would achieve a kind of miscarriage. What would become manifest in his act would be his courage or, perhaps, his stubbornness but neither the truth of what he had to say nor even his own truthfulness. For why shouldn't a liar stick to his lies with great courage, especially in politics, where he might be motivated by patriotism or some other kind of legitimate group partiality?

I V

The hallmark of factual truth is that its opposite is neither error nor illusion nor opinion, no one of which reflects upon personal truthfulness, but the deliberate falsehood, or lie. Error, of course, is possible, and even common, with respect to factual truth, in which case this kind of truth is in no way different from scientific or rational truth. But the point is that with respect to facts there exists another alternative, and this alternative, the deliberate falsehood, does not belong to the same species as propositions that, whether right or mistaken, intend no more than to say what is, or how something that is appears to me. A factual statement—Germany invaded Belgium in August, 1914—acquires political implications only by being put in an interpretative context. But the opposite proposition, which Clemenceau, still unacquainted with the art of rewriting history, thought absurd, needs no context to be of political significance. It is clearly an attempt to change the record, and, as such, it is a form of *action*. The same is true when the liar, lacking the power to make his falsehood stick, does not insist on the gospel truth of his statement but pretends that this is his "opinion," to which he claims his constitutional right. This is frequently done by subversive groups, and in a politically immature public the resulting confusion can be considerable. The blurring of the dividing line between factual truth and opinion belongs among the many forms that lying can assume, all of which are forms of action.

While the liar is a man of action, the truthteller, whether he tells rational or factual truth, most emphatically is not. If the teller of factual truth wants to play a political role, and therefore to be persuasive, he will, more often than not, go to considerable lengths to explain why his particular truth serves the best interests of some group. And, just as the philosopher wins a Pyrrhic victory when his truth becomes a dominant opinion among opinion-holders, the teller of factual truth, when he enters the political realm and identifies himself with some partial interest and power formation, compromises on the only quality that could have made his truth appear plausible; namely, his personal truthfulness, guaranteed by impartiality, integrity, independence. There is hardly a political figure more likely to arouse justified suspicion than the professional truthteller who has discovered some happy coincidence between truth and interest. The liar, on the contrary, needs no such doubtful accommodation to appear on the political scene; he has the great advantage that he always is, so to speak, already in the midst of it. He is an actor by nature; he says what is not so because he wants things to be different from what they are—that is, he wants to change the world. He takes advantage of the undeniable affinity of our capacity for action, for changing reality, with this mysterious faculty of ours that enables us to *say* "The sun is shining," when it is raining cats and dogs. If we were as thoroughly conditioned in our behavior as some philosophies have wished us to be, we would never be able to accomplish this little miracle. In other words, our ability to lie—but not necessarily our ability to tell the truth—belongs among the few obvious, demonstrable data that confirm human freedom. That we can change the circumstances under which we live at all is because we are relatively free from them, and it is this freedom that is abused and perverted through mendacity. If it is the almost irresistible temptation of the professional historian to fall into the trap of necessity and implicitly deny freedom of action, it is the almost equally irresistible temptation of the professional politician to overestimate the possibilities of this freedom and implicitly condone the lying denial, or distortion of facts.

To be sure, as far as action is concerned, organized lying is a marginal phenomenon, but the trouble is that its opposite, the mere telling of facts, leads to no action whatever; it even tends, under normal circumstances, toward the acceptance of things as they are. (This, of course, is not to deny that the disclosure of facts may be legitimately used by political organizations or that, under certain circumstances, factual matters brought to public attention will considerably encourage and strengthen the claims of ethnic and social groups.) Truthfulness has never been counted among the political virtues, because it has little indeed to contribute to that change of the world and of circumstances which is among the mosts legitimate political activities. Only where a community has embarked upon organized lying on principle, and not only with respect to particulars, can truthfulness as such, unsupported by the distorting forces of power and interest, become a political factor of the first order. Where everybody lies about everything of importance, the truthteller, whether he knows it or not, has begun to act; he, too, has engaged himself in political business, for, in the unlikely event that he survives, he has made a start toward changing the world.

In this situation, however, he will again soon find himself at an annoying disadvantage. I mentioned earlier the contingent character of facts, which could always have been otherwise, and which therefore possess by themselves no trace of self-evidence or plausibility for the human mind. Since the liar is free to fashion his "facts" to fit the profit and pleasure, or even the mere expectations, of his audience, the chances are that he will be more persuasive than the truthteller. Indeed, he will usually have plausibility on his side; his exposition will sound more logical, as it were, since

the element of unexpectedness—one of the outstanding characteristics of all events—has mercifully disappeared. It is not only rational truth that, in the Hegelian phrase, stands common sense on
its head; reality quite frequently offends the soundness of common-
sense reasoning no less than it offends profit and pleasure.

We must now turn our attention to the relatively recent phenomenon of mass manipulation of fact and opinion as it has become
evident in the rewriting of history, in image-making, and in actual
government policy. The traditional political lie, so prominent in the
history of diplomacy and statecraft, used to concern either true
secrets—data that had never been made public—or intentions, which
anyhow do not possess the same degree of reliability as accomplished facts; like everything that goes on merely inside ourselves,
intentions are only potentialities, and what was intended to be a
lie can always turn out to be true in the end. In contrast, the modern political lies deal efficiently with things that are not secrets
at all but are known to practically everybody. This is obvious in
the case of rewriting contemporary history under the eyes of those
who witnessed it, but it is equally true in image-making of all sorts,
in which, again, every known and established fact can be denied
or neglected if it is likely to hurt the image; for an image, unlike
an old-fashioned portrait, is supposed not to flatter reality but to
offer a full-fledged substitute for it. And this substitute, because
of modern techniques and the mass media, is, of course, much
more in the public eye than the original ever was. We are finally
confronted with highly respected statesmen who, like de Gaulle
and Adenauer, have been able to build their basic policies on such
evident non-facts as that France belongs among the victors of the
last war and hence is one of the great powers, and "that the bar-
barism of National Socialism had affected only a relatively small
percentage of the country."[21] All these lies, whether their authors
know it or not, harbor an element of violence; organized lying
always tends to destroy whatever it has decided to negate, although
only totalitarian governments have consciously adopted lying as the
first step to murder. When Trotsky learned that he had never
played a role in the Russian Revolution, he must have known that
his death warrant had been signed. Clearly, it is easier to eliminate
a public figure from the record of history if at the same time he
can be eliminated from the world of the living. In other words, the
difference between the traditional lie and the modern lie will more

often than not amount to the difference between hiding and destroying.

Moreover, the traditional lie concerned only particulars and was never meant to deceive literally everybody; it was directed at the enemy and was meant to deceive only him. These two limitations restricted the injury inflicted upon truth to such an extent that to us, in retrospect, it may appear almost harmless. Since facts always occur in a context, a particular lie—that is, a falsehood that makes no attempt to change the whole context—tears, as it were, a hole in the fabric of factuality. As every historian knows, one can spot a lie by noticing incongruities, holes, or the junctures of patched-up places. As long as the texture as a whole is kept intact, the lie will eventually show up as if of its own accord. The second limitation concerns those who are engaged in the business of deception. They used to belong to the restricted circle of statesmen and diplomats, who among themselves still knew and could preserve the truth. They were not likely to fall victims to their own falsehoods; they could deceive others without deceiving themselves. Both of these mitigating circumstances of the old art of lying are noticeably absent from the manipulation of facts that confronts us today.

What, then, is the significance of these limitations, and why are we justified in calling them mitigating circumstances? Why has self-deception become an indispensable tool in the trade of image-making, and why should it be worse, for the world as well as for the liar himself, if he is deceived by his own lies than if he merely deceives others? What better moral excuse could a liar offer than that his aversion to lying was so great that he had to convince himself before he could lie to others, that, like Antonio in *The Tempest*, he had to make "a sinner of his memory, To credit his own lie"? And, finally, and perhaps most disturbingly, if the modern political lies are so big that they require a complete rearrangement of the whole factual texture—the making of another reality, as it were, into which they will fit without seam, crack, or fissure, exactly as the facts fitted into their own original context—what prevents these new stories, images, and non-facts from becoming an adequate substitute for reality and factuality?

A medieval anecdote illustrates how difficult it can be to lie to others without lying to oneself. It is a story about what happened one night in a town on whose watchtower a sentry was on duty day and night to warn the people of the approach of the enemy.

The sentry was a man given to practical jokes, and that night he sounded the alarm just in order to give the townsfolk a little scare. His success was overwhelming: everybody rushed to the walls—including, at the last, the sentry himself. The tale suggests to what extent our apprehension of reality is dependent upon our sharing the world with our fellow-men, and what strength of character is required to stick to anything, truth or lie, that is unshared. In other words, the more successful a liar is, the more likely it is that he will fall prey to his own fabrications. Furthermore, the self-deceived joker who proves to be in the same boat as his victims will appear vastly superior in trustworthiness to the cold-blooded liar who permits himself to enjoy his prank from without. Only self-deception is likely to create a semblance of truthfulness, and in a debate about facts the only persuasive factor that sometimes has a chance to prevail against pleasure, fear, and profit is personal appearance.

Current moral prejudice tends to be rather harsh in respect to cold-blooded lying, whereas the often highly developed art of self-deception is usually regarded with great tolerance and permissiveness. Among the few examples in literature that can be quoted against this current evaluation is the famous scene in the monastery at the beginning of *The Brothers Karamazov*. The father, an inveterate liar, asks the Staretz, "And what must I do to gain salvation?" and the Staretz replies, "Above all, never lie to yourself!" Dostoevski adds no explanation or elaboration. Arguments in support of a statement: It is better to lie to others than to deceive yourself, would have to point out that the cold-blooded liar remains aware of the distinction between truth and falsehood, so the truth he is hiding from others has not yet been maneuvered out of the world altogether; it has found its last refuge in him. The injury done to reality is neither complete nor final, and, by the same token, the injury done to the liar himself is not complete or final, either. He lied, but he is not yet a liar. Both he and the world he deceived are not beyond "salvation"—to put it in the language of the Staretz.

Such completeness and potential finality, which were unknown to former times, are the dangers that arise out of the modern manipulation of facts. Even in the free world, where the government has not monopolized the power to decide and tell what factually is or is not, gigantic interest organizations have generalized a kind of *raison d' état* frame of mind such as was formerly restricted to the handling of foreign affairs and, in its worst excesses, to situations of clear and present danger. And national propaganda on the government level has learned more than a few tricks from business practices and Madison Avenue methods. Images made for domestic consumption, as distinguished from lies directed at a foreign adversary, can become a reality for everybody and first of all for the image-makers themselves, who while still in the act of preparing their "products" are overwhelmed by the mere thought of their victims' potential numbers. No doubt, the originators of the lying image who "inspire" the hidden persuaders still know that they want to deceive an enemy on the social or the national level, but the result is that a whole group of people, and even whole nations, may take their bearings from a web of deceptions to which their leaders wished to subject their opponents.

What then happens follows almost automatically. The main effort of both the deceived group and the deceivers themselves is likely to be directed toward keeping the propaganda image intact, and this image is threatened less by the enemy and by real hostile interests than by those inside the group itself who have managed to escape its spell and insist on talking about facts or events that do not fit the image. Contemporary history is full of instances in which tellers of factual truth were felt to be more dangerous, and even more hostile, than the real opponents. These arguments against self-deception must not be confused with the protests of "idealists," whatever their merit, against lying as bad in principle and against the age-old art of deceiving the enemy. Politically, the point is that the modern art of self-deception is likely to transform an outside matter into an inside issue, so that an international or intergroup conflict boomerangs onto the scene of domestic politics. The self-deceptions practiced on both sides in the period of the Cold War are too many to enumerate, but obviously they are a case in point. Conservative critics of mass democracy have frequently outlined the dangers that this form of government brings to international affairs—without, however, mentioning the dangers peculiar to monarchies or oligarchies. The strength of their arguments lies in the undeniable fact that under fully democratic conditions deception without self-deception is well-nigh impossible.

Under our present system of world-wide communication, covering a large number of independent nations, no existing power is anywhere near great enough to make its "image" foolproof. Therefore,

images have a relatively short life expectancy; they are likely to
explode not only when the chips are down and reality makes its
reappearance in public but even before this, for fragments of facts
constantly disturb and throw out of gear the propaganda war between conflicting images. However, this is not the only way, or
even the most significant way, in which reality takes its revenge
on those who dare defy it. The life expectancy of images could
hardly be significantly increased even under a world government
or some other modern version of the Pax Romana. This is best
illustrated by the relatively closed systems of totalitarian governments and one-party dictatorships, which are, of course, by far the
most effective agencies in shielding ideologies and images from the
impact of reality and truth. (And such correction of the record is
never smooth sailing. We read in a memorandum of 1935 found in
the Smolensk Archive—published by Merle Fainsod in *Smolensk
under Soviet Rule*—about the countless difficulties besetting this
kind of enterprise. What, for instance, "should be done with
speeches by Zinoviev, Kamenev, Rykov, Bukharin, et al., at Party
Congresses, plenums of the Central Committee, in the Comintern,
the Congress of Soviets, etc.? What of anthologies on Marxism . . .
written or edited jointly by Lenin, Zinoviev, . . . and others? What
of Lenin's writings edited by Kamenev? . . . What should be done
in cases where Trotsky . . . had written an article in an issue of
the *Communist International?* Should the whole number be confis-
cated?" Puzzling questions indeed, to which the Archive contains
no replies.) Their trouble is that they must constantly change the
falsehoods they offer as a substitute for the real story; changing
circumstances require the substitution of one history book for another, the replacement of pages in the encyclopedias and reference
books, the disappearance of certain names in favor of others, unknown or little known before. And though this continuing instability gives no indication of what the truth might be, it is itself an
indication, and an all-important one, of the lying character of all
public utterances concerning the factual world. It has frequently
been noticed that the surest long-term result of brainwashing is a
peculiar kind of cynicism—an absolute refusal to believe in the
truth of anything, no matter how well this truth may be established.
In other words, the result of a consistent and total substitution of
lies for factual truth is not that the lies will now be accepted as
truth, and the truth be defamed as lies, but that the sense by

which we take our bearings in the real world—and the category of
truth vs. falsehood is among the mental means to this end—is being
destroyed.

And for this trouble there is no remedy. It is but the other side
of the disturbing contingency of all factual reality. Since everything
that has actually happened in the realm of human affairs could just
as well have been otherwise, the possibilities for lying are boundless, and this boundlessness makes for self-defeat. Only the occasional liar will find it possible to stick to a particular falsehood
with unwavering consistency; those who adjust images and stories
to ever-changing circumstances will find themselves floating on the
wide-open horizon of potentiality, drifting from one possibility to
the next, unable to hold on to any one of their own fabrications.
Far from achieving an adequate substitute for reality and factuality, they have transformed facts and events back into the potentiality out of which they originally appeared. And the surest sign
of the factuality of facts and events is precisely this stubborn there-
ness, whose inherent contingency ultimately defies all attempts at
conclusive explanation. The images, on the contrary, can always be
explained and made plausible—this gives them their momentary
advantage over factual truth—but they can never compete in stability with that which simply is because it happens to be thus and
not otherwise. This is the reason that consistent lying, metaphorically speaking, pulls the ground from under our feet and provides
no other ground on which to stand.[22] The experience of a trembling,
wobbling motion of everything we rely on for our sense of direction and reality is among the most common and most vivid experiences of men under totalitarian rule.

Hence, the undeniable affinity of lying with action, with changing
the world—in short, with politics—is limited by the very nature of
the things that are open to man's faculty for action. The convinced
image-maker is in error when he believes that he can anticipate
changes by lying about factual matters that everybody wishes to
eliminate anyhow. The erection of Potemkin's villages, so dear to
the politicians and propagandists of underdeveloped countries,
never leads to the establishment of the real thing but only to a
proliferation and perfection of make-believe. Not the past—and all
factual truth, of course, concerns the past—or the present, insofar
as it is the outcome of the past, but the future is open to action.

If the past and present are treated as parts of the future—that is, changed back into their former state of potentiality—the political realm is deprived not only of its main stabilizing force but of the starting point from which to change, to begin something new. What then begins is the constant shifting and shuffling in utter sterility which are characteristic of many new nations that had the bad luck to be born in an age of propaganda.

That facts are not secure in the hands of power is obvious, but the point here is that power, by its very nature, can never produce a substitute for the security, or stability, of factual reality, which, because it is past, has grown into a dimension beyond our reach. Facts assert themselves by being stubborn, and their fragility is oddly combined with great resiliency—the same irreversibility that is the hallmark of all human action. In their stubbornness, facts are superior to power; they are less transitory than power formations, which arise when men get together for a purpose but disappear as soon as the purpose is either achieved or lost. This transitory character makes power a highly unreliable instrument for achieving permanence of any kind, and therefore not only truth and facts are insecure in its hands but untruth and non-facts as well. The political attitude toward facts must, indeed, tread the very narrow path between the danger of taking them as the results of some necessary development, which men could not prevent and about which they can therefore do nothing, and the danger of denying them, of trying to manipulate them out of the world.

V

In conclusion, I return to the questions I raised at the beginning of these reflections. Truth, though powerless and always defeated in a head-on clash with the powers that be, possesses a strength of its own: whatever those in power may contrive, they are unable to discover or invent a viable substitute for it. Persuasion and violence can destroy truth, but they cannot replace it. And this applies to rational or religious truth just as it applies, more obviously, to factual truth. To look upon politics from the perspective of truth, as I have done here, means to take one's stand outside the political realm. This standpoint is the standpoint of the truthteller, who for-

feits his position—and, with it, the validity of what he has to say—
if he tries to interfere directly in human affairs and to speak the
language of persuasion or of violence. It is to this position and its
significance for the political realm that we must now turn our
attention.

The standpoint outside the political realm—outside the community to which we belong and the company of our peers—is clearly
characterized as one of the various modes of being alone. Outstanding among the existential modes of truthtelling are the solitude
of the philosopher, the isolation of the scientist and the artist, the
impartiality of the historian and the judge, and the independence
of the fact-finder, the witness, and the reporter. (This impartiality
differs from that of the qualified, representative opinion, mentioned earlier, in that it is not acquired inside the political realm
but is inherent in the position of the outsider required for such
occupations.) These modes of being alone differ in many respects,
but they have in common that as long as any one of them lasts,
no political commitment, no adherence to a cause, is possible. They
are, of course, common to all men; they are modes of human existence as such. Only when one of them is adopted as a way of life—
and even then life is never lived in complete solitude or isolation
or independence—is it likely to conflict with the demands of the
political.

It is quite natural that we become aware of the non-political
and, potentially, even anti-political nature of truth—*Fiat veritas, et
pereat mundus*—only in the event of conflict, and I have stressed
up to now this side of the matter. But this cannot possibly tell the
whole story. It leaves out of account certain public institutions,
established and supported by the powers that be, in which, contrary to all political rules, truth and truthfulness have always constituted the highest criterion of speech and endeavor. Among these
we find notably the judiciary, which either as a branch of government or as direct administration of justice is carefully protected
against social and political power, as well as all institutions of higher
learning, to which the state entrusts the education of its future citizens. To the extent that the Academe remembers its ancient origins,
it must know that it was founded by the *polis*'s most determined
and most influential opponent. To be sure, Plato's dream did not
come true: the Academe never became a counter-society, and

nowhere do we hear of any attempt by the universities at seizing power. But what Plato never dreamed of did come true: The political realm recognized that it needed an institution outside the power struggle in addition to the impartiality required in the administration of justice; for whether these places of higher learning are in private or in public hands is of no great importance, not only their integrity but their very existence depends upon the good will of the government anyway. Very unwelcome truths have emerged from the universities, and very unwelcome judgments have been handed down from the bench, time and again, and these institutions, like other refuges of truth, have remained exposed to all the dangers arising from social and political power. Yet the chances for truth to prevail in public are, of course, greatly improved by the mere existence of such places and by the organization of independent, supposedly disinterested scholars associated with them. And it can hardly be denied that, at least in constitutionally ruled countries, the political realm has recognized, even in the event of conflict, that it has a stake in the existence of men and institutions over which it has no power.

This authentically political significance of the Academe is today easily overlooked, because of the prominence of its professional schools and the evolution of its natural-science divisions, where, unexpectedly, pure research has yielded so many decisive results that have proved vital to the country at large. No one can possibly gainsay the social and technical usefulness of the universities, but this importance is not political. The historical sciences and the humanities, which are supposed to find out, stand guard over, and interpret factual truth and human documents, are politically of greater relevance. The telling of factual truth comprehends much more than the daily information supplied by journalists, though without them we should never find our bearings in an ever-changing world and, in the most literal sense, would never know where we are. This is, of course, of the most immediate political importance, but if the press should ever really become the "fourth branch of government" it would have to be protected against government power and social pressure even more carefully than the judiciary is. For this very important political function of supplying information is exercised from outside the political realm, strictly speaking; no action and no decision are, or should be, involved.

Reality is different from, and more than, the totality of facts and events, which, anyhow, is unascertainable. Who says what is—*legei ta eonta*—always tells a story, and in this story the particular facts lose their contingency and acquire some humanly comprehensible meaning. It is perfectly true that "all sorrows can be borne if you put them into a story or tell a story about them," in the words of Isak Dinesen, who not only was one of the great storytellers of our time but also—and she was almost unique in this respect—knew what she was doing. She could have added that joy and bliss, too, become bearable and meaningful for men only when they can talk about them and tell them as a story. To the extent that the teller of factual truth is also a storyteller, he brings about that "reconciliation with reality" which Hegel, the philosopher of history par excellence, understood as the ultimate goal of all philosophical thought, and which, indeed, has been the secret motor of all historiography that transcends mere learnedness. The transformation of the given raw material of sheer happenings which the historian, like the fiction writer (a good novel is by no means a simple concoction or a figment of pure fantasy), must effect is closely akin to the poet's transfiguration of moods or movements of the heart—the transfiguration of grief into lamentations or of jubilation into praise. We may see, with Aristotle, in the poet's political function the operation of a *katharsis*, a cleansing or purging of all emotions that could prevent men from acting. The political function of the storyteller—historian or novelist—is to teach acceptance of things as they are. Out of this acceptance, which can also be called truthfulness, arises the faculty of judgment—that, again in Isak Dinesen's words, "at the end we shall be privileged to view, and review, it—and that is what is named the day of judgment."

There is no doubt that all these politically relevant functions are performed from outside the political realm. They require non-commitment and impartiality, freedom from self-interest in thought and judgment. The disinterested pursuit of truth has a long history; its origin, characteristically, precedes all our theoretical and scientific traditions, including our tradition of philosophical and political thought. I think it can be traced to the moment when Homer chose to sing the deeds of the Trojans no less than those of the Achaeans, and to praise the glory of Hector, the foe and the defeated man, no less than the glory of Achilles, the hero of his kinfolk. This had happened nowhere before; no other civilization, however splendid, had been able to look with "equal eyes" upon friend and foe, upon success and defeat—which since Homer have not been recognized as ultimate standards of men's judgment, even though they are ultimates for the destinies of men's lives. Homeric impartiality echoes throughout Greek history, and it inspired the first great teller of factual truth, who became the father of history: Herodotus tells us in the very first sentences of his stories that he set out to prevent "the great and wondrous deeds of the Greeks *and* the barbarians from losing their due meed of glory." This is the root of all so-called objectivity—this curious passion, unknown outside Western civilization, for intellectual integrity at any price. Without it no science would ever have come into being.

Since I have dealt here with politics from the perspective of truth, and hence from a viewpoint outside the political realm, I have failed to mention even in passing the greatness and the dignity of what goes on inside it. I have spoken as though the political realm were no more than a battlefield of partial, conflicting interests, where nothing counted but pleasure and profit, partisanship, and the lust for dominion. In short, I have dealt with politics as though I, too, believed that all public affairs were ruled by interest and power, that there would be no political realm at all if we were not bound to take care of life's necessities. The reason for this deformation is that factual truth clashes with the political only on this lowest level of human affairs, just as Plato's philosophical truth clashed with the political on the considerably higher level of opinion and agreement. From this perspective, we remain unaware of the actual content of political life—of the joy and the gratification that arise out of being in company with our peers, out of acting together and appearing in public, and out of inserting ourselves into the world by word and deed, and thus acquiring and sustaining our personal identity and beginning something entirely new. However, what I meant to show here is that this whole sphere, its greatness notwithstanding, is limited—that it does not encompass the whole of man's and the world's existence. It is limited by those things which men cannot change at will. And it is only by respecting its own borders that this realm, where we are free to act and to change, can remain intact, preserving its integrity and keeping its promises. Conceptually, we may call truth what we cannot change; metaphorically, it is the ground on which we stand and the sky that stretches above us.

[NOTES]

1. *Eternal Peace,* Appendix I.
2. I quote from Spinoza's *Political Treatise* because it is noteworthy that even Spinoza, for whom the *libertas philosophandi* was the true end of government, should have taken so radical a position.
3. In the *Leviathan* (chapter 46) Hobbes explains that "disobedience may lawfully be punished in them, that against the laws teach even true philosophy." For is not "leisure the mother of philosophy; and Commonwealth the mother of peace and leisure"? And does it not follow that the Commonwealth will act in the interest of philosophy when it suppresses a truth which undermines peace? Hence the truthteller, in order to cooperate in an enterprise which is so necessary for his own peace of body and soul, decides to write what he knows "to be false philosophy." Of this Hobbes suspected Aristotle of all people, who according to him "writ it as a thing consonant to, and corroborative of [the Greeks'] religion; fearing the fate of Socrates." It never occurred to Hobbes that all search for truth would be self-defeating if its conditions could be guaranteed only by deliberate falsehoods. Then, indeed, everybody may turn out to be a liar like Hobbes' Aristotle. Unlike this figment of Hobbes' logical fantasy, the real Aristotle was of course sensible enough to leave Athens when he came to fear the fate of Socrates; he was not wicked enough to write what he knew to be false, nor was he stupid enough to solve his problem of survival by destroying everything he stood for.
4. *Ibid.,* chapter 11.
5. I hope no one will tell me anymore that Plato was the inventor of the "noble lie." This belief rested on a misreading of a crucial passage (414C) in the *Republic,* where Plato speaks of one of his myths—a "Phoenician tale"—as a *pseudos.* Since the same Greek word signifies "fiction," "error," and "lie" according to context—when Plato wants to distinguish between error and lie, the Greek language forces him to speak of "involuntary" and "voluntary" *pseudos*—the text can be rendered with Cornford as "bold flight of invention" or be read with Eric Voegelin (*Order and History. Plato and Aristotle,* Louisiana State University, 1957, p. 106) as satirical in intention; under no circumstances can it be understood as a recommendation of lying as we understand it. Plato, of course, was permissive about occasional lies to deceive the enemy or insane people—*Republic,* 382; they are "useful . . . in the way of medicine . . . to be handled by no one but a physician," and the physician in the polis is the ruler (388). But, contrary to the cave allegory, no principle is involved in these passages.
6. *Leviathan,* Conclusion.
7. *The Federalist,* No. 49.
8. *Theologico-Political Treatise,* Chapter 20.
9. See "What Is Enlightenment?" and "Was heisst sich im Denken orientieren?"
10. *The Federalist,* No. 49.
11. *Timaeus,* 51D–52.
12. See *Republic* 367. Compare also *Crito* 49 D: "For I know that only a few men hold, or ever will hold, this opinion. Between those who do and those who don't there can be no common deliberation; they will necessarily look upon each other with contempt as to their different purposes."

13. See *Gorgias* 482, where Socrates tells Callicles, his opponent, that he will "not be in agreement with himself but that throughout his life, he will contradict himself." He then adds: "I would much rather that the whole world be not in agreement with me and talk against me than that I, *who am one*, should be in discord with myself and talk in self-contradiction."

14. For a definition of thought as the silent dialogue between me and myself, see especially *Theaetetus* 189–190, and *Sophist* 263–264. It is quite in keeping with this tradition that Aristotle calls the friend, with whom you speak in the form of dialogue, an *autos allos*, another self.

15. *Nicomachean Ethics*, Book 6, especially 1140b9 and 1141b4.

16. See Jefferson's "Draft Preamble to the Virginia Bill Establishing Religious Freedom."

17. This is the reason for Nietzsche's remark in "Schopenhauer als Erzieher": "Ich mache mir aus einem Philosophen gerade so viel, als er imstande ist, ein Beispiel zu geben."

18. In a letter to W. Smith, November 13, 1787.

19. *Critique of Judgment*, Paragraph 32.

20. *Ibid.*, Paragraph 59.

21. For France, see the excellent article "De Gaulle: Pose and Policy," in *Foreign Affairs*, July 1965. The Adenauer quotation is from his *Memoirs 1945–1953*, Chicago, 1966, p. 89, where, however, he puts this notion into the minds of the occupation authorities. But he has repeated the gist of it many times during his chancellorship.

22. In the words of Montaigne: "If falsehood, like truth, had but one face, we should know better where we are, for we should then take for certain the opposite of what the liar tells us. But the reverse of truth has a thousand shapes and a boundless field."

[2] STATIC AND DYNAMIC

SOCIETY

A View from Megalopolis

Modern western man understands himself as a dynamic being, restlessly engaged upon transforming his environment, improving his conditions of existence, recasting his thinking about reality in novel terms. In all this, we feel, we are different from other human types. Part of the self-understanding of dynamic, modern, western man is his awareness of how he contrasts with his polar opposite, static man. The static type, as we see him, is content to live in a changeless environment; he abhors innovation and in fact has no endowment for it. His life is governed by tradition; his production techniques, his beliefs, his social arrangements, the authorities he acknowledges—all these are traditional. In the static world, each generation's life is a replica of its predecessor's.

From his habitat, Megalopolis, dynamic man surveys the world. He finds his polar opposite holding sway in "static" ancient civilizations and the Ages of Faith, as well as in the "static" enclaves of contemporary civilization—rural subcultures, tribal societies. But then modern man also recognizes intermediate stages. Kindred spirits are beckoning across the gulf of time; we see modern dynamism prefigured in classical Athens and Rome, in the Italian Renaissance, in the Reformation. Since the sixteenth century, we note, dynamism gradually became dominant in the West as the traditional way of life crumbled under the cumulative onslaught of restless, Faustian, dynamic innovators. The process was slow at first, but its tempo quickened more and more until in the last few generations it became vertiginous. At present, dynamic man finds himself living in an exploding environment, figuratively if not literally.

The contrast "dynamic" and "static" man reflects a feeling of superiority mingled with some nostalgia. Perhaps, dynamic man feels, life was happier in the traditional world; and it may in fact be happier today in the organic, rural "community" than it is in the depersonalized city. But, we hold, one must renounce this static type of happiness for other, greater satisfactions. There are the higher values: comprehensive knowledge, mastery over nature, comfort, safety, moral refinement, and individual freedom. These can be achieved only through dynamism. Having tasted the higher values, dynamic man would be unhappy in the primitive Eden of the static world. He must take the drawbacks of the "higher" mode of existence, its insecurity, conflict, frustration, and disorientation, in stride. There is no turning back. Once dynamic personalities emerge in a static, traditional cultural environment, they seek either to shake it up, disrupt it, or else to leave it for a dynamic environment, if one is accessible. People move from the rural to the urban environment, but not in the inverse direction. That is the path of progress and modernization.

Change according to the modern view is in any case the supreme law of human existence. The static cultures themselves are not free from it. Once they accumulate a surplus of energy not claimed by the struggle for subsistence, they can use it to get out of stagnation and become dynamic. This will happen if dynamic personality types emerge and acquire enough power to challenge the dominant, traditional way of life. But static cultures do not let this happen easily. They shield themselves from innovation and victimize the innovators.

Be this as it may, dynamic man nevertheless observes constant spontaneous "evolutionary" change—even in basically static cultures. What distinguishes static from dynamic culture is not the absence of change as such, but only the absence of a specific type of change: deliberate, "rational" innovation. This is what "traditionalism" connotes for us.

The traditional type of man appears subjectively unaware of

change but objectively caught up in it. His traditions themselves, as we discover in retrospect and from the outside, change imperceptibly all the time. They pass through higher and higher stages of elaboration or else lose their force and disintegrate.

Besides indigenous evolution or decay, we also recognize in the "static" world another type of change, resulting from interaction. Traditional cultures are seen as constantly intermingling, and thus influencing one another.

Explanations of change in terms of "influence" are deterministic. The concept is taken from astrology: It refers to an active agent producing an irresistible and inescapable effect upon a passive one. The "influence" relationship excludes rational choice and deliberation. Thus it can be a vehicle of change in the static world as viewed from Megalopolis. "Influences" account for the "diffusion" of elements among static cultures, as well as for "acculturation" of static cultures as a result of contact with dynamic cultures. The outcome is predetermined: Contact with the dynamic culture corrodes and kills the static one.

That change in the static world can only occur in passive, unconscious forms (through "evolution" and "influence"), the dynamic point of view explains by a fundamental fact: Static cultures leave no room for "individuality." Static man is not an "individual." Both in the application of his intelligence and in the exercise of his will, he follows collective patterns. He thinks what he has been taught to think; he does what the group, or the dominant authorities of the group, expect him to do. In any case, his thinking and action are subject to guidance by authority. He can take no independent initiative in forming his beliefs about the world, in transforming his material environment, or in modifying the power structure of his society. All the opportunities that exist in these regards go unrecognized and unused in the static world, for lack of individuality.

Dynamic man, by contrast, is essentially an individual. He assesses his world not according to what he has been taught to think but according to what his own independent exploration of that environment reveals to be the case. He does not do what the group or the powers that be expect him to do but what is apt to enhance his own, individually experienced values. Mere authority does not count for him. Thus every possible hypothesis about reality gets scrutinized; every avenue toward the realization of values gets explored. Thought patterns that do not stand up to critical inquiry will be discarded; social arrangements that deny basic individual values will be rejected or modified. And what the exercise of critical intelligence and reforming passion leaves standing will still remain on trial. Dynamic society does not codify anything once and for all; exercising his freedom to choose one alternative, dynamic man does not relinquish his prerogative to choose others that may appear preferable at some later time.

There is a good deal of distortion in this view from Megalopolis; the polar contrast in terms of which modern urban man understands and defines himself is not consistent with the scholar's idea of traditional, "static" periods and cultures. To the anthropologist and historian, prehistory reveals extraordinary dynamism rather than stagnation. No technical innovation was more momentous than, say, the domestication of animals or the cultivation of grasses. No social revolution had a more shattering impact than the displacement of matriarchal by patriarchal institutions. And these changes did not just happen in spontaneous, "evolutionary" fashion. The basic inventions may have had a fortuitous origin, but it certainly took "dynamic" insight and intelligence to adopt and develop them. And the institutional innovations were "dynamic" events through and through—they were willed by groups aspiring to power and perceiving novel ways to acquire it.

It is the same with pre-modern, seemingly static and tradition-bound historical periods. To the historian, the Middle Ages, despite their traditionalist features, are full of dynamism. The habit of dating the birth of modern dynamism back to *the* Renaissance or *the* Reformation leads to some rather absurd consequences. As we study these things more closely, we see that both "Renaissance" and "Reformation" steadily move backward in time. Dante, Petrarch, and Chaucer in the fourteenth century were clearly "renaissance" men. In fact, the synthesis of Aristotelian philosophy and Catholic theology in thirteenth-century high scholasticism was already a kind of renaissance. But wait a moment—all this had already started in the twelfth century, with Abelard and Gilbertus Porretanus, if not before. What is more, in the ninth century, there had been a Carolingian "renaissance." And why not go back to the fourth century with Basil, Gregory of Nazianz, Augustine?

Likewise, the Reformation did not start with Luther or even with his immediate precursors. There had already been a Franciscan "reformation" in the thirteenth century and, before that, a Hildebrandian in the eleventh.

All these so-called renaissances and reformations were anything but "evolutionary" events. Cultural and institutional changes did not just happen; they represented conscious, deliberate innovations, based upon individual awareness of values. This type of change is ubiquitous. It is not an exclusive appanage of Megalopolis, or even of exceptional cultural periods that strike the contemporary public mind as somehow peculiarly "modern."

We shall have to further qualify the contrast between "dynamic" and "static" culture when we consider the problem of "individuality" and "freedom." The independence and autonomy of the individual as a characteristic of the dynamic culture is clearly overdrawn in the current image of Megalopolis as outlined. Just as anthropologists and historians discover "dynamic" elements in "static" culture, sociologists are aware of the limitations that modern dynamic urban culture puts upon the individual's autonomy. With all due regard for the crucial role played by critical inquiry and political freedom in modern democracies, it is still a vast exaggeration to say that the individual denizens of Megalopolis arrive at their beliefs about reality through independent, critical investigation, or that collectively binding decisions in the modern democratic world reflect every individual's autonomous pursuit of individual values.

Scientific inquiry, to begin with, is so specialized an activity that only small groups of insiders can have autonomously derived beliefs about reality—and then only about very small segments of it. Outsiders must follow authority—and in this respect everybody in Megalopolis is an outsider, even scientific experts when it comes to problems not lying in their area of competence. If the outsider is lucky, he will hit upon genuine authorities whose ways of operating in fact correspond to the canons of the scientific method. If not, he will be taken in by charlatans. But he cannot judge for himself which is which, and in any case he does not and cannot acquire and develop his personal beliefs in critical, controlled, scientific fashion. Megalopolis may be thought of as a collective entity exploring reality through science, but individual Megalopolitans can do so only vicariously. And the more they insist upon critical, scientific fact-finding as the only road to truth, the more dependent will they be and the less will they be able to exercise their own intelligence autonomously.

When it comes to the practical aspects of life—changing the environment, modifying social relationships—the autonomy of each individual again turns out to be a myth. Here, too, the individual must accept guidance from authorities selected and attested for him through institutional channels.

The *modus operandi* of some of the authoritative and authority-producing institutions of the modern world indeed allow for the free exercise of the critical intellect. Such are the universities in which authoritative competence in medicine, law, and the like is acquired and attested (and note that these institutions are of pre-modern, medieval origin). But this type of authority has a monopolistic character; it is reserved for the members of closed corporations. It is to them that the individual must turn in seeking competent guidance and service.

Another form of authority, political leadership, is acquired and attested in modern democracies in a more competitive fashion: The individual has some choice about which authority to follow. But there the source and acquisition of authority are more the consequence of suggestion and manipulation than of the free, critical exercise of autonomous individual intelligence. The idealized model of collective decisions reflecting every individual's value positions is wide of the mark. Voting decisions, for example, are typically heteronomous: In order to make his decision count, the individual must restrict himself to alternatives already enjoying wide support by others.

It appears, then, that there is no all-or-nothing trait differentiating dynamic from static societies. There is authority limiting individual autonomy in the former, and deliberate innovation is not absent from the latter. Still, the contrast conveyed by the view from Megalopolis does undoubtedly exist, although in a less sharp form. What is its nature? Is it perhaps a quantitative difference, a matter of degree?

This is plausible. Deliberate innovation plays a large role in modern urban civilizations, in the form both of technological invention and of directed social change (political and institutional reform or revolution). In pre-modern times we find relatively little of this, or rather we find it intermittently, embedded within long stretches of traditionalism.

Pre-modern cultures are characterized by the tendency of vast innovations to become traditionalized. The traditional agricultural and industrial techniques of antiquity preserve the results of pre-historic and paleohistoric technological revolutions. The modern process of technological change does not work like this; new techniques do not become traditional.

Pre-modern religious belief systems also show the peculiar trait of the traditionalization of innovation. Here, too, settled traditions point back to outbursts of innovation. The heads of traditional pantheons are typically usurpers who have succeeded in displacing earlier deities. At the origin of the great world religions (Judaism, Buddhism, Christianity, Islam), we find huge apostasies: "covenants" nullifying earlier loyalties, founders shattering their peoples' religious traditions. This kind of anti-traditional innovation becomes the fountainhead of stable traditions that are adhered to with fierce loyalty from generation to generation.

But here we notice something peculiar. Whereas the technology of Megalopolis does not tend to traditionalize innovations, its political life sometimes does. All the great modern western revolutions (the "Glorious Revolution" of England, the American, French, and Russian revolutions) became the source of political and ideological as well as institutional traditions.

Traditionalism, as we see, exists everywhere. It is apparently ubiquitous, just as is innovation. But there is less of it in the dynamic than in the static society.

This quantitative difference, however, is not the whole story. Above all, we should not look upon tradition as a survival in modern society of vestiges of the static past, bound to disappear under the impact of dynamism. There are some stable traditional elements that are not marginal relics but are central to the life of our modern society as it unfolds in its dynamic way.

Tradition and Invention

Traditional attitudes and forms of behavior persist in various spheres of modern urban life. We have just referred to traditionalism in politics; other examples of it in religion and social custom come easily to mind. All these phenomena, however, are somehow marginal. We do have our political traditions, but they provide only a general framework for the political process; the substantive decisions that are made have no traditional character. As to the religious tradition, it does not pervade life in the dynamic society. It is being pushed into the background by an accelerating secularization. And traditional social custom, ritual, etiquette, and the like, where still observed, regulate intercourse among individuals largely outside their main fields of activity.

There is, however, a central element of culture that does have an essentially traditional character in every society, dynamic as well as static: This is language. Language as the basic technique of communication is a traditional phenomenon. The acquisition of the mother tongue, as we observe it *in vivo* in contemporary society, illustrates what tradition is and how it functions.

Language is a traditional skill transmitted in early childhood within the family to every normal member of the language community. Training is provided mainly by the parents; thus the culture preserves the skill through the nexus of successive biological generations. Every contemporary parent couple transmits the same code of its offspring. We are concerned here with a decentralized, undirected, spontaneous encoding process producing a behavior pattern that is uniform throughout the group and remains fixed from one generation to another. It is this type of cultural encoding we call "tradition."

Not all traditional encoding processes are mediated by biological parents: Traditional skills are often transmitted through a master-pupil generational nexus. Also, not all traditional codes are imprinted upon every member of a given society. Some are restricted to specialized skill groups. What is essential to traditional encoding is its undirected spontaneity and the persistence of the coded pattern through a series of generations.

This persistence should not be understood in an absolute sense. Traditions are not changeless. They undergo imperceptible evolutionary change and can also be modified by deliberate innovation. The point is only that the traditional encoding process provides no regular institutional channels for innovation. It cannot do so because traditional encoding, as noted above, is not performed by any public institutional center. It is the entire generational group possessing the code and living by it that provides for its perpetuation. Thus traditional codes are "objective social facts" in the Durkheimian sense. Without being changeless, they are refractory to directed change and reform.

In addition to the traditional encoding of behavior patterns, we find various types of institutionalized, nontraditional encoding. The two are apt to appear in combination. In static societies, where traditional encoding is dominant, it may be supplemented by institutional, essentially nontraditional encoding. Dynamic societies, in which institutionalized encoding of behavior is prevalent, must incorporate traditional encoding patterns in their system of socialization and behavior coordination.

Code preservation as well as code changing occurs in both the traditional and the institutional mode. Contrary to what one might suppose, the rigid preservation and standardization of behavior codes cannot rest on *mere* tradition; for tradition, and hence traditional codes, are always fluid. Their fixation requires an institutional framework which is not provided by traditional encoding as such. On the other hand, code changing of a major, systematic sort also calls for some institutional framework.

All this does not mean that institutional authority itself is necessarily nontraditional. There are many traditional institutions both in static and in dynamic societies. In fact, so traditional an institution as the family is instrumental in the encoding of language. The point is only that traditional institutional authority merely mediates traditional encoding; it is not its source. When the encoding of a behavior pattern originates with an authority, traditional or nontraditional, the encoding as such has a nontraditional character: It goes beyond mere tradition.

Let us consider briefly some characteristics of the traditional encoding process. The following seem to be the most important:

a. Traditional encoding is essentially *conflictless*. The learner of the traditional skill is fully motivated to acquire it; he identifies himself with the transmitter of the code. Public, institutionalized coding processes such as the regulation of conduct by laws and ordinances do not have this characteristic. They are not conflictless.

b. Traditional encoding rests on a personal nexus. It takes place within face-to-face groups. This contrasts with impersonal, voluntary encoding mediated in our culture by literature and other public media.

c. Traditional encoding has a socializing function intimately connected with its skill-transmitting function. By acquiring skill or competence, the traditional learner becomes a fully accepted member of the encoding group, and acquires the dignity associated with membership.

d. Traditional encoding creates corporate groups with in-group solidarity and loyalty. Nontraditional institutional encoding such as legal regulation does not have this "incorporating" character. There are, however, certain forms of nontraditional encoding that do create in-groups with corporate loyalty. An example of this is encoding by voluntary action groups such as political movements. This kind of encoding, however, tends to *become* traditionalized.

e. When encoding is not of traditional origin but has a tradition-forming potentiality, as is the case with nontraditional political or religious movements, it also has the characteristic features of traditional encoding noted above: conflictlessness, person-to-person mediation, socializing, and incorporating efficacy. But these features have a precarious existence in nontraditional groups striving to found an enduring tradition. Such groups are prone to internal division and conflict. Their tradition-building impulse may prove abortive.

f. Traditional encoding does not necessarily produce uniform, repetitive, stereotyped behavior patterns. Traditionally encoded *rituals* do, of course, have this character, but traditional communication and production *techniques* (language, craft, and lore) do not. In the case of the latter, the traditional code has to be applied in creative and autonomous fashion. Thus the fact that the traditional code of language regulates speech does not render speaking a stereotyped, habitual activity. Apart from ritual occasions, speaking is improvisation. In primitive societies, to mention another example, hunting is a traditional lore, but the hunter must judge the situation in the light of his own experience and work out his strategy creatively. In fact, the masters of traditional crafts often show originality of the highest order. Thus traditional encoding is not counterposed to dynamic, individual creativity. It is counterposed to impersonal, nonsocializing, institutional encoding and hence also to "innovation" in the sense of institutionalized code changing.

g. Traditional codes, whether "ritual" or "technical," are incorporated into behavior not as a preferable set of alternatives among other possible ones but as the *only* possibility, the "natural" way of doing things. The idea of alternative codes either does not enter consciousness at all or is shocking and traumatizing. It is a shock to discover that other people speak a different language or have different belief systems and rituals. Still, communities living by a traditional code, or at least their individual members, can come to terms with certain forms of code diversity. This is particularly likely to happen when the codes are essentially homologous, as is the case with communication codes (languages). The individual members of a language group can learn other languages outside the normal channels of traditional encoding, without giving up their own. It is more difficult to come to terms with nonhomologous code diversity.

h. Traditional encoding is not incompatible with cultural pluralism. Although traditional codes represent the only possibility, the natural way of life, for the encoding group, traditional societies may accept the fact that other encoding groups with different codes exist alongside them. They are not necessarily impelled to break up the codes of these other societies and impose their own upon them. In fact, such cultural imperialism implies nontraditional institutional encoding of the "traditionalizing" type, referred to above. This is incompatible with purely traditional encoding.

In modern urban culture, pervasive, fully traditional encoding is found only in the realm of language. Apart from language, traditional encoding exists only in such social segments of modern urban culture as preserve old traditions or seek to found new ones, as well as in certain traditional phases of educational (skill-encoding) processes. In static societies, traditional encoding has much wider application. In particular, the production process is largely dominated by it.

In modern urban society, only one skill, the language skill, is really pervasive. In primitive societies, productive skills are pervasive too; before specialization and division of labor, all members of the society are expected to be competent in all production skills. These skills are transmitted within the family environment, essentially as is the language skill in all societies, including ours.

The pervasiveness of production skills, that is, omnicompetence and lack of division of labor, is not absolute even in "primitive" societies. Already on the primitive level there is division of labor between the sexes; males become socialized by learning man's skills, females by learning woman's. Also, some professional specialization, for example, in magic and related skills, appears early. But productive specialization, even where highly developed, is encoded in static societies in traditional fashion. Specialized production is the domain of traditional *crafts*.

Productive activities in modern dynamic society are differentiated from those of static societies, not so much by specialization and division of labor as by the tendency of traditionally encoded production techniques (crafts, lores) to disappear. Instead of these, we have more or less specialized and skilled "jobs." These require nontraditional, institutionalized modes of encoding, such as drilling, mechanical disciplining, or else training, not to turn out one or another kind of *product* but to handle certain types of *apparatus* or *machinery*.

Drilling in industrial discipline is wholly nontraditional: It lacks the characteristic features of traditional encoding, such as conflictlessness, socialization, and the rest. The unskilled worker (the classical "proletarian") can only develop patterns of socialization and incorporation unrelated to the production code, and in fact antagonistic to the encoding institutional authority. Higher skill specialization, to be sure, has certain "craft" aspects: On this level, we do find professional "socialization," together with some measure of antagonism toward the encoding authority. The encoding of higher industrial skills actually occurs, in part, in traditional forms. But it cannot be wholly or predominantly traditional: The industrial environment is changing too fast for that. The encoding must provide readiness for systematic code changing.

Whereas in the industrial milieu the lowest type of encoding, drilling, is the least traditional, the highest type, scientific training, includes the *greatest* admixture of traditionalism. Scientific activity as such is nontraditional or anti-traditional in terms of its content. It is oriented toward discovering new facts, developing new theories, finding new practical applications. But the scientific method is a permanent encoding pattern, transmitted and perpetuated in traditional fashion. It is an evolving code in that the scientific method is being constantly refined in the course of time: Critical standards are becoming more rigorous, and so on. But the method itself is not encoded by a nontraditional authority; it is perpetuated by a traditional community. The method has a revolutionary origin: Europe has had its scientific revolution associated with the names of the great innovators of the seventeenth century—Galileo, Kepler, and the rest. But it was a traditionalizing revolution.

It may be added that the traditionalizing revolution from which modern science originated, like all other traditionalizing revolutions, has preserved large elements of earlier traditional codes. The scientific language, for example, is to a large extent that of classical mathematics, a traditional discipline going back to pre-modern times.

Of course, I am using the term "traditional" here in a special sense that does not refer to the encoding of fixed beliefs resting only on suggestion or of stereotyped patterns of behavior representing mere arbitrary convention. Traditional encoding certainly can carry contents of this sort, but so can nontraditional encoding. The nontraditional origin of encoding does not in itself guarantee rationality, absence of suggestion and manipulation, respect for the autonomy of the individual, and so on; conversely, traditional encoding does not exclude these things. The individual person's intelligence can be stultified and his freedom annulled both in traditional and in nontraditional ways, while both traditional and nontraditional encoding can stimulate creativity and autonomy. But in any case, the term "traditional," as here used, merely refers to the formal features of the encoding of patterns of thought and behavior, notably the conflictless, decentralized, and socializing preservation of continuity, as we see it in the case of language. It has nothing to do with stereotyping and rigidity as such.

Although traditional encoding is a decentralized process, the encoded behavior sometimes has to be directed by central institutional authority. It is only in quite primitive societies that *all* behavior codes are self-executing in the sense that code-enforcing authority is diffused throughout the society. This is the case with the "code" of oral language in all societies, including the most dynamic ones; the technical production codes of relatively advanced pre-modern societies, too, are largely self-executing in this sense. But it is different with behavior codes of a political character— those related to the handling of interpersonal and intergroup conflict and those related to the preservation of the group's integrity. The political codes of all except the most primitive societies are administered through hierarchical authority channels.

Now the selection and mode of operation of the hierarchical authorities may be traditionally encoded. If so, the conferral and functioning of authority is both socializing and conflictless. The key authorities merely mediate a pre-existent code. The traditional authority of the king, judge, and priest is of this sort. The civil or ritual law exists objectively; it is only that it cannot be administered on the basis of diffused authority.

Centralized authority is also needed to direct collective activities of society-wide dimensions (hunting expeditions, predatory raids, wars, or vast technical enterprises such as dam building). Here authority of a different sort is needed, the authority of the "dux" rather than of the "rex," to use Bertrand de Jouvenel's distinction. This sort of authority tends to be nontraditional insofar as the selection of the authority-wielder is concerned. It is essentially "charismatic" authority.

This term needs some clarification. There is much terminological confusion about "charisma" as defined by Max Weber. He stresses mainly the nontraditional character of charismatic authority. The charismatic leader in Weber's sense is primarily a usurper in whom people believe because he is successful and who is successful because people believe in him. But Weber does not only use this essentially pragmatic criterion in his characterization of charismatic authority. He also introduces a different idea—the unique nonroutine, nonprofane nature of charismatic authority, its being derived from contact with supernatural, sacred powers (the etymological root of the word clearly points to *this* characteristic). Hence "charisma" in Weber refers to two very different things—to nontraditional ascendancy mainly based upon success, and to a nonprofane, "sacral" nimbus that can very well be vested in a traditional corporation or in a dynasty. And on top of it all, charisma can also be "routinized," thus losing both its nontraditional and its sacral aspect.

Clearly this is too ambiguous a concept to be of much use for typological or analytical purposes. In using the term, I restrict its meaning to the first component mentioned, nontraditional authority conferred upon a person by a group whose members have implicit faith in him as an individual, whether in addition to this he does or does not also have traditional authority. The charismatic leader in my sense may—but need not—be a usurper; he can be king or priest, not like any other king or priest, however, but unique. He has a superhuman aura about him; he is divinely appointed, a prov-

idential person; but these supernatural qualities are different from
the supernatural, sacral authority of the king or priest. Charisma in
this sense is a personal attribute spontaneously recognized rather
than institutionally conferred. It cannot be passed on or bequeathed
to a successor; it certainly cannot be routinized.

The *techniques* used by the charismatic leader of the "dux" type
can be traditional, as the warrior's or hunter's lore usually is in
primitive societies. Even so, of course, a traditional "craft" is not
like ritual knowledge; this kind of code must be applied creatively.
But the "dux" need not be an innovator. He may exercise his authority, like the traditional king or priest, entirely within the framework of traditional codes.

Nevertheless, public, hierarchical authority, even if traditional,
always involves an element of potential tension and conflict. To be
sure, the traditional authority of the king, judge, and priest is recognized and obeyed voluntarily, and so is that of the leader ("dux").
But traditional codes that are centrally administered do not necessarily represent the "only possible," "natural" way of doing things.
Those who administer the codes must reckon and deal with deviations. They also may become aware of a range of possible alternatives in applying the code. Thus consistency emerges as an explicit
problem for political authorities. Legal and ritual codes, when centrally administered, tend to lose their purely traditional, customary
character. They are likely to become formalized, fixed, elaborated,
in order to ensure consistency. We may see in this tendency a kind
of secondary encoding, a re-encoding, which transcends traditional
encoding as such. The fixing and standardization of a traditional
code is an inherently controversial undertaking. It draws the line
between orthodoxy and heterodoxy.

The "orthodox" cannot be equated with the "traditional." Pure
tradition knows no orthodoxy-heterodoxy distinction. Orthodoxy
presupposes, to begin with, discrimination between various strands
of traditional thinking or behavior, sanctioning a privileged one and
rejecting the rest. But there is more to it than that. When a traditional code becomes an "orthodoxy," it changes its character. It
loses its naturalness and imposes a deliberate commitment to one
choice, excluding other possible ones. Orthodoxy tends to stimulate
both debate and competition. It is the seedbed of holier-than-thou
attitudes and also of intellectual, ritualistic, or ascetic virtuosity.

The formal codification of an orthodoxy requires central political authority. This authority is of the sacral "rex" type but goes beyond purely traditional sacral authority. It has a nontraditional charismatic element, even though its purpose is to preserve a tradition. The charismatic qualification of the codifier of orthodoxy is that of a sacral "teacher" of a community, a qualification that cannot be acquired in traditional ways. It must be conferred by acclamation.

The same type of charisma is found also in the reforming, code-shattering, or code-originating "teacher," the prophet. Prophetic teaching exemplifies "traditionalizing" revolution: It subverts an existing orthodoxy and founds a new one.

We find this distinction between orthodoxy and heterodoxy not only in static but also in dynamic social and political environments. Voluntary action groups such as revolutionary political movements are regularly impelled to define their orthodoxy and draw a line against deviations. This involves charismatic authority of the "teacher" type. The founders of revolutionary movements possessing a formalized creed function as charismatic "teachers" besides being charismatic "leaders" exercising authority of the "dux" type. Lenin and, in his heyday, Stalin, were recognized both as teachers and as leaders.

The "dux" type of authority is not related either to the administration of traditional behavior codes or to their codification, although the chief of the warrior group also has to act incidentally as judge (or in some other "sacral" capacity). The exercise of leadership, as noted above, may leave the existing technical codes (the craft or lore of hunting, war, etc.) unaffected. But leaders do not always look upon the traditional craft or lore as the only possible, natural way of getting results. They may look for, and find, novel alternatives.

Here the problem is not consistency but efficiency. Crises, pressing circumstances, may impel the leaders directing collective undertakings to modify traditional codes in order to solve problems with which traditional methods cannot cope. Thus leadership is a potentially dynamic factor even in a generally static, traditional environment.

Change and conflict come into tradition-bound societies mainly through the channels of central, hierarchical authority, particularly in connection with the latter's charismatic, nontraditional aspects. That traditional encoding is conflictless and socializing does not mean that the societies in which collective behavior patterns are predominantly traditionally encoded are always harmonious "communities" from which conflict, force, and coercion are absent. This state of harmony tends to exist only to the extent that the traditional codes are self-executing, which makes for social equality and absence of conflict. With hierarchical authority, however, distinctions of rank and coercive regulations come in. Also, the large-scale, organized use of violence typically leads to the creation of stratified social structures—the enslavement of defeated groups, the establishment of sharp class and caste differences.

Still, the conflictlessness of tradition and its socializing function do make themselves felt to some extent when stratification becomes traditionally encoded. Lower classes and castes are not necessarily rebellious. They may adopt a conservative traditionalist outlook and identify themselves with their status. Acute social conflict tends to arise in societies largely ruled by tradition when loss of status, enslavement, and the like occur through the application of nontraditional social and political techniques. Debt slavery is more likely to lead to endemic social conflict than enslavement or caste differentiation based upon conquest.

Most of the traditional and nontraditional encoding, code-administering and code-changing processes, and authorities discussed so far exist in some form both in static cultures and in our own dynamic urban society, although their incidence and mode of application show some characteristic differences. Thus tradition in our cultural setting is mostly of the self-executing type; traditional code-administering authority is nearly extinct. This kind of authority is typical of static cultures, although at times nontraditional charismatic authority also appears in the latter.

But now we have to turn to those forms of code setting, code administration, and code change that are specific to the dynamic society and differentiate it from the static one. These forms will turn out to be neither traditional nor charismatic. In fact, I think the dynamic society can be defined as one in which the existing institutional system provides for encoding, code administration, and code change occurring in nontraditional but at the same time also in noncharismatic form.

This definition does not postulate the absence either of traditional encoding or of charismatic authority. It only implies that it is not these things that give a society a specifically dynamic character. Cultural dynamism, we postulate, is based upon behavior coding that is neither as permanent as the traditional nor as discontinuous as the charismatic one.

Our definition will appear odd at first glance. Is not charismatic leadership the most dynamic of all, both in its mode of exercise and in its effects? In a sense it certainly is. No use of political power can bring about as great a change in as short a time as the revolutionary manifestations of political charisma. But then there is also a static side to charismatic power: its *traditionalizing* propensity, its tendency to produce a formalized, rigid orthodoxy. There is dynamism as an enduring characteristic only where the existing institutions favor deliberate innovations that will be kept under control. *Ex ante,* there must be a rational expectation that the change will be for the better; *ex post,* it must be possible to scrutinize the effects of the change. But when innovations become traditionalized, they are removed from control. This is likely to happen when innnovations occur under charismatic auspices. The group then will invest so much passionate hope in the change that it will not tolerate any critical examination of its effects.

Controlled change is easier to maintain in the field of production than in the political field. When a society moves away from the traditional mode of production, it is likely to adopt new production codes in piecemeal fashion, making it possible to eliminate those that do not work or those for which better alternatives become available. Our urban culture has developed institutional mechanisms for controlling the process of technical innovation that works tolerably well, though not ideally. It is in the field of production that modern urban society is most consistently dynamic in the sense of using nontraditional codes without traditionalizing them.

The major institutional setting for controlled technological innovation is the market. Technological innovation rests in the first place upon intellectual accomplishments, knowledge, inventiveness, originality, and so on. But the question is how a discovery or invention will enter into the production codes of the society. For this, institutional channels reflecting a certain power and authority structure are needed. In the modern western industrial societies, the autonomous market fulfills this function: In it the decisive power element is represented by economic bargaining power. The socialist countries also have market mechanisms for developing and administering production codes, but their markets have no autonomy. They are controlled by the political authorities. Political power is the main regulator of code change.

It is a momentous and much debated question whether it is the autonomous or the controlled market mechanism that is conducive to the highest degree of economic dynamism. Looking at indices of economic growth, one could get the impression that the controlled economy of the socialist countries was for a number of years more dynamic than the western autonomous market economy. The socialist economies indeed show remarkable growth rates, particularly during the period of building their heavy industry. But global growth indices cannot measure certain other aspects of dynamism, notably rationally controlled development and innovation. From this point of view, the autonomous market economies now seem to be superior.

In the political field, western urbanized societies have also developed distinctive institutional frameworks for dynamic, controlled innovation. The basic type is constitutional democracy, a form of government peculiarly suited for nontraditional as well as noncharismatic code setting and code administration. In democratic systems, law—to mention only one type of code—does not subsist "objectively," as law is conceived of in traditional societies. There are authority channels for innovating, adding new elements to the code, or codes, of the legal regulation of conduct. But this process again is controlled.

In principle, no part of modern legal systems has "traditional" validity in the pure and simple sense that deliberate change is ruled out. In practice, however, the control over change in legal matters everywhere includes a considerable element of traditionalism. To a great extent, the standard applied in controlling change is continuity and consistency rather than efficiency. This standard is applied in particular to democratic systems. Totalitarian systems allow more room for "efficient" innovation in the legal sphere. But they tend to subject the process of change to control by the standard of ideological orthodoxy. In this way, a charismatic element is introduced into the coding process.

Generally speaking, no contemporary urbanized society is as consistently dynamic (as here defined) in its political as in its economic encoding and code-administering practices. The basic element of dynamism, nontraditional as well as noncharismatic coding, is always there, but not without some more or less considerable admixture of traditional or charismatic elements.

This is inevitable. It is in developing an ever perfectible and perfected machinery for controlling the material environment that Megalopolis has achieved its triumphal breakthrough to dynamism, that is, rationally controlled change. We are far from being able to handle relations among human beings in this dynamic fashion. Perhaps this goal is utopian beyond realization.

Traditional as well as charismatic codings and modes of experience are deeply embedded in our psyche and in the fabric of our culture. At present we cannot undertake to render the world more rational by eliminating or disregarding them altogether. And it seems to me that it would be better not to try too hard. We may lose too much—our sense of identity, our feeling of being at home in the world, our capacity for admiration. Real progress toward a more rational world may not point toward more and more pure dynamism but toward something else—a synthesis of dynamism, traditionalism, and charisma.

DAVID KETTLER

[3] POLITICAL SCIENCE AND
POLITICAL RATIONALITY

The recent appearance of important books by Charles Lindblom and V. O. Key, as well as the interesting anthology compiled by Carl J. Friedrich, signal the fact that within the last few years the concept "rationality" has again become respectable among American political scientists. This welcome development creates an opportunity for re-examining the relationship between the concerns and achievements of political theory in the traditional sense and the kinds of procedures and interests which have been occupying many productive political scientists. In the present study, the re-examination will begin by locating the theme of political rationality within the context of the older political theory. Then attention will turn to an account of the reasons why and the ways in which the theme, with its full range of associations, is directly pertinent to the present state of the discipline. Finally, an aspect of the rationality theme will be explored in a way intended to illustrate, fairly specifically, how the perspective of political theory can influence and assess the work of disciplined factual inquiry.

Historical Introduction: Political Theories
and Political Rationality

Political theorists working in the great tradition share a common presumption. It is that the amazing range of phenomena associated with man's political experience can somehow be seen or structured so as to "make sense" to a man caught up in that experience as actor, victim, or amazed observer. "Making sense," in this view, has two important aspects. First, it interconnects—as the expression does in colloquial speech—consideration of how things work with an examination of how such workings can be justified or made justifiable. Second, there is the common requirement that the consideration and examination be disciplined by procedures and standards competent to ascertain truth, and that this truthfulness be itself capable of being publicly established.

The major writers whose works are usually studied in histories of political theory address their inquiries to two sorts of primary concerns: first, under what conditions can a claim to political power be said to be justified and sustainable and, second, how can proper care to public matters be secured, a care that, so far as possible, what is done will satisfy rational standards? These themes will here be designated as, respectively, the problem of "authority" and the problem of "political rationality"; and this essay focuses on the second of them. For purposes of this historical overview, the requirement for a rational definition of standards will be given a merely formal interpretation: A rational approach is any that meets the standards of disciplined, truth-oriented discourse of the time, or credibly puts forward a claim for acceptance by initiates into disciplined intellectual effort. None of this precludes a later philosophical assessment of any or all such approaches according to critical standards of adequacy. At this point, the objective is simply to propose a typology for putting in order the historical record concerning theories of "political rationality," i.e., the use of political power for the maintenance and/or creation of order corresponding to the requirements of rationality.

The question arises whether the themes of "authority" and "political rationality" do not refer to the same set of problems, both being concerned with the application of supposedly rational criteria to the facts of political life. In the literature of political theory three basic sorts of approaches to this issue appear: (1) Some, like Plato in the *Republic*, define authority in terms of political rationality: those may rule who will rule wisely, because they will rule wisely; (2) others, like Calvin, define political rationality in terms of authority: that which is done by those who may rule is done well, because they have done it; and (3) the great majority in the tradition distribute themselves along a continuum between these two possibilities. The ties between the two themes are interesting and important, but each may be separately considered. In a recent book, Charles Lindblom states the distinction well:

> We depart in this book from a long established inquiry that asks . . . [what] is an effective way to guard the guardians, protect liberty or democracy, obstruct tyranny, make power responsible. . . ? We ask questions that respond to another kind of concern: [what is] . . . a good way to make decisions? to calculate and to weigh alternative courses of action? to achieve rationality in some sense? to avoid foolish decisions?[1]

Seymour Martin Lipset's well-known distinction between legitimacy and effectiveness refers to the same matters, although the scope of inquiry into them is, in accordance with his conception of disciplined political inquiry, deliberately more limited than is usual in the traditional literature.[2]

In one important respect the theme of political rationality, as developed here, has wider boundaries than comparable concepts developed by the writers just cited. Uses of power which maintain and foster the conditions said to support authority will, where this is applicable, be themselves considered under the heading of political rationality. A hypothetical example may clarify this point: A political theory contends that authority properly derives from selection by a divinely inspired priesthood. It contends, further, that political rationality recommends fostering the greatest happiness of the greatest number and that this requires an authoritative ruler. A decision by a ruler to support and safeguard the priesthood will, according to the proposed usage, be classed under political rationality. It derives from the theory of authority, in a sense, but the ruler's authority is not conditioned upon such a decision. A decision to destroy the priesthood would, in the hypothetical theory, be considered authoritative but not rational. The distinction between authority and rationality, as now drawn, retains the capacity for examining an argument like that of Kant, where much is said about rational or wise rule, but authority theoretically founded without regard to that wisdom. But it also calls attention to the fact that even writers who come very close to requiring only that power be authoritative—like some democratic theorists—tend to urge and expect a pattern of use which will maintain the system of authority itself. And such urging and expectation raise most of the interesting questions comprehended under the topic of political rationality.

Two aspects distinguish the theme of political rationality, and the questions associated with each can be provisionally and tentatively associated, respectively, with the normative or evaluative and the empirical sides of the matter. The first concerns the conception of rationality itself: What are the proper constituents of order? Ordered to what or what sorts of principles? How can the standards be explained and defended by reason? For the second side of the issue, one broad question states the basic concern: What is there about the way things are said to be, about the way in which the political is to be seen or structured, that makes it likely that rational outcomes will be produced? Political theories addressing themselves to this broad theme, then, may be classed according to different ways of conceiving the ends and character of rationality and according to different ways of discerning the locus of rationality in political reality. As a tactical matter, priority will here be given to the second sort of classification, a typology of loci of rationality.

This is not because useful distinctions cannot be drawn among diverse views of rationality itself. One will become important as the analysis proceeds, and can be briefly explained now. When rationality is identified with certain specific contents—ultimate ethical injunctions, metaphysical propositions about reality, and the like —the theory of rationality is said to be "substantial"; when the conception of the rational stresses certain sorts of procedures and general rules of inquiry—rules of scientific procedure, logic, and so on —it is classed as "formal." Whether the pure types can arise is fortunately not now in question. For historical use, these types can only serve as polar points defining a continuum along which actual theories may be located.[3] Discussions of rational standards as such, however, tend to be vague, complex, and often evasive or manipulative, so that a direct approach to this theme in the literature is often fruitless and comparisons especially hard to make on terms which those being compared would consider fair. Classifying diverse conceptions of the locus of rationality provides a useful way into the materials, then, apart from its intrinsic interest. Putting the matter less formally and more nearly in the familiar language of the tradition, the question involves provision for wisdom in the counsels and determinations of public authorities.

This question was central for the first major writer in the tradition, Plato. He considered it so important that in the *Republic* he dramatized it by the perhaps simplistic (or ironic) solution of saying, in effect, that to secure wisdom in decisions, it is necessary to let the most wise govern. This most direct approach to the matter has had recurrent appeal; although it is clear that many who invoke it probably do not mean to be taken quite seriously as arguing that the direct exercise of power by those best capable of rational thought can in the real world solve the problem of carrying into effect actions which reason would approve. More often, such formulas as "enlightened despotism" or "technocracy" or rule by "experts"—and these almost always represent some variation on the Platonic theme—mean little more than that the person employing them is far more interested in the detail of rational policies than in the broad range of questions characteristic of political theory. They are stopgaps inserted to occupy a space in the structure of the argument. In any case, there is in the literature a characteristic type of response to the problem of political rationality that actually does build on the Platonic foundation, and usually it then proceeds to stress the educational process (in the broadest sense) by means of which rulers are bred to the rule of reason.

Closely allied to this type of solution is one according to which the need is to make the ruler amenable to wise counsel. Plato himself in many of his expressly political writings most commonly stressed this type of statement, and saw that the critical problem faced by this approach is how to structure matters so that rulers will be inclined to listen to reason and capable of implementing it. The normal procedure has been to rely on the force of exhortation itself, and it is important to recognize that the great bulk of political writings of all sorts in the history of the culture consists of such exhortatory literature. Much of this has been neglected, because students of political theory have been so much occupied with problems of authority that the implications and presuppositions of exhortation as a political phenomenon have not been adequately explored. But the exhorter faces two difficulties. If he is straightforward, he finds that he is without effect unless he tells his ruler what he wants to hear; if he resorts to trickery, he is challenged to justify his pretended authority to govern the duly constituted governor of society. Hobbes clarified and attempted to solve both of these difficulties—although it was David Hume, rather than Hobbes himself, who spelled out the implications of the Hobbesian approach.[4] The task, as seen from this point of view, is to free the ruler from irrational forces—above all from boundless insecurity and fear—and thus to let him feel free to pursue his own rational self-interest as ruler, which corresponds to the general demands of reason. Then a counselor can successfully function, and does not need to disguise his wise advice in the symbols of an authoritative language or hide behind other tools of manipulation. In the language of Hobbes' important distinction, he can in fact be a counselor rather than exhorter.[5] Such frank counsel, then, does not raise the problem of authority, because the counselor serves as aide and not as secret controller of the ruler.

But even this brief exposition of the Hobbesian type of answer already points beyond it to the general type which, in its many subtypes, is the most widespread among political theorists. If a secure sovereign is said to find it in his interest to rule rationally, then the inclination toward rationality is in fact being seen as in some sense implicit in the function of ruling itself, when properly construed or constructed; and the advice of the wise counselors must be understood merely as making actual a potentiality already given within the political process as such. If the Platonic, and in some measure even the Hobbesian types, see political rationality as a transcendent force, external to the world of the political as such and needing somehow to be constantly imported into it—like a god in a theatrical rigging device—this third type of approach perceives a locus of political rationality somewhere within the complex of structures and processes which it imagines to comprise the very substance of political reality. Political rationality is then (or can become) an immanent force, not a transcendent one. Without calling on "wise men" as rulers or counselors, this approach hopes to find a bias toward rationality built into a decisive part of the political world.

A typology of such efforts can be suggested by a few illustrations of the diversity to be encountered. In the context of the problem of "authority," legislative assemblies have usually been discussed as ways of institutionalizing the "consent" supposed to be the sole legitimate source of authority. That is, they have been related primarily to the issues normally grouped under the term "representation." But from Aristotle on, assemblies have also been discussed from the standpoint of their ability to apprehend reason, "two heads" being said to be "better than one."⁶ This aspect of their work is often discussed under some heading such as "deliberative function," although it might usefully be identified as "conciliar," to indicate the tie between conceptions of consultative or deliberative counsels that are unconnected with conceptions of authority founded on representation or consent and those currently more familiar. This conciliar issue is often at the heart of discussions which mistakenly (i.e., confusingly) try to make do with the language of representation alone. Much talk about reapportionment comes to mind; although the source of the confusion actually is, as will be discussed below, the contemporary difficulty of discussing problems of rationality apart from purely formal considerations of the sort that figure importantly in theories of representation. But the earlier literature is less diffident, and the main sorts of immanent approaches can be illustrated from the history of Liberalism alone.

In the writings of Locke and other constitutionalists, it is quite clear that a major problem is to envision a structure which builds in a high measure of probability that rational decisions will be made: i.e., that legislative and magistrative action protects rights, and that administration or legislature promotes the general welfare and provides for the common defense. These Liberals will, of course, differ among themselves as to how this can be expected to happen. Some—and Locke himself tended in this direction—will repose primary confidence in the lawmaking, law-adjudicating, and administrative processes themselves: Among these, there is seen to be something inherently rational about the pursuit of these activities, the performing of these functions, or the playing of these roles, when they are properly designed. Others, like Montesquieu and his followers, rely on a compound of social and governmental processes, on socially rooted conflict and competition built into the organization of governmental institutions themselves. Still others within the basic tradition ascribe an inherent tendency toward rationality to a nonpolitical societal process, usually economic in character, with the governmental arrangements as such seen to serve simply as auxiliaries.

Very broadly speaking, then, these examples suggest three types of immanent approach to the locus of rationality: (1) an inclination toward rationality located in certain ways of organizing the work of governing (here the example was the assembly or counsel);

(2) the locus of rationality in certain roles or functions within the governmental process (legislating, magistrating, administrating, for examples); and (3) rationality immanent within processes not themselves governmental, but supposed to stand in relation to government as base to superstructure (allusion here was to confidence in socioeconomic processes, as in Manchester liberalism or Social Darwinism). It is clear that once again the description of these ideal types serves as an aid to the consideration of any specific writer, rather than as a substitute for it; seldom does a complex argument rest exclusively on one or the other of these types of analysis. A writer like John Stuart Mill, for example, rests his case on general education (process), on preferential voting for the university-trained (Platonic), on open voting to prevent irrational influences (Hobbesian), on liberty of discussion (nongovernmental process), on representative government (organization), as well as other factors.

Then, too, numerous examples can be given to show the need for further refinement of the categories. Thus, there are arguments for the wisdom of one against the confusion of many, and many detailed patterns of organization have been put forward as the proper means to rationality—including the familiar arguments in behalf of bureaucratic and hierarchical "rationalization."[7] The leadership function has often been closely linked with some inherent tendency toward rationality, and recent American discussions of "presidential leadership" or "party responsibility" clearly rest, at least in part, on some complex assumptions about the kinds of policy results anticipated from one or the other kind of institution. Most varied of all have been the diverse processes which have been, at one time or other, held inherently to move toward rationality. One version of the societal model especially common today emphasizes processes of negotiation, conflict, and mutual adjustment among a plurality of interested groups; but there are also contemporary forms of Rousseau's conception of a political-communal process expressly distinct from and hostile to the interest-linked societal one, or from the processes internal to the government as such. For Marx, the locus of rationality lay in the revolutionary movement of the class-conscious proletariat, and his spiritual heirs have found themselves dividing the legacy between those who chose the revolutionary movement, and those who stayed with the working-class movement as it actually developed. Other striking varieties could be cited, but present purposes do not require a detailed working out of the scheme. It is enough that a vocabulary for dealing with the theme has been developed.

The Contemporary Status of the Problem

I have no exquisite reason for't, but I have reason good enough.
                                                        —*Twelfth Night*

The temptation is to dismiss all that has gone before as prehistory, and to restate matters so as to put the question into more easily manageable form. As the various schemes have been stated, they cannot be subjected to comparative evaluation through empirical methods. To characterize all the diverse sorts of outputs as "political rationality," it might be said, simply obfuscates the admitted fact that these different theorists often had radically different things in mind when they spoke of the "rational." The trick then would be to create operational indices from the various sorts of value standards vaguely lumped together as "rationality" and then to proceed, through rigorous empirical inquiry, to discover what factors under which conditions are most likely to support one or the other pattern of values. As for the choice among values, this view would conclude, that is a matter for individual or political decision, where rational thought—in the forms of scientific procedure and conceptual criticism—can do nothing more than to clarify alternatives.

That response, probably taken as commonplace by many political scientists, represents the most important of several basic challenges to be met by any contemporary effort to carry on the work of "the enterprise" of political theory. Two are most directly pertinent here. The first arises out of the *functionalization of political ideas* and the second, already anticipated above, is *epistemological*. From the standpoint of functionalization, what is at issue is the growing awareness that political ideas have an ideological function, that they are usually developed and employed as weapons in political struggle.[8] In considerable measure this understanding has been strengthened by the simple fact that in the course of the nineteenth century explicit ideologies came to be ever more important components of political life. Combined with the Marxist use of ideological analysis as a means for discrediting opponents, Freudian insight into processes of rationalization and illusion, and anthropological findings concerning the role of myth in society, the awareness of ideology has threatened to destroy the self-respect—so to speak— of political theory. Although the proposition "political ideas are political weapons" does not logically imply the contention that "*all* political ideas are *nothing but* political weapons,"[9] the psychological association is close enough, and many contemporary writers on politics are satisfied to treat all comprehensive political doctrines as mere ideologies—matters for sociological inquiry into provenance and function only.

The epistemological challenge strikes even more deeply at the roots of claims traditionally advanced in behalf of the political theory enterprise. Increasingly since the sixteenth century the assumptions and methods of the physical sciences have come to be recognized as the models for the disciplined use of reason; and since David Hume many philosophers of knowledge have contended that respect for that model precludes all pretension to secure true rational knowledge about the proper objects of human choice. Scientific thinking, from this point of view, can acquire true (or highly probable) knowledge about what *is* or *appears to be;* it can say nothing about *what ought to be* or "*really*" *is*. All that disciplined thinking can do in the realm of norms is, first, to create clarity and consistency within any given scheme of values, and, second, to show probable conditions for and consequences of actions governed by one or another preference. Accordingly, on this view, the basic claims made in behalf of comprehensive political theory of the traditional sort are without foundation. "Political theory," then, may properly refer either to a testable set of propositions explaining actual political events as do theories in the well-established sciences, or the term may refer to a coherent scheme of value preferences which cannot claim to be "true" in any rational sense. Most influential political scientists today profess adherence to such an approach, and any attempt to ascertain the contemporary relevance of the political theory enterprise and its traditional formulation of questions, like that of "political rationality," must make some sort of peace with this epistemological challenge. And this would appear to be no simple task.

To speak of a locus of "rationality" rather than of institutionalized "values" signifies several important things about the discussion in which this happens. It indicates, first of all, that conclusions are intended to serve as justifying explanations or recommendations. Secondly, such a formulation acknowledges the authority of political theory within the disciplined study of the political; that is, it expressly permits concerns about the meaning and purpose of political life to set the tasks for political inquiry. Such usage proclaims, and in some measure helps to preserve, thirdly, the autonomy of political theory.

The third of these requires amplification. When the talk is of "values," the tendency is to let the requirements of empirical research govern the definition of the quality being investigated: The variable must be one which can be operationally measured. The practical consequence is that the values whose implementation is given careful empirical attention are those for which unambiguous, hopefully quantitative, indices can most easily be constructed. This improperly foreshortens examination of an important question that philosophical and rational analysis of value problems ought to consider on its own merits: What sorts of values are capable of being given rational consideration, and in what form can they best be expressed? Methodological discussions of operationalism quite properly do not discuss such issues; they ought not be permitted, either, to usurp by default the place of such discussion. The appropriateness of operationalism to rigorous empirical research is not being challenged. No matter what conclusion may be reached about the character of rationally discussible values, rigorous empirical research into the conditions and consequences of their actual appearance will have to proceed through operational indices contrived with as much ingenuity as can be mustered.[10] It may also be, however, that issues will be thrown up for which ingenuity will not suffice, and where rigorous empiricism will have to tolerate reliance on less precise modes of inquiry, disciplined by appropriate standards. Insistence on the terminology of "rationality" in this matter, in short, symbolically reaffirms the proposition that political science ought properly to be the respected and functionally autonomous handmaiden of the comprehensive humanistic effort to secure as rational an orientation as possible to the political.[11]

But this expanded reaffirmation can in itself only explain what would be involved in continued use of traditional language. It cannot itself persuade that reinvigorating the enterprise of political theory is a desirable objective to pursue, despite the confusions and impostures to which such pursuit has sometimes given rise. Nor can it itself provide any assurance that the task is possible, that the search for "rationality" will be more than ritualistic or *ipse dixit* sanctification of some merely ideological scheme, that the challenges to the enterprise can be rationally met. These tasks require, first of all, an understanding of the present situation in disciplined thought about political matters.

It is in fact not true that political scientists in the United States today neatly divide between those who decry modern scientific method in the name of some earlier philosophic doctrine and those who scorn as "theologians" or "technicians" any whose work transgresses the bounds of empirical theory building and testing. A considerable proportion, rather, proceed as if there were no philosophical obstacle in the way of recommending "rational" policies or institutions. When challenged on philosophical grounds, such writers will characteristically—when they do not blandly confess their limitations with uninhibiting modesty—take refuge in some variety of instrumentalism. These recommendations, they will say, are meant to be compelling only to one who accepts the values they are designed to promote; and their source is the personal preference of the writer, the stated or assumed preferences of those to whom the recommendations are addressed; or—approaching more closely to traditional grounds—the consensus, underlying assumptions, or animating principles of the political system, society, or culture. Not every work by such writers will expressly concern a problem of rationality; but they will be quite comfortable in the use of terms with normative "surplus meaning"; they will think of their work as having "implications" for political choice, and they will defer to political theory as the queen of the discipline—if also with some of the irony with which practical men defer to queens.[12]

Before characterizing the recent work of the political theorists themselves, it will be helpful to mention some of the factors other than conventionalism that sustain the kind of activity just described. There is an intimate link between politics and political science. Political practitioners, however skeptical about "mere" theorists, expect scientific thinkers to have answers or to know how to get them; and those who enter the discipline have often seen their vocation as being in some vital sense related to a concern for the public good. This does not mean that citizens and politicians welcome advice or heed it; but they expect from men of thought reassurance that what they are doing is right, and, above all, a place to turn when they are disoriented by events. And the familiarity of the list may dull the awareness but cannot change the fact that the twentieth century has been steadily unsettling to established principles of orientation. Men have had to live with the danger that a failure of rationality—by any important international actor—can burn mankind; with the unconditional assertion of "unreasonable" demands by populations that could hitherto be counted on; with pressure to guarantee against mistakes by supplementing or replacing improvisation with planned control and thereby avoiding the irreversible and fatal. Assumptions about the sense of things and sureness of touch in handling them are subjected to constant jarring: Conditions foster a sense of precariousness. There is no one sort of reaction to such a state of affairs, of course, and it is an empirical question to discover what actually happens and how it comes about. Some will doubtless withdraw their attention from the disorienting scene and passively accept as fated fact whatever happens there; others will seek reassurance in simple, certain, comprehensive interpretations and firm guides to action; still others will respond with clamorous and urgent demands on those who profess, in any sense, to know. And all such responses, except the passive one, make demands on the political scientist to contribute to the task of making sense of things, of pointing the rational way.

In such a setting, and given the fact that political scientists are themselves also a part of the population which responds in the diverse ways sketched above, it is not surprising that the requirements of scientific asceticism (however celebrated on ritual occasions) are commonly disregarded or evaded. The formulas commonly used to make it possible to devise plans for achieving certain objectives, without claiming that those objectives are in any sense "true" or otherwise in need of rational defense, steadily lose in credibility. It makes less and less sense to describe the objectives as mere matters of personal preference: The occasions multiply when both author and audience are convinced that the recommendations deal with life-or-death matters, and when their implementation demands great risks and sacrifices. Similar considerations confound the attempt to perform as technical consultant. Disorientation makes it less likely that clear guidelines will be given the "expert": he will often have been called in precisely to remedy an incapacity to formulate such guidelines. Moreover, with issues believed to be so fateful, bureaucratic self-effacement becomes ever less tolerable. When retreat turns to principles presumed to be a matter of consensus or logical presupposition of the system, then it is again clear that a threshold has been passed into the traditional domain of presumptuous political theory.

The great danger of disingenuous or naïve instrumentalism is that it tempts one uncritically to accept a Platonic or transcendent way of embodying rationality within political life. If the proposal being offered simply implements desires already present, then it can surely be put into effect without "politics," through the knowing direction of those initiated into the expertise. The most modest instrumentalism then comes to function in political life like the most imperious "rationalism." At worst, then, this course is attended by intellectual confusion about what is being done, inadequate criticism of standards being employed, and political ineffectuality. Of course, it does not need to come to the worst. It is men out of precisely this group who are, through encouragement, criticism, and direct contribution, fostering the revival of a political theory at once pertinent and intellectually respectable.

Work not intended by its authors to offer normative recommendations will also, when dealing with matters where guides are being sought, serve a normative function. Although sometimes offered as a sweeping challenge to all claims of value-free science, this point can be far more reasonably offered in support of a call to modesty and responsibility. A recent statement by Jack L. Walker expresses this viewpoint:

> Ideas and other beliefs have manifold consequences, some intended and others wholly unexpected; writings meant by their authors to be purely descriptive may still lead their readers to draw normative conclusions. . . . Regardless of the writer's intention, I would argue that the facts he presents and the explanations he proposes may prompt his readers to make certain normative inferences.[13]

Nothing in this argues that the discovery or rational defense of norms is identical with the work of science. The connections between the rigorous development of verifiable propositions and the concerns of the political theory enterprise are more complex.

First, there is the widely conceded point (although resisted by some) that political scientists select problems to be investigated on the basis of their own value preferences: They inquire into that which interests them. This does not call into question the scientific integrity of the work, of course. "The scientific method," it has been well said, "is precisely for the purpose of protecting us from our-selves so that we can be free to study areas in which we have ex-ceedingly strong biases."[14] But the fact that the inquiry is structured, at least initially, by a normative principle of selection, provides the foundation for a level of meaning added to the scientific-explana-tory one. This foundation is reinforced, especially where writers undertake inquiries into complex problems, by an all but irresistible temptation to supplement rigorously established propositions, which tend to be modest in scope, with approximations, projections, and guesses, which increasingly partake of the normative-interpretative character of traditional political theory—or, it may be said, are sub-ject to the forces which shape ideologies.[15]

But even assuming that this sort of nonscientific or ideological input cannot be practicably eliminated, the question still is: By what *right* do readers "draw normative conclusions" where none are intended, and does the political scientist have any responsibility for that when it happens? Here reference to a historical model may help. David Hume is commonly honored as patron saint of the gen-uine scientific attitude. His work is cited as the *locus classicus* for the facts-values distinction, and for the "noncognitivism" of matters of value. What is overlooked is that Hume treated the "knowledge of ignorance" concerning rational prescription as a rational argu-ment in support of naturalistic standards supplemented by civilized convention. When rational grounds for challenging conventional authority are cut away, the task of securing ethical and political orientation is turned over to the description of how the world ac-tually is. The skeptic about rationalist pretensions, then, denies that there are reasons for doubting an educated conventional view. Hume was no libertine or relativist.[16] It was a critic and opponent of Hume who laid down the rule "that questions of fact or mere explanation should be considered apart from the questions of esti-mation and choice"; and this was argued precisely to support a "science of morals" to counter the primacy of the fact defended by Hume.[17]

The point of the historical reference is not that Hume is some sort of "authority" because long dead, but rather that he and his opponents correctly saw what is involved in a position like his, and were prepared to take and give responsibility for it. Given the human need for the kind of orientation that the old moral philoso-phy or the enterprise of political theory was prepared to give, it is in fact quite proper to press on to "normative conclusions" from accounts which purport to show how things really are, when all other aids are systematically denigrated and denied. The locus of "rationality"—or its sole reasonable functional equivalent—is then quite unabashedly found in the process that generates custom, or civilized opinions. Whether this is an adequate approach is not now at issue. Hume is cited for his insight into what is, in some sense, entailed by a factual account of the universe which men encounter as morally charged, and to which they seek orientation. In his capacity as strict experimentalist and rigorous logician, he does not encounter the world in that mode; but to choose to act as experimentalist and logician is part of such an encounter. Hume is sharply insistent on the special play-character of that aspect of his work, and responsibly aware of the interconnections between this and his capacity as practicing, recommending, and judging man; and he does not imagine that they can or ought to be more than temporarily independent of one another. Seen in this perspective, the work of the most rigorously scientific political scientist also requires the supplement of a critical, probing, so-what?-asking political theory of the traditional sort. Otherwise the intellectual functions that such theory attempts to subject to rational discipline will be performed either by an unexamined and unchosen *de facto* Hume-ism, or by whatever uncontrolled arbitrariness seizes hold.

Such narrowing of the real choice forms the central theme of contemporary rational defense of the traditional enterprise. Some of the most attractive recent exponents of political theory in the traditional sense have, of course, gone about their business without paying much attention to the presumed crisis of the enterprise, and this has been all to the good in their cases. But the issues keep pressing, and sterile repetitions of a stereotyped facts-values discussion bore or even paralyze all who take part; and so it is important to call attention to explicit efforts to deal with contemporary challenges to political theory in a rational and coherent way. Recent essays by John Plamenatz and Sheldon S. Wolin point promising directions.[18] In an explanatory but not apologetic manner, then, the most credible account of the enterprise sees the diverse theories it comprises as illustrations, in Plamenatz' words, of man's need "to place himself in the world, to come to terms intellectually and emotionally with himself and his environment."[19] They are not reducible to propositions which can be empirically tested and verified; nor are they simply postulated grammars to be subjected to rigorous analytical scrutiny. Each important political theory must be seen as a distinctive effort to interpret the meaning of man's political experience, to explicate a set of problems, to ascribe significances within a clamor of happenings, to expound a vision of order and possibilities.[20] Each is informed by a moral perspective, as well as by a social and historical angle of vision, but is not reducible to either aspect. The enterprise of political theory pursues truth in the sense of political wisdom, not truth or validity in the sense of the most widely accepted contemporary theories of knowledge—and appreciation of one activity does not entail a denigration of the other. If political theory is to be considered as a rational enterprise, however, there must be some sort of public criteria of truthfulness, there must be a discipline. It is clear that political theory, seen as interpretation of meanings, cannot pretend to provide univocal certainty: Possibilities remain fluid; the search for standards, continuing; the angles of vision, multiple. But the reasonings must have some specifiable character, and the more "adequate" must be distinguishable from the less.

Justice cannot be done here to the diverse efforts to move in this direction; that would require a detailed critical review of recent ethical theory. The primary task of this essay will be served if it can be shown that the undertaking is directly and specifically pertinent to the prime concerns of political scientists, that it shows promise, and that it can proceed without requiring a Luddite assault on modern science or some fideist suspension of rational judgment. All that has gone before has been directed to the first of these objectives—except insofar as the attempt to offer reasons here has itself involved application of some principles of rationality adequate to such a task. Next will follow attention to one contemporary approach considered particularly fruitful. The concluding section of this chapter will return to the theme of "locus of rationality" to consider, in an illustrative and exploratory way, how a contemporary effort to carry on the enterprise of political theory can deal with this traditional topic.

Despite very important differences and conflicts among the various contemporary approaches to rationality, a common paradigm can be traced: Rationality is conceived in a formal rather than substantive way; it involves recourse to certain intellectual procedures in an interpretative but essentially practical encounter with some given situation, with the procedures selected being said to be recognizable as implicit in the very fact of the encounter itself, when full consciousness of the situation is attained. A neo-Kantian approach appears particularly well suited to give an account of how rational political theory is possible.

In a persuasive effort to make such an approach comprehensible to contemporary analytic philosophy, James Ward Smith offers an elegant and clear statement. "There are 'musts' in our intellectual life," he begins, "which are neither the 'musts' of logic nor the 'musts' of incontrovertible evidence."[21] These "musts" constitute the "advice" or "recommendations" that make up political and moral philosophy and also underlie the "coerciveness" of any sort of evidence, in however precise a science. As the use of the term "advice" suggests, Smith sees acts of *decision* as the ground for any encounter with the world; these are decisions about "interpretation," about the "distribution of emphasis." The question, then, is whether such decisions are themselves subject to rational justification. Smith argues that it is a mistake to assume that modes of justification appropriate to propositions in the technical sense (i.e., logical and empirical propositions) are the only ways in which the rational "temper of deciding" can manifest itself. Rather, he argues, "justification finally always relates to our actions, our decisions, our recommendations, and our hopes, fears, and purposes" (p. 9). He concludes, then:

> Political philosophy is misconceived as a search for demonstrations, proofs, or certainties. What we need from political philosophers is sound advice as to how to make rationally justified decisions when we are dealing with hunches, guesses, and hopes [p. 31. . . . It] is concerned with isolating those basic commitments apart from which our ways of behaving as a group and our common purposes in action make no sense [p. 59].

There is circularity of a sort here: Justification of a given "distribution of emphasis" can itself proceed only in terms of an interpretation. But, Smith maintains, precisely the fact of this predicament provides guidance to proceeding "sanely and rationally" (pp. 42, 48). So, for example, it is possible to reject arguments which purport to have the kind of coerciveness appropriate to logical proofs or empirical verification. Secondly, this fact warns against over-general recommendations which underestimate the extent to which there are "many truths about man . . . many ways of interpreting what we do" (p. 57). He writes:

> Political theory bulges at the seams with arguments about the truth or falsity of bloated general propositions where in fact it should be examining the conditions under which one kind of advice is appropriate rather than another [p. 54].

But these two arguments themselves rest on a strategy of justification. They implement a decision as to how the concept rationality will be applied. There is underlying them a conception of where the question "why?" ceases to make any sense (pp. 70ff). Ultimately, reason proceeds from a showing of "the way the world is," and the very decision to proceed by giving reasons itself sets limits to the ways in which the world will be seen. The task is, according to Smith, to proceed through case studies to discover the difference between "responsible" and "irresponsible" rules for justifying recommendations. The philosopher must cultivate self-consciousness of what he is about, and govern his work by these insights.

For Smith, the most striking and universal attribute inherent in the rational attitude is "fallibilism." On this basis he proceeds to what he calls a "methodological defense of democracy" (pp. 109ff). "The 'matter' of political and moral philosophy," he writes, "is after all precisely people's methods of going at their problems in action" (p. 132). Smith sees democracy as the way of solving political problems consonant with the requirements of rationality. It can be rationally justified, in his view, because:

(1) separation of church and state acknowledges that political matters cannot be solved by deduction;

(2) separation of science and state similarly rejects recourse to induction;

(3) checks and balances provide defense against those who pose as bearers of truth;

(4) the principle of decision by poll recognizes that there is no "pompous" reason to deny the wishes of the majority; and

(5) equality of opportunity and freedom to participate acknowledge the same quality in the situation of political judgment.

This line of argument is, of course, familiar from the writings of theorists like Karl Popper and David Spitz;[22] and it has been more subtly worked through by these others. It is offered here simply to show how Smith applied his basic approach.

Moreover, it is not possible to accept as fully adequate Smith's implementing of his categorical dictum to come to self-consciousness as a guide to responsibility. There are important things about the way the world is which he does not perceive. Recommendations in the political sphere involve a curious and tragic paradox: Although their defense is couched in the language of fallibilism, their application may be secured through the use of the most dreadful instruments of coercion.[23] They must thus be tentative statements made in full knowledge that they may have the most categorical and irreversible consequences. That property of a certain sort ought to be protected by force, for example, is a tentative judgment supported by fallible arguments—and by definitive prison sentences. All discussions about political theory, thus, must be conducted with a live sense of human sufferers listening in.

Smith, like many who write on these topics, is deficient in such imagination. He notes:

> The tabloids scream of murders, rape, and theft; but the street on which I live is a quiet, law-abiding, happy place. My street is typical; that is why it has never, so far as I am aware, been in the news. The foundations of democracy are the foundations of that street and of the life that is led upon it [p. 121].

It is not cynical to comment that the income level and secure social status of the inhabitants probably contribute a little. Such comment is justified, first, by Smith's own point that exploring limiting conditions is essential to rational consideration, and, second, by his observation that logic and empirical evidence, although they cannot establish the correctness of any interpretation, can "uncover mistakes" (p. 48). Smith's argument does not require that the comment about "foundations" be taken as an empirical proposition, of course—although in his concluding comments defending the need for democratic dogma as supplement to reason because "most people do not think" (p. 209), he comes perilously close to proceeding as though it did. But this is not the point of the argument. All that is being said is that an adequate account of that street must bear in mind those who do not and cannot live by its rules and the reasons for this, and what is done to those others to shelter that street. Failing to do this is to suffer the kind of distortion that Marx and others have properly attacked through a pejorative application of the concept "ideology."[24] As this is written, Negro youths maraud through the streets of Chicago. It would be an impertinence and irrelevancy to urge upon them now the maxims of Mr. Smith's street.

Smith's fundamental recommendation, to move to responsibility through expanding self-consciousness, requires continuing and expanding implementation, although his cautions about the status of findings continue to be pertinent. Sheldon Wolin has suggested that the continuing tradition of the political theory enterprise, as conveyed in the great literature, probably provides the most reliable frame of reference for new theorizing,[25] and such rootedness in the enterprise does offer one important addition to the self-awareness required. For the rest, the task is one of continuous exploration, using such aids to the definition of mistakes as reason can provide, and developing whatever resources are needed to build and extend the sense of responsibility, to act in full respect for the integrity of the enterprise.[26]

If it be objected that such terms as "responsibility," "integrity," and the like are figments, the rejoinder must be that the history of human thought provides presumptive evidence that there are identifiable patterns of behavior, norms of a role which may be so labeled. Whether they should be identified by some more "neutral" terms comes back to the accumulated weight of the argument set forth in this essay as a whole, and bears its central thrust: that the alternative to the pursuit of reason for men engaged in intellectual pursuits is a tacit vindication of custom and the power which helps to render it operative, and thus an implicit threat to the possibility of intellectual pursuits themselves. This threat may and probably will not be clear and present. Decent scholars develop a Hume-like reliance on custom precisely during times when custom gives men like themselves secure and sheltered roots. But when, as in the Germany of the 'thirties, the customary friendliness to scholarly pursuits is destroyed, the absence of a consciously-fostered tradition of rationality is felt. Then the relatively more "rootless" sorts of intellectuals most likely to develop comprehensive approaches in the sense of the "enterprise" will be better oriented. Some may indeed be found among the wreckers, if captured by perverse and dark trends also present within the tradition; but others will be the backbone of the opposition. These two facts do not balance out: Those who succumb to dark heresies may aid but will not initiate or propel the attack on reason; the defense of reason in contrast may well get its sustaining impulse precisely from the intellectuals in the tradition. The confrontation between Miguel de Unamuno and the Fascist general, Millan Astray, in 1936, embodies all the points involved: The general summed up when he shouted, "Down with the Intellectuals! Long live Death!"[27] The dangers and risks attendant on the style of the intellectuals have been much denounced by writers during the fifties; but such denunciation is itself a recurrent phenomenon within the tradition.[28] Even when put in the most sweepingly general terms, its import ought not to be misunderstood: The challenge to the presumptions of rationalist dogmatism must be seen as a constantly necessary self-corrective; it must not be permitted to destroy.

The pursuit of reason, then, uncovers a "temperament of deciding," some standards of error, and respect for a tradition and role. These are formal and functional attributes; the content of the rational must be sought in the interpretation of issues more specific than the possibility of political theory itself.

The Locus of Rationality. Prospects for Research

You hardly ever even hear the word "wisdom" mentioned. . . . In almost four years of college . . . , the only time I can remember ever even hearing the expression "wise man" being used was in my freshman year, in Political Science! And you know how it was used? It was used in reference to some nice old poopy elder statesman who'd made a fortune in the stock market and then gone to Washington to be an advisor to President Roosevelt. . . . I'm not saying that happens to everybody, but I just get so upset when I think about it I could die.   —*Franny and Zooey*, by J. D. Salinger

The prime danger which bedevils discussions of rationality in politics is some variant of Platonic transcendentalism. The outputs of political processes can be accounted rational only, it is then argued, if men governed by the rational temper make political decisions, and also fully control their implementation. Rational administration is to take the place of politics. To argue in this way, it is not necessary to have some grand and completed scheme of rationality in mind. Sometimes the area to be attended in this "rational" way is expressly identified as a restricted segment of the whole, defined by some presumed highest necessity (national security, for example, or economic prosperity) or by an alleged consensus on the ends to be sought. Other times, the quasi-Platonic strategy is disguised in the language of "coordination": no one wise man, it is then said, can expect to know all or to promote all defensible interests; but cooperation and communication among all those involved can produce coherence and rationality. Reasoning must be put in command. The prime objection to such an approach can already be found in the *Politics* of Aristotle. Political rule properly involves considerations other than the rational solution to this or that problem—including, for example, a care for the instruments of ruling—and it rules through a coercion quite different from the "coerciveness" of right reason in the context of rational dispute.

From the standpoint of the contemporary conception of reason set forth above, moreover, it is clear that the role and identity requisite to sustaining prime loyalty to reasoning are different from those normally associated with participation in political rule.[29] But lest it appear that what is said here amounts to a lament that things just aren't "up" to the perfection of men of reason, it should also be noted that reason as conceived here is not a prime innovator of values: It calculates, balances, orders, conserves; but that to which it reacts in a disciplined and disciplining way are the passions and aspirations and activities of living men. Making sense of political life presupposes existence of a fabric of activities in which the activity of investigating rationality only forms one strand. Denial that this is the reality of things may result in terroristic efforts to force the recalcitrant materials of political life into an impossible mold. But this is, after all, not as probable as feared by some commentators; intellectual errors are a less potent political factor than is sometimes fancied, as is unfortunately also true of intellectual discoveries. A more likely outcome is a debasement of the concept "rationality," its use to justify or disguise events and decisions conforming in fact neither to the inadequate theory of the transcendental theorist nor to the standards of an adequately rational assessment.

An extreme reaction against transcendent views of the locus of rationality produces, curiously enough, much the same debasement of critical standards. When immanent theories are developed into a sort of theodicy, the rational comes to be equated with any decision or outcome that may happen to be produced by those in authority. Political rule is then said to be always rational, in the only sense of that term considered acceptable. For fairly obvious reasons, such a position is often not argued but simply assumed by many (including, predictably enough, many in the highest places) who equate accession to power with an access of rationality (and not merely access to "intelligence").

One source of such an assumption is the refusal to distinguish between authority and rationality. It is held then, in effect, that a showing of authority automatically carries with it a presumption of rationality, even if the theory of authority itself rests, for example, on a principle of consent which has no self-evident connection with the rationality of decisions. In cases of this latter sort, matters often shift from unexamined assumption to explicit argument. Because it is impossible to discover certain rational truth about matters of judgment and interpretation, it is held, the authoritative processes provide all the rational defense possible for any given course of action. Such arguments, for the most part, refer to some species of democratic representation held to be peculiarly legitimized by the theory of consent. Two points need to be made about this sort of contention. First, even if the conception of rationality relied on were fully adequate, there would remain the need to cope with and account for the expectation that these authoritative processes will yield decisions supporting the processes themselves: Problems of minority rights and a majority decision to abolish majority rule illustrate this point. Second, however, the conception of rationality is not adequate. Men who profess adherence to it do not operate in accordance with it, either in their private lives or in their advocacy of political recommendations.[30] That reason is fallible is important, of course, but that it has no recourse save deference to majority opinion is a position quite literally indefensible—not because it cannot be argued without circularity; this quality it would share with all justifications of rationality; but rather because it cannot be circularly defended without blatant misstatement of fact: Men simply do not consider the opinion of a majority as adequate reason for all or even most of their judgments. The issue of political rationality and its possible sources within the political system, then, remain distinct from the issue of political authority.

None of this is intended to argue that there are no valid insights embodied in even the extreme transcendentalist or immanentist positions just criticized. The objection has been to an unwarranted telescoping of complex arguments, oversimple and overgeneral assumptions of self-evidence. If "Platonic" institutions have a place in political life, it is necessary to justify and specify them, to show the conditions under which and the reasons why they might be expected to serve the ends of rationality. If rational outcomes may be the product of processes little influenced by deliberate application of habits of rational judgment, this too must be established and fenced about with the findings of disciplined inquiry. That this or that institution will provide the greatest possible assurance of rationality under specified circumstances is, of course, always finally a judgment of political theory, a recommendation based on interpretation and not as such subject to verification by empirical techniques or logical scrutiny. But the reasons urged in behalf of the judgment must each be subjected to the most rigorous applicable test, and for such a judgment the full list of reasons must include accurate statements about matters which can indeed be put in the form of testable propositions. The autonomy of political theory is no license for ignorance about the way things are; it is no excuse for shoddy or sentimental guessing about things that can be known. Political theory thus welcomes every improvement in accurate measurement of the measurable, every logical clarification of the needlessly obscure. What political theorists really need from political scientists with other gifts and interests is more serviceable information, answers to questions properly put.

Much has been written on the problem here under review. Political theory has distinguished a number of important and relevant questions; disciplined factual inquiry has collected some answers. But there has been something shamefaced about it: Writing of this sort has been set down as somehow "journalistic," and the writers have excused their concern with these matters as somehow extramural, the indulgence of a public-spirited hobby; or they have been written off by professional colleagues as newspaper columnists, dilettantes, or propagandists. Such attitudes are destructive in two directions: They distort the emphases within the profession by deterring many of the most gifted and independent-minded from taking on the most significant investigations and by penalizing those who do, and they tend to lower the quality of the work done on such questions, because—in the manner of a self-fulfilling prophecy—they often relegate it to charlatans and hirelings or to the off-guard leisure hours of the qualified. And such destructive attitudes are grounded on a fundamental misunderstanding of the genius of disciplined political inquiry. There is no possibility of discussing in detail here the many important achievements which indicate that such misunderstanding is not universal and may be, in fact, diminishing, despite the dogmatism of some. Three conflicting lines of inquiry will be briefly described and some reasons given for the need to pursue and eventually to integrate all three.

The attempt to specify and defend the dimension of the problem seen by Plato and Hobbes can be identified with writers as seemingly diverse as John Dewey, Karl Mannheim, Walter Lippmann, and C. Wright Mills.[31] They undertake to explain precisely how and why the rational temperament is necessary for the production of policy outcomes of which reason can approve and they offer detailed recommendations for ways to infuse political power with such intelligence, or at least see the necessity of so doing. Dewey attempts to account for and to enhance the problem-solving capacity of democratic "publics"; Mannheim contends that in a critical epoch of "reconstruction" a planning intelligentsia must and can gain access to the political elite; Lippmann seeks to show the conditions under which a political leadership responsible to rational principles can emerge and maintain itself; and Mills charges his "power elite" precisely with a structural incapacity to heed reason, and he explores ways of meeting the conditions under which, in his view, mechanisms like those envisioned by Dewey will operate. If these efforts can still be generally classed as transcendent, they approach the Hobbesian model more closely than the Platonic, and reveal considerable awareness of the need to account for the possibility of links between reasoning and political rule. They do not simply assume that the two are identical.

Frequently offered in direct rebuttal of such an approach are works by prominent exponents of immanentist views. The books of Friedrich Hayek exemplify this development, as does the far more moderate and masterful recent statement by Charles Lindblom.[32] These object, first, to what they take to be a false conception of what rational coping with problems can look like, arguing that a rational strategy proceeds by specific incremental management of problems as they come up in answerable form and not by sweeping efforts to solve problems or anticipate future ills. And, second, they attempt to show that rational results in this can be attained—perhaps best or only attained—by processes which Hayek and his associates tend to equate completely with market-like mechanisms, and which Lindblom sees in a much subtler and more diverse array as processes of "partisan mutual adjustment." With such work, the development of this sort of position has come far from mystical assurances about the beneficent design of the divine plan or closely related dependence on analogies to mechanical physics of checks and balances, which both can now be seen as metaphorical allusions to precisely the sorts of processes being detailed in the contemporary literature.[33]

The third major possibility requiring further exploration has been pursued in interesting ways by some Marxist writers, although most Marxists are properly classed as "Platonists" of a rather obvious sort, and although neither Marx nor his followers can lay sole claim to this approach.[34] If the first group cited here emphasizes the need for securing access to political power for trained intelligence, and if the second stresses the capacity of properly conceived peculiarly political processes to produce rational results, the third to be mentioned concentrates on the contribution to rationality of novel political forces thrusting themselves on the scene with great spiritual force, tearing open long-standing conventions, destroying established power alignments, and forcing consideration of radically new perspectives. In the works of Rosa Luxemburg, such a conception looked to revolutionary processes themselves, the dynamics of revolutionary happenings, to achieve such results; Marxists like Lukacs and Trotsky and many non-Marxists variously associated with contemporary "New Left" or "New Politics" tendencies concentrate on the impact and inner processes of movements, either outright revolutionary or otherwise profoundly radical; and some theories of dictatorship, in virulent and defiantly irrational form, but also some moderate proponents of complex theories of the American presidency, for example, pay special attention to leadership as role and process.[35] The problem for all such writers is, of course, to define boundaries between such creative disruptions and redefinitions and meaningless destruction.

Much needs to be done before any one of these possibilities can be excluded; and it seems likely that a way will have to be found to combine them. A *prima facie* case can be made for attending to each: The demonstrated capabilities of a technocracy armed with computer technology and empowered by the fears and uncertainties of lay politicians militate against dismissing the first as irrelevant; persuasive accounts of some political systems brilliantly synthesized by Lindblom and supported by other researchers working along pluralist lines give importance to the second; and the phenomena of rising revolutionary expectations and the manifest accomplishments of movements associated with them give weight to the third. Whether one of these approaches can provide enough flexibility to comprehend the insights of the others remains to be seen. At the moment, it appears, further discussion must begin with the assessment of Lindblom. But these and other dicta are not the decisive thing. What matters is that political theory can give direction and meaning to this whole discussion and is vitally interested in its progress. These, then, appear from a standpoint of political theory as the most promising and important developments in political science today.

In *Magister Ludi,* Hermann Hesse tells of a time when all mental discipline is rigorously applied to problems of an immensely complex and endlessly fascinating game, a game expressly divorced from all contact with ordinary life. He explains well the emergence of this discipline from the revulsion among the intelligent youth against the flabbiness and imprecision of an intellectual life preoccupied with questions about the presumed "meanings of things." It stems from a revulsion against an "age of the newspaper columnist." Hesse writes:

> The young people who now set out to pursue cultural and social studies no longer understood by this a dilettante's sampling of this and that at the universities, where the remains of an earlier cultivation were passed on by well-known and long-winded professors, lacking all authority. They were now to be committed to a course of study as rigorous, perhaps even more rigorous and systematic as that formerly pursued by engineers and technicians.[36]

But having clearly stated the motives which produced the new discipline, Hesse goes on to show its sterility. Over against it, he then sets the vitality of the irrational. The point of this essay has been to show, first, that Hesse offers a choice based on a false disjunction. The alternatives need not be those between rational sterility and some irrational fever. Second, however, it is necessary to realize that developments within disciplines like political science can come to the point where such a choice is all that is available. Disciplined political inquiry has power to prevent such an abandonment of reason in intellectual life. Its power to affect events in other spheres is, of course, immeasurably less.

[NOTES]

The research upon which this paper rests received financial support from the Assigned Research Program of The Ohio State University. An early draft of the essay was subjected to helpful criticism by faculty seminars at Ohio State and at the State University of New York at Binghamton.

1. Charles E. Lindblom, *The Intelligence of Democracy. Decision Making through Mutual Adjustment* (New York, 1965), pp. 206–207n. Substituting the general question "what is" for Lindblom's quite specific inquiry about the worth of "fragmented decision-making" misrepresents Lindblom's approach on a point not pertinent to that being here made. Lindblom attaches great importance to limiting questions to specific alternatives and to avoiding such general formulation of questions.
2. Seymour Martin Lipset, *Political Man* (Garden City, N.Y., 1963), pp. 64f. "Effectiveness means actual performance, the extent to which the system satisfies the basic functions of government as most of the population and such powerful groups within it as big business or the armed forces see them. Legitimacy involves the capacity of the system to engender and maintain the belief that the existing political institutions are the most appropriate ones for the society." Note that the attempt to define "effectiveness" without presuming to define "basic functions of government" makes it hard to sustain the distinction. See below, concerning the attempt to define "rationality" in terms of "authority," pp. 82–83.
3. A distinction between "substantial" and "formal" rationality plays an important part in the work of Max Weber, but it is not put there in a form fully useful for the sort of historical survey here intended. Because Weber tends to equate "rationality" with a particular range of more or less formal alternatives, he actually treats "substantial" rationality as an unanalyzed residual category used to refer to standards less rigorously calculating than the truly formal, but too close to rational process to be called "irrational." As is almost universally true in the history of thought on these questions, he becomes clearer whenever he discusses one or the other sort of rationality in specific relationship to the actual social and intellectual processes said to generate it. Hans Gerth and C. Wright Mills, eds., *From Max Weber* (New York, 1958), pp. 228, 331.
4. David Hume, *A Treatise of Human Nature*, ed. by L. A. Selby-Bigge (Oxford, 1958 ed.), pp. 537–538.
5. Thomas Hobbes, *Leviathan*, ed. by Michael Oakeshott (New York, 1962), pp. 191–197, 282, 361–362.
6. For a recent statement, see J. Roland Pennock, "Reason in Legislative Decisions," *Rational Decision*, Nomos VII, ed. by Carl J. Friedrich (New York, 1964), pp. 103–104.
7. To avoid possible misunderstanding, it should be noted that the processes usually designated as "rationalization" since Max Weber, but confusingly labeled "formal rationality" by Karl Mannheim, and set over against "substantial rationality," are here given no special preference. They are, in the usage of this essay, social processes embodying and presumed to satisfy the standards of a certain conception of rationality. From the present historical perspective, neither the adequacy of that conception nor the efficacy of the processes is better established than the beliefs associated with Plato's phi-

losopher-king. Cf. Karl Mannheim, *Man and Society in an Age of Reconstruction* (London, 1960), pp. 51f.

8. For a compelling statement of this matter, see Karl Mannheim, *Ideology and Utopia* (New York, 1946).

9. See, e. g., Robert K. Merton, "Karl Mannheim and the Sociology of Knowledge," in *Social Theory and Social Structure* (Glencoe, 1957), pp. 490ff., and Ernst Grunwald, *Das Problem der Soziologie des Wissens* (Vienna-Leipzig, 1934).

10. Psychologists appear more aware than political scientists often seem to be that all measurable data are indices and that it is a separate question to ascertain whether commensurable quantities (votes or responses to public opinion sampling) are in fact homogeneous in the sense of being indicators of similar processes. Edwin N. Barker, "Humanistic Psychology and Scientific Method" (paper presented to the Third Annual Meeting of the American Association of Humanistic Psychology, Chicago, Illinois, 1965. Mimeographed).

11. Such calm statement of the situation would itself render this discussion suspect to many apologists for the earlier traditions of political theory. The challenges have generated a disputation at once tedious and hysterical. Among the symptoms of hysteria, according to an early listing by Freud, are a deadening of certain modes of perception (hemianesthesia), contraction of the field of vision, and violent, purposeless (epileptiform) convulsions. Anyone familiar with the uninformed hostility to science, cultural provincialism, or violent outbursts that too often mar the affirmations of humanism in political theory may be tempted to further extensions of the psychiatric metaphor. And, as if in symbiotic relationship to the hysterics, the critics of the tradition in turn repeatedly charge the same frantic windmills.

12. Reference is to writers like Arthur Macmahon, Harvey C. Mansfield, Earl D. Latham, and many others interested in political structures and in policy areas.

13. Jack L. Walker, "A Reply to 'Further Reflections on "The Elitist Theory of Democracy,"'" *American Political Science Review*, LX (1966), 391.

14. Barker, *op. cit.*, p. 10.

15. For a fine analysis see William E. Connolly, *Political Science and Ideology* (New York, 1967).

16. David Hume, *Enquiries Concerning the Human Understanding*, ed. by L. A. Selby-Bigge (Oxford, 1902), pp. 41f. A persuasive contemporary statement of a position close to Hume's is by Michael Oakeshott, *Rationalism in Politics* (New York, 1962); cf. David Kettler, "The Cheerful Discourses of Michael Oakeshott," *World Politics*, XVI (1964), 483–489.

17. Adam Ferguson, *Principles of Moral and Political Science* (Edinburgh, 1792), II, 3. See David Kettler, *The Social and Political Thought of Adam Ferguson* (Columbus, 1965), Chap. 5, especially p. 136n23.

18. John Plamenatz, *Man and Society* (New York, 1963), Introduction, and Sheldon S. Wolin, *Politics and Vision* (Boston, 1960), Chap. 1.

19. Plamenatz, *op. cit.*, p. xix.

20. Plamenatz writes: "The putting and answering of questions of this sort is an activity not less rational and not less difficult than scientific enquiry, and neither more nor less useful." *Ibid.*; and cf. Wolin, *op. cit.*, pp. 11–15.

21. James Ward Smith, *A Theme for Reason* (Princeton, 1957), p. 5.

22. Karl Popper, *The Open Society and Its Enemies* (Princeton, 1951), and David Spitz, *Democracy and the Challenge of Power* (New York, 1958).

23. E. V. Walter, "Power and Violence," *American Political Science Review,* LVIII (1964), 350f., clarifies the relation between power and violence.

24. For an illuminating group of papers on this theme see *Ideologie,* ed. Kurt Lenk (Neuwied, 1961). See also Connolly, *op. cit.* Connections between the ideology theme and questions here discussed are further explored in David Kettler, "Sociology of Knowledge and Moral Philosophy: The Place of Traditional Problems in the Formation of [Karl] Mannheim's Thought," *Political Science Quarterly* (1967).

25. Wolin, *op. cit.,* p. 25.

26. Connolly, *op. cit.,* develops an interesting, less ambitious conception of "responsible ideology."

27. The film *To Die in Madrid* presents Unamuno's statement and photographs of the event. A summary and excerpts appear in Alvah Bessie's review of the film in *Ramparts,* V (1966), 59–60.

28. For the scholar-intellectual distinction and an example of one sort of denunciation, see Daniel Bell, *The End of Ideology* (New York, 1961), pp. 393f.

29. Cf. Robert K. Merton, "The Intellectual in Bureaucracy," in *Social Theory and Social Structure, op. cit.,* pp. 162f.

30. See Lindblom, *op. cit.,* pp. 247f.

31. John Dewey, *The Public and Its Problems* (New York, 1927); Karl Mannheim, *Man and Society . . .* and *Freedom, Power and Democratic Planning* (New York, 1950); Walter Lippmann, *The Public Philosophy* (New York, 1955); and C. Wright Mills, *The Power Elite* (New York, 1957).

32. Friedrich A. Hayek, *The Road to Serfdom* (Chicago, 1944) and *The Counter-Revolution of Science* (Glencoe, 1950); and Lindblom, *op. cit.*

33. Often in the older literature the metaphors and quite detailed analyses stand side by side. This is widely acknowledged for Montesquieu, Adam Smith, and James Madison. It is no less true of Hegel.

34. What is involved is development of insights contained in Rousseau's work. For Marx's most interesting discussion of these problems see his early political essays, especially "Debatten über das Holzdiebstahlgesetz" and "[Kritik des Hegelschen Staatsrechts]" not yet available in English, but presented in an excellent collection, *Frühe Schriften,* ed. by Hans-Joachim Lieber and Peter Furth (Stuttgart, 1962), I, 208–426.

35. Rosa Luxemburg, *Reform or Revolution* (Bombay, 1951) and *The Russian Revolution* (Ann Arbor, 1961); Georg Lukacs, *Geschichte und Klassenbewusstsein* (Berlin, 1923), especially pp. 261f.; Leon Trotsky, *Terrorism and Communism* (Ann Arbor, 1961). See also the complex and sensitive statement in Leszek Kolakowski, *Der Mensch ohne Alternative* (Munich, 1961), especially pp. 200–215. Best known among the recent American writings stressing the leadership function of the presidency are the Kennedy-age interpretations by Arthur Schlesinger, Jr., and James Macgregor Burns.

36. Hermann Hesse, *Das Glasperlenspiel* (Zurich, 1943), I, 50 (translation supplied).

[4] CHANGING CONCEPTIONS OF POLITICAL LEGITIMACY: ABANDONMENT OF THEOCRACY IN THE ISLAMIC WORLD

Students of Islam have often noted the rigidity of the Islamic creed. In the eyes of Muslims the Qur'ān, the revealed word of God, contains all that has happened and all that will happen, the perfect solution to all questions of belief and conduct. It is supplemented by the traditions (*Hadīths*) about the sayings and actions of Mohammed, God's messenger and prophet; and Qur'ān and traditions together are the sources of the sacred law of Islam (*Sharī'a*) which is infallible and unchanging. And yet, both the early and later stages of Islamic law show development and change, adaptation and growth, and these adjustments to the realities of life are especially pronounced in regard to the question of who should rule the community and by what right such rulership should be exercised—the question of political legitimacy. The purpose of this essay is to trace the stages in this process of doctrinal change and relate it to changes in Islamic society. The paper is thus analytical and theoretical rather than descriptive—it contains no facts unfamiliar to Islamic or Middle East scholars.

I

Mohammed had organized his followers in a political community which has been called variously a theocracy or nomocracy. It was a commonwealth at once religious and political in which God and his revealed law were the supreme authority and where Mohammed, his apostle, was the Lord's vice-regent on earth. The prophet's political power was derived from his religious mission; the primary purpose of government was the promotion and protection of the new religious faith. Even more than in other societies of the ancient Middle East, the Islamic community at Medina therefore knew no distinction between the temporal and the spiritual, between church and state. There existed no separation between man's obligations as a believer and his duties as a citizen. The temporal and the spiritual power were one and the same. The Islamic state was governed by God's law revealed to Mohammed, his deputy. The latter functioned both as religious prophet and temporal head of the community. Mohammed had founded what one observer has called a "theocratie laique."[1]

The Prophet died in A.D. 632 without designating a successor and the Qur'ān was similarly silent on the question of how to appoint a new ruler. It is likely that Mohammed refrained from choosing a successor because he recognized the strength of Arab tribal tradition according to which the members of the tribe themselves elected a chieftain primarily on the basis of his qualities as a leader and his ability to inspire personal loyalty among his followers. In line with this principle, an assembly of Medinans elected Abū Bakr, Mohammed's faithful friend, as their new leader, and he was called the successor (*caliph*) of the Prophet. Abū Bakr's political power was as complete as that of Mohammed though he did not claim to be a divinely inspired prophet. The first caliph nominated his successor, Omar, and this nomination was accepted and confirmed by the community of Medina. The third and fourth caliphs were also elected; however, violence now played a considerable role in the succession. Of the four caliphs following Mohammed, only the first died a natural death; the other three were murdered in office.

A somewhat greater measure of stability was reached with the fifth caliph, Mu'āwiyah, who four years before his death nominated his son as his successor, thus founding a dynasty (the Umayyads) and formally introducing the hereditary principle. This precedent was followed for the next four hundred years. By the time the Abbasid dynasty in Baghdad replaced the Umayyads in the year 750, hereditary autocratic rule had become firmly established, a practice leaning heavily upon the ancient Persian concept of kingship by divine right. "The prince, isolated from the uniform herd of his subjects, consecrated by divine designation for his office, legitimized by his descent from a long line of kings, guarded by an elaborate etiquette, . . . this type of despot," notes von Grunebaum, "now merged successfully with the theocratic representative of Allah and much less successfully, with the Arab chieftain of olden days."[2] Whereas early tradition had considered the caliphate as an elective office, with precedent pointing to a minimum of five electors, the number of electors was eventually reduced to one, a change that amounted to an implicit acceptance of the hereditary principle with the predecessor appointing his successor. The myth of election continued to live alongside, drawing strength from the oath of allegiance paid to the new prince in the capital and throughout the growing Islamic empire.

Islamic constitutional doctrine developed gradually as a rationalization of practice followed during the first two centuries of Islam. "The theory as embodied in the works of Mohammedan theologians and jurists was elaborated in order to suit already operating facts."[3] According to this theory, the ultimate source of political authority was God who had provided for a ruler (*imām* [leader] or caliph) to be obeyed by the people in order to ensure peace and protect the faith. It was God who established princes and deprived them of power as he saw fit, though the representatives of the community chose the caliph, acting, as it were, in God's name. The candidate for the caliphate had to be of legal age, a freeman of the masculine sex, in full possession of his physical and mental faculties, knowledgeable in the divine law as well as in the art of war and, last but not least, a descendant of the *Quraysh,* the tribe to which the Prophet had belonged. The functions of the caliph were to govern the Muslim community as the successor of the Prophet and to protect and enforce the holy law. By accepting his office, the caliph promised to exercise his powers within the limits of the law and he confirmed this promise in a contract—*bay'a*—with the representatives of the community. If he violated this contract, the people were absolved of allegiance and could elect another ruler.

This was the theory as it evolved in its early form and for which theological sanction was found and read into the Shari'a—the Qur'ān and the traditions. The former contained a number of injunctions to obey the messenger of God, Mohammed, and others set in authority over the community.[4] In the case of the traditions—the usages ascribed to Mohammed—there is considerable evidence to indicate that some of them were manipulated to suit the interests of the ruling group almost from the beginning. Inasmuch as the doctrine of the contract between ruler and ruled made no provision for removing a bad caliph short of revolution, the door was opened to those who stressed the danger of chaos that would follow from calling a ruler to account and who insisted on practically unquestioning obedience. This dread of anarchy was reinforced by the political instability, which was real enough. Disorder was fed by the uneasy coexistence of many different ethnic and cultural groups in the same empire, by the continuing strength shown by tribal kinship groups undermining the loyalty exacted by the central government, and by the existence of many sons in the polygamous families of the ruling dynasty encouraging rivalries and intrigues. In such a situation, characterized by frequent assassinations and palace revolutions, many scholars serving the caliphs emphasized the need for submissiveness to the powers that be. Endeavoring to give this teaching theological grounding and to work it into the mainstream of Islamic law, they produced sayings of the Prophet in defense of their tenets, "and as time went on these became more and more categorical and detailed." The tradition, Sir Hamilton Gibb concludes, "was being invaded by forgeries on a vast scale, sometimes by editing and supplementing genuine old traditions, more often by simple inventions."[5] Ignaz Goldziher, the most outstanding critical student of the Hadīth, does not hesitate to speak of "pious fraud."[6]

The majority of the traditions relating to political conduct had the basic aim of buttressing an uncompromising doctrine of civic obedience. A few examples are indicated—many of them bear a striking resemblance to the teachings of early Christianity that similarly aimed at shoring up civic order and stability: "The Apostle of God said: 'Whoso obeys me, obeys God, and whoso rebels against me, rebels against God; whoso obeys the ruler, obeys me; and whoso rebels against the ruler, rebels against me.'"[7] All earthly authority was seen as being of divine appointment, with a tyrant functioning as God's punishment for man's sin: "The Prophet said: 'Do not abuse those who rule. If they act uprightly, they shall have their reward, and your duty is to show gratitude. If they do evil, they shall bear the burden, and your duty is to endure patiently. They are a chastisement which God inflicts upon those who he will; therefore accept the chastisement of God, not with indignation and wrath, but with humility and meekness.' "⁸ The occasional tradition affirming the right and duty of Muslims to disobey and rebel against a ruler violating God's law was thus effectively checked by the introduction of those far more numerous sayings that branded the creation of disorder without adequate justification as a mortal sin. Reform movements and rebellions insisting on the religious orthodoxy of the ruling dynasty were suppressed—a subject to which we will return.

The prestige and power of the early Abbasid caliphs was great. But the enormous Arab empire that the first caliphs had built did not last. Spain broke away under an independent ruler in 756. By the year 909, Morocco, Tunisia, Egypt, and Syria in effect had become separate states, some claiming their own caliphate. The orthodox theory had finally to be abandoned when in the middle of the tenth century the caliph of Baghdad became a prisoner and pensioner of a military clique. Effective power was now wielded by the sultan, a military chieftain, whom the caliph was forced to invest with a show of legitimacy. The caliph still performed certain ceremonial functions but essentially he had become a figurehead. A *de facto* separation between church and state had come about and the jurists once again adjusted the theory to the new reality.

Abandoning any attempt to defend and maintain the dignity of the caliph, the religious teachers (*ulamā*) and jurists now taught that anyone in effective possession of political power had to be obeyed, no matter how irregular his assumption of power or impious and barbarous his conduct. The Islamic community, no longer tied to any particular constitutional scheme, was held to be intact as long as the secular government formally recognized the Sharī'a, consulted the ulamā, and conditions existed enabling individual Muslims to obey the holy law. The sultan's power was legitimized by the legal fiction of deriving his authority from that of the caliph; the new practice and the teaching of the theologians and jurists defending it were declared to be binding since the community had accepted it. The saying credited to Mohammed, "my community will never agree upon an error," reinforced the hold of precedent. "Where the legists were forced to succumb to facts," notes a student of the sociology of Islam, "they called in aid the doctrine that *ijmā'*, the agreement, actually the acquiescence of the community, justifies whatever happens in Islam."⁹

The fact that Islamic constitutional practice and theory had traveled a long way was frankly acknowledged by al-Ghazāli (1064–1111), a scholar often acclaimed as the greatest Muslim after Mohammed. In his eyes the circumstances of the time required the acceptance of the ignominious position of the caliph and of the fact that government now was a consequence solely of military power:

> The concessions made by us are not spontaneous, but necessity makes lawful what is forbidden. We know it is not allowed to feed on a dead animal: still, it would be worse to die of hunger. Of those that contend that the caliphate is dead forever and irreplaceable, we should like to ask: what is to be preferred, anarchy and the stoppage of social life for lack of a properly constituted authority, or acknowledgement of the existing order, whatever it be? Of these two alternatives, the jurists cannot but choose the latter.[10]

Actual power was in the hands of the sultan, al-Ghazāli admitted, though the validity of his government depended upon the sultan's oath of allegiance to the caliph. However, since al-Ghazāli accepted the practice of the day according to which the caliph was appointed by the sultan, the function of the caliph was clearly reduced to being that of a symbol of unity, divine guidance, and historical continuity.[11]

Eventually the fiction of the sultan's delegated authority became so apparent that it was abandoned altogether. The legitimacy of the sultan was divorced from that of the caliph, success in assuming and maintaining the rulership being the only criterion. The Egyptian judge Ibn-Jamā'ah (1241–1333) realistically described this state of affairs:

> The sovereign has a right to govern until another and stronger one shall oust him from power and rule in his State. The latter will rule by the same title and will have to be acknowledged on the same grounds; for a government, however objectionable, is better than none at all; and between two evils we must choose the lesser.[12]

The above was written a few years after the Mongols had stormed Baghdad in 1258 and had put the caliph to death. From that time on the institution of the caliphate was essentially extinct, a development noted by the famous fourteenth-century Arab philosopher of history, Ibn-Khaldūn. To be sure, the Mamlūk rulers of Egypt for two and a half centuries kept a descendant of the last Abbasid caliphs as a puppet, and the Turks, capturing Cairo in 1517, were said to have transferred the caliphate to the Ottoman line. But while the caliphate thus lived on in name until the twentieth century, its meaning had changed completely. In the late Ottoman period, the title "caliph" was increasingly assumed by sultans wanting to embellish their authority.

This, then, was the pattern of Islamic government that developed after the destruction of the Baghdad caliphate. Any *de facto* ruler declaring his fealty to the Sharī'a had a claim on the obedience of his Muslim subjects. The clerical class, the ulamā, at times denounced the unrighteous ways of a sultan, but by and large they staunchly supported the government and warned against civil disorder. In practice as well as in theory, neither the ulamā nor the individual was held to have rights as individuals or groups that could be asserted against the ruling authority. Inasmuch as Islam had not produced a separate religious establishment that could successfully challenge the state, no conflict developed between church and state as in medieval Christianity. Reinforced by the poverty of the Muslim countries and their economic and social stagnation, the dominant trend was one of unrelieved political quietism, supported and encouraged by religious arguments. No matter how evil a ruler, the subject's duty was to obey. "The *civitas Dei*," writes von Grunebaum, "had failed and the Muslim community had accepted its failure."[13]

II

The development sketched out so far is that of the general body of orthodox Muslims known as *Sunnis*. But alongside this mainstream Islam has abounded in smaller tributaries—sects and heresies that had their own theological views as well as different conceptions of political rule. At times these sects were able to gain a hearing and eventually achieve a compromise with the majority Sunni position. In other instances, however, the challenge was sufficiently radical so as to make peaceful resolution of differences impossible. Such was the case with a movement that has been called the earliest sect of Islam, the so-called *Khawarij* or Kharijites (seceders).

The early Khawarij were Bedouins who as untamed nomads resented the encroachments of the new Islamic state upon the freedoms of their tribal society. This spirit of rebellion first burst out in open revolt during the reign of the fourth caliph, Ali. Later, disturbed over what they regarded as the irreligious and lax behavior of the Umayyad caliphs, these "Puritans of Islam" continued to spread terror among their opponents, often killing women and children as well as male Muslims who disagreed with them. The Khawarij regarded themselves as saints under moral obligation to revolt against sinful government and its supporters. God alone in their eyes was entitled to complete fealty. Applying the strict standards of the Prophet, they concluded that the Umayyad caliphs were unbelievers and therefore had to be fought.

The doctrinal teaching of the Khawarij was far from unified, with heresiologists listing as many as twenty-one subsects.[14] Some of these, it appears, stressed the freedom of the human will and opposed the concept of predestination. In a manner strikingly similar to the teachings of the revolutionary Anabaptists of the sixteenth century,[15] the Khawarij insisted that man was responsible for his own actions, that God wishes the good and not the bad, and that it was therefore right and necessary to kill all impious and tyrannical rulers and those following them.[16] Some court theologians, in turn, did their best to counter this view by embracing the necessity of believing in fate. All acts, they said, must necessarily occur as decreed by God, and this included the cruel deeds of tyrants, whom it was wrong, therefore, to resist.[17]

Both the Khawarij and their opponents created their own traditions to provide doctrinal support for their respective positions. For example, the Prophet was asked, according to a tradition invoked by the Khawarij: " 'Your cousin Mu'awija commands us to do this and that, should we obey him?' 'Obey him,' spoke the Prophet, 'in obedience to God, oppose him in his opposition to God.' "[18] Against this and similar traditions justifying resistance to irreligious rulers, court theologians invoked sayings of Mohammed praising unconditional obedience. Still, the Khawarij for a time had many followers. They benefited from the social tensions building up between the Arab aristocracy, the individualistic Bedouins, and the non-Arab converts. All upright Muslims, they taught, had the same rights in the Islamic community, whether rich or poor, freeman or slave, Arab or non-Arab. The legitimacy of their leader, the imām, depended upon his personal merit, and if he erred his followers had the divine right to remove him.

Like some segments of early Calvinism, the Khawarij were puritanical in their approach to daily living. They forbade music, singing, tobacco, and liquor. "The complete orientation of Khariji life," writes a recent student, "was to eschatological ends. There was among them a strong desire to die, for life in this world was to them a panorama of shallowness and deceit; nothing was of any value in it. The only thing worth pursuing in this profane world was a life of purity and asceticism in preparation for the next world."[19] Since most of the Khawarij were ordinary people, busy with earning their meager living, this great stress on piety also resulted in promoting the prestige of the learned, leading at times, as later in Calvin's Geneva, to the dictatorship of the religious teachers, in this case the ulamā.[20]

By the end of the eighth century the Khawarij movement had been militarily crushed, though small colonies of them survive to this day in Libya, Algeria, Oman, and Zanzibar. However, their fanaticism, their egalitarianism and its anarchical consequences in the meantime had helped push their opponents to the other extreme of increasingly deprecating the right of rebellion against unjust authority. Just as St. Paul, Luther, and Calvin reacted to the antinomianism of the early Christians and of the sixteenth-century Anabaptists, respectively, by emphasizing the duty to obey the powers that be, the orthodox theologians under the Abbasids, strengthened by the Persian tradition of divine-right kingship, taught that any revolt, no matter how extreme the provocation, was the most heinous of crimes. This doctrine, writes Sir Hamilton Gibb, "came to be consecrated in the juristic maxim, 'Sixty years of tyranny are better than an hour of civil strife.' "[21]

Also benefiting from widespread social unrest during the first century of Islam was the emergence of another, far more important, Islamic sect, the *Shi'a.* Shi'ism began as a legitimist political movement which demanded that the caliphate be entrusted to the house of Ali, Mohammed's son-in-law and paternal first cousin. Soon, however, the Shi'ites attracted the support of the underprivileged classes, especially in the garrison cities planted by the Arabs in conquered lands. These Muslims of non-Arabic descent, writes Bernard Lewis, rallied to a form of Islam "that challenged the legitimacy of the existing Arab aristocratic state. Their aspiration was for an order in which all Muslims would be equal and Arab birth would no longer carry privileges."[22]

In a situation where church and state were closely interwoven, this challenge to the existing social system necessarily led to theological schism and the formation of sects. Common to many of the Shi'ite sects was the belief in a divinely illuminated leader who would lead the oppressed out of their misery—a messianic figure or *Mahdi* (the rightly-guided one). Practically all the Shi'ites attributed superhuman qualities to their *imām*, a political and religious leader who, unlike the caliph of the orthodox Sunnis, could define and modify religious dogma and doctrine. The imām of the Shi'a was appointed by his predecessor rather than elected; he was sinless and infallible and could not be deposed.

The most extreme of the early Shi'ite sects was one known as the *Ismā'īlis*. Because of the secretive, quasi-masonic character of the movement, an amalgam of Shi'ite and Persian and Syrian gnostic sects, our knowledge of the movement's doctrines and activities is limited. It appears that the Ismā'īlis found their main support among laborers, artisans, and other depressed classes. Laws, they taught, were merely invented and enacted to hold down the masses and serve the interests of the ruling class. Those who possessed access to the secret body of the knowledge of their sect were not required to obey the law of the land. The Ismā'īlis exalted rebellion against the Sunni caliphs while at the same time they enforced the strictest obedience to their own imām, endowed with supernatural powers.

A later branch of the Ismā'īlis flourishing in the tenth and eleventh centuries was the popular revolutionary movement of the Carmathians, which was characterized by strongly eschatological views. "The time of manifestation is near," says one of the few surviving original manifestoes, from the year 1018, "the moment of the sword, the upheaval, the massacre of the impious and their forcible annihilation, is approaching rapidly."[23] Another offshoot, the "Assassins," staged frequently dramatic killings of prominent opponents in mosques and in the court, one of their most famous victims being the vizier and scholar, Nizām ul-Mulk, who was assassinated in 1092. "By dying in the line of duty," writes a student of the Assassins, "they were using their bodies to purify their souls for the realms of light."[24] The modern successors of the Assassins, fully pacified and respectable, are the Ismā'īlis following the leadership of the Aga Khan.

The Carmathians, as noted, were especially successful among the urban artisans, where they used the craft guilds to maintain their influence long after their more ambitious military challenges had been defeated. These guilds in time became the stronghold of Islamic mysticism (*Sūfism*) which fused Christian, Shi'ite, and gnostic images, and had a strong appeal to the underprivileged masses.

Eventually the sūfi orders became formally Sunni and relinquished much of their early revolutionary zeal. However, occasionally insurrections broke out led by guilds or sūfi preachers like the great revolt of the Ottoman dervishes in the early fifteenth century or the guild insurrections in seventeenth-century Istanbul.[25]

Throughout the first eleven hundred years of its existence, Islamic political life thus had its share of rebellions. An orthodox doctrine that stressed the duty of practically unconditional obedience to the powers that be was accompanied by heresies and sects that taught and practiced the duty and rightfulness of revolt against impious or oppressive authority. These two seemingly contradictory phenomena, of course, are related. Muslim political doctrine and Islamic political institutions failed to assure a peaceful resolution of differences over social and economic issues and an orderly succession, regional and tribal loyalties remained strong, and governments most of the time showed themselves incapable of inspiring the loyalty of their subjects by facing and solving the society's social problems in an equitable manner. In this situation, aggravated by geographical isolation and a poverty of resources, rebellions and military mutinies were constant and frequent occurrences. In Algiers, for example, between 1671 and 1818, fourteen of the thirty rulers achieved power through a military rebellion and by assassinating their predecessors.[26] These rivalries, internal wars, assassinations, and rebellions signify the failure of Islamic political institutions while at the same time they assured the survival of Islam. "Traditional Islam," notes an astute observer, "survived for more than a millennium in a harsh and uncertain environment because it was capable of converting constant tension and conflict into a force for constant political renewal and social survival."[27] Rebellions, many of them inspired by religious motives, acted as a safety valve that attacked and undermined political authority but also often helped to renovate it. The same impulse propelled the theocratic Mahdist movements of the eighteenth and nineteenth centuries.

III

The centuries-long tradition of autocratic rule and political quietism, interrupted from time to time by futile rebellions, lasted in the Islamic world until the French Revolution. Facilitated by the fact that the revolutionary slogans of liberty, equality, and popular sovereignty were expressed in non-Christian terms, and that the revolution was soon followed by a steady European penetration of the Near and Middle East, the ideas of the French Revolution successfully breached the walls of the ancient citadel of autocracy. Almost immediately began that process of westernization which is still in progress more than 170 years later and which has created the turbulence and upheaval—political, social, and intellectual—to be observed today in all parts of the Islamic world—from North Africa to Pakistan and Indonesia.

Contact with the West and the subsequent European penetration brought with them important economic and social changes. Transport and communications improved, the import of cheap western manufactured goods undermined the traditional craft guilds, urbanization and industrialization weakened tribal and family ties. At the same time, Islamic society began the difficult task of trying to absorb the West's cosmology without disrupting entirely its own system of beliefs and values.

The uneasy coexistence of two radically different world views could be seen almost anywhere. When in 1805 Mohammed Ali assumed power in Egypt following the withdrawal of Napoleon's troops, the document recording his investiture said: "According to time honored tradition and also according to Islamic law, every nation has the right to install rulers and depose them. Oppressive rulers deviate from the true path of the law, hence the right of nations to depose them."[28] Stated here were the doctrines of popular and national sovereignty that the author of this document tried to integrate into the tradition of Islamic law—an endeavor still unfinished today.

Constitutional government was the next item on the agenda. Tunis received a constitution in 1861, and the first Ottoman constitution was promulgated in 1876. The effective life of these attempts at constitutional government was short, but an important precedent had been set. For the first time in Islamic history, membership in the political community was defined in nonreligious terms. All citizens, regardless of their faith, were granted equality before the law. The stated purpose of government no longer consisted merely in the implementation of God's holy law.

A further shaking-up of the Islamic world came as the result of European imperialism. In 1881 France occupied Tunis, in 1882 England entered Egypt, and further acts of penetration soon followed in other places. How were the Muslims to view government by foreign Christian rulers? When a Mongol conqueror in 1258 destroyed Baghdad, and the caliphate, the ulamā assured him that a just unbeliever was preferable to an unjust believer.[29] And a Muslim jurist taught, after the Norman conquest of Sicily from the Muslims, that even a Christian ruler must be obeyed if he grants religious toleration of his Muslim subjects.[30] But the situation now was different. The European rulers not only were foreign conquerors and infidels, but in addition they were harbingers of a new type of economy and of an alien culture that aggressively attacked all aspects of Islamic society, introduced a foreign system of education, and threatened the very nerve center of Islam—the Sharī'a. In these circumstances, the old notion that all power comes from Allah was increasingly hard to maintain and a new legitimation of power seemed needed. The intellectual confusion and distress were compounded by the abolition of the caliphate by Ataturk in 1924.

Islamic intellectuals reacted to this new reality in a number of different ways. Taking an over-all view, which encompasses the last one hundred years, and slightly simplifying the picture in order to facilitate classification and analysis, we can distinguish four main groups: (1) Modernists, who aim at integrating western-style democracy into a rejuvenated Islam. (2) Traditionalists, represented mainly by ulamā, who see no need for doctrinal change and who, as in earlier centuries, are willing to go along with any system of government. (3) Fundamentalists, who seek to return to the theocratic foundation of early Islam. (4) Secular nationalists, who may still appeal to the Islamic predilections of the masses but who seek modernization and a new secular foundation for the legitimacy of government.[31]

The first group—modernists—owes much to the thinking of two nineteenth-century Muslim scholars and statesmen—Jamāl al-Dīn al-Afghāni (1839–1897) and Muhammed 'Abduh (1849–1905). The former is usually called the father of Pan-Islamism, the latter is best known for his attempt to reconcile reason and science with the Islamic religion. Both men denounced fatalism and political quietism, and challenged the authority of the medieval schools. Where the orthodox jurists and ulamā invoked the doctrine of ijmā (the principle of consensus) in order to put the stamp of infallibility and unchangeability upon Islamic doctrine, essentially denying the right of individual interpretation (*ijtihād*), the two reformers insisted on reopening the "gate of ijtihād" and rejected the view that Islamic law was a static body of doctrine. 'Abduh, in particular, advocated the adoption of representative government that would have the task of adapting the Sharī'a to modern conditions. "Representative government and legislation by representatives chosen by the people," he wrote, "are entirely in harmony with the spirit and practice of Islam from the very beginning."[32]

Twentieth-century modernists, many of them western-educated Muslim intellectuals, have continued to argue that Islam and democracy are compatible, if not identical. They point to the bay'a as a kind of primitive social contract and to the prophet's practice of consulting important members of the aristocracy of Medina (shūra). But, as Bernard Lewis has said, this endeavor of implanting modern political ideals in the Islamic tradition is "usually based on a misunderstanding of Islam or democracy or both."[33] The political practices of a tribal society do not fit the complexities of the twentieth century. The idea of elected representative bodies legislating in spiritual matters offends the very basis of Islam. The attempt to reconcile democratic ideals and Islam has served the needs of Muslim intellectuals trying to restate their faith in terms of the fashionable ideology of the day and it has fostered pride in the Muslim past. It has not, however, provided guidance in solving the political problems of modern nation-building. Writing in 1945, Sir Hamilton Gibb expressed the hope that Muslim intellectuals would turn to creative thinking, "removed from the intellectual confusions and the paralyzing romanticism which cloud the minds of the modernists of today."[34] This expectation, as we shall see soon, has been fulfilled only in part.

The traditionalists, our second category, by and large have reacted to the political and intellectual challenge of the West with a minimum of perturbation. Frequently still isolated from modern currents of thought, lacking an organizational base for political action, and continuing the age-old tradition of working with any government, no matter what its form, most of the ulamā have cooperated with the new nation-states and their secular rulers. They have adjusted themselves to the powerful currents of nationalism, even though orthodox Islam recognizes neither geographical nor ethnic boundaries, the community of faith standing against the unbelievers being the only distinction. In Egypt the ulamā have condemned the violent tactics of the Muslim Brotherhood, which used

force in opposing the secularizing government of Naguib and Nasser.[35] The ulamā of Pakistan have accepted with good grace the
country's failure to achieve an Islamic constitution for which the
ulamā and their allies had worked for many years. The prestige of
the ulamā, especially in the rural areas, is still high, but their ability
to influence the thinking of those elite groups holding the reins of
government is practically nil. The ulamā do not want to re-establish
the caliphate. "Their ideal," concludes Leonard Binder, "remains
the medieval pious sultanate, in which the ruler recognized and cooperated with the ulamā to the extent that Muslim personal-status
law was maintained, religious endowments respected, and outward
official piety upheld."[36]

The third type of response to the revolutionary impact of western thinking has been fundamentalism, represented in the realm of
theory by the Syrian-born religious scholar Muhammad Rashīd
Ridā (?–1935). Like the modernists, Ridā attributed much responsibility for the ills of Islamic society to the medieval ulamā who
had legitimized tyranny and despotism, but in contrast to the
modernists, he strongly opposed western democracy and nationalism
and instead advocated a revival of the caliphate. The original Muslim state, under the so-called "Rightly guided Caliphs," in his eyes
was "the best state not only for Muslims but for the entire humanity."[37] "The fact," comments Nadav Safran, "that a political system had admittedly worked correctly for only forty out of thirteen
hundred years did not for a moment lead him to look for weakness
in its procedural arrangements, but to search instead for villains and
wicked plotters."[38]

Ridā's thinking exhibited similarities to the ideology of the puritanical Mahdist movements of the eighteenth and nineteenth centuries—the Wahhābis of Arabia and India and the uprising of the
Sudanese Mahdi, Muhammad Ahmad (1844–1885). All of these had
the same theocratic aims and the preoccupation with purifying the
faith.[39] More recently, fundamentalism has found a powerful expression in the movement of the Muslim Brotherhood, an organization founded in 1928 by the elementary schoolteacher Hasan al-
Bannā, a student of Ridā. The program of the Brotherhood is somewhat vague, but several points stand out. The movement wants the
establishment of an Islamic state, governed if possible by a caliph,
which would realize the rules and injunctions of the Sharī'a. Adul-
tery, usury, drinking, and gambling are to be suppressed vigorously;

marriage and procreation are to be encouraged. Narrow nationalism is regarded as a "hideous pestilence";[40] instead, the Brotherhood advocates the union of all Islamic countries and the driving out of any European influence through a holy war (*jihād*). After achieving the liberation and union of all Islamic populations wherever they may be, the Brotherhood seeks the conquest and conversion to Islam of the rest of the world.[41]

The Brotherhood denies the legitimacy of secular governments that neglect the economic, social, and moral teachings of Islam and exhorts its followers to fight such a government by all available means. The acknowledgment of the sovereignty of God and His law alone can legitimize rulership. The head of the state is to implement the Sharī'a, which is held to be clear and unambiguous. No opposition is tolerated and interpretations of the holy law that differ from those of the Brotherhood are to be suppressed. "When the righteous dispute with the unrighteous and each party advances the same verse in its support, we sit with folded hands instead of smiting the shameless misinterpreter and restoring right where it belongs."[42]

The Muslim Brotherhood is active in several countries of the Near East. A Pakistani movement with a similar fundamentalist program and in touch with the Brotherhood is the *Jama'at-i-Islami* party, led by Maulana Maududi. In the eyes of Maududi, Islam "is the antithesis of secular Western democracy. The philosophical foundation of Western democracy is the sovereignty of the people." Lawmaking is their prerogative. Islam, on the other hand, "altogether repudiates the philosophy of popular sovereignty and rears its polity on the foundations of the sovereignty of God and the viceregency (*Khilafat*) of man."[43] The Islamic polity, Maududi says, might be called a "theo-democracy," that is "a divine democratic government, because under it the Muslims have been given a limited popular sovereignty under the suzerainty of God."[44] Since the great mass of the people neither know the holy law nor can perceive their own true interests, the executive will represent the general will of the Muslims. Maududi's constitutional proposals, especially those concerning the question of who should have final say as to whether a law or the conduct of the ruler corresponds to the commands of the Sharī'a, have changed several times.[45] In 1952 he accepted the suggestion of Muhammad Asad, a European journalist who converted to Islam in the 1920s and has achieved some prominence as a Muslim political theorist, whose proposals for an Islamic constitution included a supreme court with the jurisdiction of deciding the repugnancy of acts of the legislature of the Sharī'a.[46]

The fourth and last category of contemporary Islamic political thought is that of secular nationalism; a friend of Muhammad 'Abduh, the Egyptian national leader Ahmad Lutfī al-Sayyid (born in 1872) can be considered its first articulate spokesman. Lutfī rejected the idea that religion could be a basis for political action. Egyptian nationalism, he insisted, had to be based on the nation's interest and not its beliefs, even though religion could be a helpful element in achieving unity of outlook. Islamic law had oriented the Muslims toward accepting despotism and theocracy; these two were a greater menace than even the British occupation, which by its nature was temporary.[47] A similarly radical position has been developed by Lutfī's countryman, 'Alī 'Abd al-Rāziq (born in 1888). In a book, *Islam and the Principles of Government*, published in 1925, 'Alī advocated a complete separation between religion and politics. The caliphate, in his eyes, had no basis in the Qu'rān; it had been a source of tyranny, oppression, and internal discord and was unnecessary for either the spiritual or temporal life of the Islamic community. The ruling classes had taught the necessity of the caliphate in order to protect their privileges; in the twentieth century Muslims should evolve their system of government in the light of their present needs and the modern ideas of humanity. Islam, said 'Abd al-Rāziq, represented a spiritual, religious community; it had nothing whatsoever to do with questions of political rule.[48]

'Abd al-Rāziq's book was condemned by the theologians of Cairo's al-Azhar, the center of contemporary Islamic learning, but when the same thesis was propounded in more popular form twenty-five years later, in 1950, by Professor Khālid Muhammad Khālid, a ban pronounced by the ulamā of al-Azhar was overruled by an Egyptian court, a sign of the changing temper of the times. Openly acknowledging his intellectual indebtedness to Voltaire, Rousseau, and Thomas Paine, Khālid called the Islamic priesthood a reactionary, totalitarian body that had dragged the people "into an abyss of servility and subjection."[49] Theocratic government, whether in Christianity or Islam, had always been the worst possible type of tyranny. Religion, Khālid concluded, "must remain as the Lord has always wanted it to be—namely, prophethood, not empery; guidance, not government; and preaching, not a sword. The detachment of religion from politics and its soaring high above it is the surest way of its remaining pure, bright and blissful."[50]

Khālid's ideas, including his advocacy of socialism, are similar to the theoretical foundations of Egypt's policies under Naguib and Nasser. The officers overthrowing the decadent monarchy in 1952, relates Naguib, did not want to turn their backs on the Islamic faith, but they felt that the message preached by the Prophet had to be interpreted with due regard to the great changes that had occurred since those early days. "There is nothing in the Koran," writes Naguib, "that calls for theocratic government." A cosmopolitan country like Egypt had to be governed "by means of a secular republic in which the rights of minorities shall be respected so long as the minorities, in turn, respect the Islamic way of life."[51] President Nasser, too, has stressed that Egypt cannot ignore "the existence of an Islamic world, with which we are united by bonds created not only by religious belief, but also reinforced by historic realities."[52] At the same time, it is quite clear that his allusions to Islam are primarily a matter of foreign policy rather than ideology. Thus, while the constitution of 1956 had declared Islam to be the religion of the state, the new provisional constitution of 1958, drawn up after the union with Syria that included a sizable Christian minority, made no reference to Islam. The basis of Nasser's claim to legitimacy, as we shall see again later, is secular.

IV

Which of these four schools of thought—modernism, traditionalism, fundamentalism, secular nationalism—is currently dominant? To which of these Muslim ideologies belongs the future? The answer to these questions is again intimately related to the basic social trends observable in present-day Islamic society. The period following the abolition of the caliphate in 1924 had witnessed a general trend toward secularism. The governing elites of the Arab countries were oriented toward a secular future; the idea of Pakistan, of a state based on Islamic identity, first suggested by Muhammad Iqbal in 1930, did not become a living force until the 1940s. The educational monopoly of the ancient religious institutions like al-Azhar in Cairo and Deoband in India was being curtailed if not terminated.[53] All Muslim countries, with varying degrees of thoroughness, rewrote their codes of law in conformity with French, Swiss, Italian, and British models. The Shari'a was being pushed aside in one area of social life after another until it was largely restricted to the realms of personal status—family, marriage, divorce, inheritance— and even in the sphere of family law western ideas were introduced by way of various ingenious expedients.[54] The reformers did not so much seek to learn the will of God as they were guided by the needs of social welfare.

The 1940s and the years following the end of World War II, on the other hand, saw a revival of Islam. Confidence in the ideals of the West was shaken by Fascism and the war, which seemed to have brought western democracy to the brink of destruction. The increased political pressure of the western powers, the presence of foreign troops, and eventually the creation of Israel, increased nationalism. Since the masses of the people were still predominantly Muslim and since the nationalistic leaders sought to mobilize these masses, nationalism increasingly was infused with religious elements. In the Near East Islam was described as the product of the Arab national genius.[55] North African nationalism, in particular, not troubled by the presence of an Arab Christian minority, appealed to religious feeling. The North Africans, writes one scholar, "viewed Islam as their bastion of strength. All hope of success lay in the rehabilitation of Islam to serve as a basis for national unity."[56]

On the Indian subcontinent Islam saw a powerful resurgence through the creation of Pakistan. It was the awareness of the religious and social differences between Muslims and non-Muslims that brought Pakistan into being; Islam has continued to provide a force for integration and cohesion.[57] To be sure, the search for an Islamic constitution, which occupied Pakistani intellectuals for close to ten years, ended in failure. Prolonged debates between the various schools of Islamic thought, which ran the gamut from Maududi's fundamentalism to the secular nationalism of Liyaqat 'Ali Khan, over the source of sovereignty, the permissibility of legislation, and the question of how to judge the conformity of legislation with the Shari'a, ended in a compromise that essentially represented a victory for the secularists. The constitution of 1956 provided for a democratic state based upon Islamic principles. The lack of sanction for a nation-state in Islamic theology was ignored; the reconciliation of popular sovereignty with the sovereignty of the Shari'a was side-stepped. No law was to be enacted contrary to the holy law of Islam, but the legislators themselves were entrusted with deciding whether they were in fact contravening the injunctions of Islam. Two years later this constitution was suspended and General Mohammed Ayub Khan, ruling since October, 1958, has followed an essentially secular course. Still, the forces of Islam are strong in Pakistan and they have necessitated concessions on Ayub Kahn's part. The new constitution of 1962 again required that the head of state be a Muslim and in the making of laws the president and the legislature were to seek the counsel of an Advisory Council of Islamic Ideology to help them determine whether a proposal was repugnant to Islam.[58]

The strong hold of religious sentiment on the thinking of the Muslim masses has benefited fundamentalist extremism. At the end of World War II the Muslim Brotherhood had at least one million followers in Egypt and several other Near Eastern countries, and despite harassment and repression the movement continues to show strength. "The potential following of such movements," notes Manfred Halpern, "continues to grow as nationalist reforms speed the process of modernization and thus inescapably incite the political consciousness of an ever larger number of tradition-bound men by involving them in untraditional and unresolved problems."[59] At a time when the old value system is crumbling under the impact of technology and mass communications are reaching ever wider circles, fundamentalism seems to offer salvation and meaning in life by striving to resurrect an idealized past. To the submerged masses, as yet without a stake in the modern world and disappointed by the achievement of political self-determination that frequently has failed to bring about a substantial improvement in their lot, a militant messianic radicalism glorifying passion and struggle has considerable appeal. Since 1945, several secular nationalist leaders in Egypt, Iran, and Pakistan have been assassinated by fundamentalist extremists; in 1965 another plot against President Nasser was uncovered and an attempted assassination foiled. Clearly, Islam, even though often expressed merely in ritual without any deeper comprehension of its meaning, still is a force to be reckoned with; "the appeal of Savonarola," concludes a French scholar, "is not yet exhausted in these countries."[60]

And yet, it is doubtful that fundamentalism and other forms of neo-orthodoxy in fact have a future. The forces of secularization increasingly undermine religion. Urbanization and industrialization break up tribal life and weaken the traditional family; the state apparatus almost everywhere is in the hands of secular nationalists who may still use traditional symbols and an Islamic vocabulary but who increasingly adhere to a secular path. Religious leaders, unable to confront the realities and problems of a country challenged by western technology and power with a meaningful program, ever more lose their prestige and influence to the new secular leadership. Islam is neither persecuted nor abolished; it is simply being by-passed as no longer relevant.

The revolution of rising expectations adds urgency to the task of modernization. But religion not only does not offer solutions, but frequently is invoked so as to become a force obstructing progress. At a time when Pakistan had to absorb more than six million refugees from India, when more than 25 percent of all children up to the age of four died of malnutrition, the country was caught in a constitutional morass, drafting and redrafting an Islamic constitution that had no bearing at all upon the critical problems facing Pakistan. Riots between rival Muslim sects continue to claim lives every year, and the recent armed conflict with India over Kashmir was aggravated by the ulamā who preached a jihād against the Hindu infidels. Both in Pakistan and Egypt the unchecked population explosion will frustrate all attempts at achieving economic and social advancement, yet the Maududi movement and the Muslim Brotherhood oppose birth control and brand it a plot of the western imperialists who seek to reduce the number of Muslims in the world.

The struggle for independence everywhere weakened political authority and the legitimacy of the state. The task of the patriot was to defy the alien state and to subvert it to the best of his ability. The most urgent job now is to reverse this trend, to build political cohesion and stable government that will be able to deal with the problems of nation-building and social change, as well as to find a new basis for legitimacy. The constitutions of most of the Islamic countries still provide that Islam be the religion of the state and that the head of state be a Muslim, but such provisions are of a largely deferential character. They cannot guarantee national integration or legitimize political power. Sovereignty can no longer be derived from the Sharī'a. Political authority, to be considered legiti-

mate, must successfully address itself to the problems created by
the uprooting of the old structure of society.

Many governments in today's Islamic world quite consciously
stress the tie between modernization and legitimacy, while at the
same time they often dismiss the western democratic idea of rival
parties competing for the allegiance of the voters as unsuitable for
regimes struggling to accomplish rapid social change. Speaking of
Nasser's Arab Socialist Union, the regime's official agent for mobiliz-
ing mass support, an Egyptian writer stressed that this movement
was not an ordinary political party but represented the whole people. "The people," he continued, "are not limited by partisan principles but are gathered together around their national goals to
achieve the mission of Arab nationalism and to stimulate their efforts for the sound political, social and economic construction of the
nation."[61] The authoritarian character of these regimes sometimes
is defended as a transitional phenomenon to more democratic practices once modernization has been accomplished; in other instances,
the revolutionary government is held up as a new and superior type
of democratic system, similar to the totalitarian democracy discussed in the writings of J. L. Talmon. A strong leader, endowed
with charismatic qualities, becomes the focus of loyalty and inspires
his followers with an enthusiastic picture of the nation's future.
David Apter calls the fully developed form of such a system "mo-
bilization regime." It relies on a "political religion" to bolster the
legitimacy of the leadership. Such a regime, he says, "represents the
new puritanism. Progress is its faith. Industrialization is its vision.
Harmony is its goal."[62]

Strong-man regimes like those of Nasser or Ayub Khan are facilitated by the traditional subordination of the individual to the state
or community in Muslim political practice and by the Islamic respect for power. Leadership has usually been regarded as legitimate
when it could maintain itself in power. Hence an Egyptian maga-
zine that deprecated the importance of the 1956 plebiscite con-
firming Nasser as President of the Republic was absolutely in the
mainstream of Islamic thought when it wrote: "In itself it will be
only the normalization of a situation whose fundamental legality
has never been seriously challenged. In the Muslim world the justification for leadership has been ability and capacity. The form of
leadership is secondary and relatively unimportant."[63]

Still, power and force alone are not enough to inspire loyalty. Hence the appeal to nationalism, social reform, and modernization, accompanied by a religious ceremonial in order to bolster legitimacy. Islam, despite the seeming rigidity of its doctrine, has been quite adaptive in the past and it may well adjust itself to this new situation as well. It may in time become what much of Christianity has already become; that is, a body of private religious beliefs, fulfilling the psychological needs of some individuals and contributing to a sense of national heritage, but without practical implication for the conduct of the state. Though such a new kind of Islam may be radically different from anything history has known so far, it would be presumptuous to maintain that such a religion should no longer be called Islamic. "Throughout its history," notes John S. Badeau, "Islam has been in constant interplay with the processes of society and the result has been a working compromise between Muslim and non-Muslim elements that reflects the conditions of cach era. To say that Islam is changing its role today is not necessarily to say that it is on the verge of disappearing—only that once more compromise is taking place, the final form of which cannot yet be determined."[64]

[N O T E S]

1. Louis Gardet, *La Cité Musulmane: Vie Sociale et Politique,* 2nd rev. ed. (Paris, 1961), p. 31.
2. Gustave E. von Grunebaum, *Medieval Islam: A Study in Cultural Orientation* (Chicago, 1961), pp. 155–156. For a discussion of ancient Oriental theories of political rule, see Henri Frankfort, *Kingship and the Gods* (Chicago, 1948).
3. Thomas W. Arnold, *The Caliphate* (Oxford, 1924), p. 11. See also Anwar G. Chejne, *Succession to the Rule in Islam* (Lahore, 1960), Chap. IV.
4. Notably, 4:62.
5. H. A. R. Gibb, *Mohammedanism: An Historical Survey,* 2nd ed. (New York, 1962), p. 75.
6. Ignaz Goldziher, *Vorlesungen über den Islam* (Heidelberg, 1910), p. 48.
7. Quoted in Arnold, *op. cit.,* p. 48.
8. Abu Yūsuf, Kibāb el-Harac, p. 11, quoted in H. A. R. Gibb and Harold Bowen, *Islamic Society and the West,* I: *Islamic Society in the Eighteenth Century* (London, 1957), 28.
9. Reuben Levy, *The Social Structure of Islam* (Cambridge, 1962), p. 290.
10. Kitāb al-Iqtisad (Cairo, A.H. 1320), p. 107, cited and translated by David

de Santillana, "Law and Society," in *The Legacy of Islam,* Thomas Arnold and Alfred Guillaume, eds. (London, 1943), p. 302.

11. Cf. Leonard Binder, "Al-Ghazāli's Theory of Islamic Government," *The Muslim World,* XLV (1955), 229–241.

12. Cited (without indicating the source) by Santillana, *op. cit.,* pp. 302–303.

13. Von Grunebaum, *op. cit.,* p. 169.

14. Elie Adib Salem, *Political Theory and Institutions of the Khawarij* (Baltimore, 1956), p. 28.

15. Cf. my article "Some Theology About Tyranny," *Smith College Studies in History,* XLIV (1964), 86–87.

16. Al-Shahrastani, *Religionsparteien und Philosophen-Schulen,* German trans. of *Al-Milal wa-'l-Nihal* by Theodor Haarbrücker (Halle, 1850), pp. 144–145.

17. Ignaz Goldziher, *Mohammed and Islam,* trans. Kate Chambers Seelye (New Haven, 1917), pp. 103–104.

18. Abu Dāwūd, II, 131, cited by Ignaz Goldziher, *Mohammedanische Studien* (Hildesheim, 1961), II, 93 n. 5.

19. Salem, *op. cit.,* p. 103. See also Julius Wellhausen, *Die religiöspolitischen Oppositionsparteien im alten Islam* (Berlin, 1901), p. 16.

20. Claude Cahen, "The Body Politic," in *Unity and Variety in Muslim Civilization,* Gustave E. von Grunebaum, ed. (Chicago, 1955), p. 137.

21. H. A. R. Gibb, "Constitutional Organization," in *Law in the Middle East,* Majid Khadduri and Herbert J. Liebesny, eds. (Washington, D.C., 1955), I, 15.

22. Bernard Lewis, "Some Observations on the Significance of Heresy in the History of Islam," *Studia Islamica,* I (1953), 47.

23. Quoted in Bernard Lewis, *The Origins of Ismā'īlism* (Cambridge, 1940), p. 83.

24. Marshall G. S. Hodgson, *The Order of Assassins* ('s-Gravanhage, 1955), p. 83.

25. Louis Massignon, "Guilds (Islamic)," *Encyclopaedia of the Social Sciences* (New York, 1935), VII, 216; Bernard Lewis, "The Islamic Guilds," *Economic History Review,* VIII (1937), 20–37.

26. Charles-André Julien, *Histoire de l'Afrique du Nord* (Paris, 1952), II, 292, cited by Manfred Halpern, *The Politics of Social Change in the Middle East and North Africa* (Princeton, 1963), pp. 20–21.

27. Halpern, *op. cit.,* p. 10.

28. Cited by Jamal Mohammed Ahmed, *The Intellectual Origins of Egyptian Nationalism* (London, 1960), p. 8.

29. Levy, *op. cit.,* p. 296.

30. Bernard Lewis, "Communism and Islam," in *The Middle East in Transition: Studies in Contemporary History,* Walter Z. Laqueur, ed. (New York, 1958), p. 319.

31. For a critical discussion of various other schemes of classifying "the crisis of the Islamic intelligentsia," see Leonard Binder, *The Ideological Revolution in the Middle East* (New York, 1964), pp. 24–31.

32. Muhammad 'Abduh, *Tafsir al-Manār,* II, 167f., cited by Nadav Safran, *Egypt in Search of Political Community* (Cambridge, Mass., 1961), p. 72.

33. Lewis, in Laqueur, *op. cit.,* p. 318.

34. H. A. R. Gibb, *Modern Trends in Islam* (Chicago, 1947), p. 105.

35. Christina P. Harris, *Nationalism and Revolution in Egypt: The Role of the Muslim Brotherhood* (The Hague, 1964), pp. 222–223.

36. Binder, *Ideological Revolution,* p. 37.

37. Muhammad Rashīd Ridā, *al-Khilāfah aw al Imāmah al-'Uzmā* (Cairo, 1923), p. 116, cited by Safran, *op. cit.,* p. 80.

38. Safran, *op. cit.,* p. 80.

39. For the origins of Wahhābism in Arabia, see the writings of H. St. John Philby; a recent discussion of the Sudanese Mahdi is P. M. Holt, *The Mahdist State in the Sudan: 1881–1898* (Oxford, 1958).

40. Muhammad al-Ghazāli, *Our Beginning in Wisdom,* trans. Isma'il R. el Faruqi (Washington, D.C., 1953), p. 37.

41. Cf. Ishak Musa Husaini, *The Moslem Brethren: The Greatest of Modern Islamic Movements,* trans. John F. Brown et al. (Beirut, 1956), p. 67.

42. Ghazāli, *op. cit.,* p. 20.

43. Sayyid Abul A'la Maududi, *The Islamic Law and Constitution,* ed. and trans. by Khurshīd Ahman (Lahore, 1960), p. 147.

44. *Ibid.,* p. 148.

45. Cf. Leonard Binder, *Religion and Politics in Pakistan* (Berkeley, 1963), Chap. 3.

46. Cf. Muhammad Asad, *The Principles of State and Government in Islam* (Berkeley, 1961).

47. Cf. Safran, *op. cit.,* pp. 90–97; Ahmed, *op. cit.,* pp. 86–107.

48. See 'Ali Abd al-Rāziq, *L'Islam et les sources du pouvoir,* trans. L. Bercher, *Revue des Etudes Islamiques,* VII (1933), 353–391; VIII (1934), 163–222.

49. Khālid Muhammad Khālid, *From Here We Start,* trans. Isma'il R. el Faruqi (Washington, D.C., 1953), p. 36.

50. *Ibid.,* p. 146.

51. Muhammad Naguib, *Egypt's Destiny* (London, 1955), p. 150.

52. Gamal Abdul Nasser, *Egypt's Liberation: The Philosophy of the Revolution* (Washington, D.C., 1955), p. 86.

53. Cf. Kenneth Cragg, *The Call of the Minaret* (New York, 1956), p. 23.

54. J. N. D. Anderson, *Islamic Law in the Modern World* (New York, 1959), pp. 81–91.

55. Sylvia G. Haim, ed., *Arab Nationalism: An Anthology* (Berkeley, 1962), p. 55. See also her article "Islam and the Theory of Arab Nationalism," in Laqueur, *op. cit.,* pp. 280–307.

56. Ibrahim Abu-Lughod, "Retreat from the Secular Path? Islamic Dilemmas of Arab Politics," *Review of Politics,* XXVIII (1966), 458.

57. This point is stressed in somewhat exaggerated form by Wilfred Cantwell Smith, *Pakistan as an Islamic State* (Lahore, 1951), p. 13.

58. *The Constitution of the Republic of Pakistan* (Karachi, 1963), art. 6 (1). See also Richard V. Weekes, *Pakistan: Birth and Growth of a Muslim Nation* (Princeton, 1964), and Khalid Bin Sayeed, "Religion and Nation Building in Pakistan," *The Middle East Journal,* XVII (1963), 279–291.

59. Halpern, *op. cit.,* p. 153.

60. Jacques Berque, *The Arabs: Their History and Future,* trans. Jean Stewart (New York, 1964), p. 256.

61. Muhammad Hamid al-Gamal in a book published in 1960, cited by Malcolm Kerr, "Arab Radical Notions of Democracy," St. Anthony's Papers, no. 16: *Middle Eastern Affairs,* 3 (London, 1963), 35.

62. David E. Apter, "Political Religion in the New Nations," in *Old Societies and New States*, Clifford Geertz, ed. (New York, 1963), p. 78.
63. *Egyptian Economic and Political Review*, II (May, 1956), 17, cited by Morroe Berger, *The Arab World Today* (Garden City, 1962), p. 306.
64. John S. Badeau, "Islam and the Modern Middle East," *Foreign Affairs*, XXXVIII (1959), 61–62.

[5] CONSTITUTIONALISM IN THE SIXTEENTH CENTURY: THE PROTESTANT MONARCHOMACHS

My purpose in this chapter is to suggest that the political doctrines of the monarchomachs represent a distinct and important phase in the emergence of modern constitutional ideas. This component of their thought has been ignored or understated in the scholarly literature because the monarchomachs have traditionally been viewed from the standpoint of the right of resistance and the theory of political obligation, from which standpoint the differences between their idea of constitutionalism and that of their medieval predecessors are not very easily detected. But the traditional view of the monarchomachs is, in my opinion, one-sided and misleading. The constitutional component seems to be not only the more interesting but also the deeper aspect of their thought since their doctrine of resistance presupposes it. And although the monarchomachs rely very heavily on medieval constitutional formulae, their use of this tradition involves new emphases and new connections that are characteristically modern in their tone and clearly anticipate ideas that we normally associate with the assertion of parliamentary supremacy in England in the succeeding century. My contention, therefore, is that the political thought of the monarchomachs is an important transition in the movement from medieval to modern constitutionalism, and that further study of their contribution would give us a clearer understanding of how this transition came about and what alterations it involved.

The constitutionalism associated with the Germanic kingships of the early Middle Ages was generally limited to the right of active resistance—by the whole community or any part—against a ruler who, in his judgments or his edicts, had come into serious conflict with the sense of justice embodied in the folk tradition. The supremacy of law, in other words, was not guaranteed by regular institutional controls. As long as he could maintain the effective consent of the community, a king could act upon his own discretion, for even if he were expected to consult with the magnates or wise men of the realm before making any great decision, he was not bound to do so, and was also free, at least in principle, to choose his advisers as he pleased.[1] Moreover, the acknowledged right to resist, or even overthrow, a king for alleged injustice or incompetence does not seem to have been regarded as an act of the community, done in its corporate capacity, against a ruler whose authority, as a mandatory of the people, could be revoked by them for cause. An "unjust king" was simply set aside *de facto* and a successor confirmed by some form of acclamation and rendering of homage.[2] Hence the notion of supremacy of law in the early Middle Ages was not associated with two ancillary concepts that are fundamental to modern constitutionalism—the idea of a sovereign community from which all authority derives, and the institutionalization of this sovereignty through control of governmental power by the people or their representatives.

With the transition to the more complex and organized institutions of the high and later Middle Ages, both of these ideas appeared. From the eleventh century on, the idea of popular sovereignty became an increasingly important principle in the jurisdictional conflict between church and state. All of the civilians interpreted the *lex regia* of the *Institutes* to mean that the emperor's authority derived from a grant of the community. Many, although by no means all, held this grant to be revocable for cause on the ground of a private law analogy between the people as principal and the emperor as agent.[3] And there were even some who believed that the people had retained, in principle at least, some share of legislative power.[4] Similar conclusions, of course, could be and sometimes were reached by those who took Aristotle rather than the *Corpus Juris* as the starting point for political discussion. And perhaps the most radical statement of popular sovereignty in the Middle Ages is the *Defensor Pacis* of Marsilius of Padua, according to which the entirety of legislative power remains in the people or its *pars valentior.*

The idea of institutional controls upon royal exercise of power was, on the other hand, closely associated with the growth of representative bodies, the most powerful of which, in the fourteenth and fifteenth centuries, were the English Parliament and the Estates of Aragon. From the thirteenth century on, it was a commonplace of customary lawyers that a king could neither impose new taxation under ordinary circumstances, nor make new statutes or abrogate old ones without the consent of the realm, which came to mean the consent of the Estates. And in the writings of Sir John Fortescue, a monarchy thus limited is given formal classification as a *dominium politicum et regale* as opposed to a simple *dominium regale*, and it is praised as that form of government which best maintains the supremacy of law.

The important point for present purposes, however, is that these conceptions of the later Middle Ages do not, at least in their secular applications, add up to the juridical formula of modern constitutionalism. Among the civilians and Aristotelians, the principle of continuing popular sovereignty is, to begin with, a somewhat exceptional position, the standard view being roughly that of St. Thomas Aquinas, for whom sovereignty is jointly shared by king and people. But quite apart from this, and even more important, the idea of popular sovereignty is used almost exclusively to determine the ultimate locus of political authority in the conflict between church and state rather than to examine the structure of a governmental system. Hence, among the civilians and the Aristotelians the principle of popular sovereignty is very rarely connected with the idea of institutional controls, and then only in a tangential and allusive way.

Conversely, the idea of a monarchy limited by the rights of the Estates is not connected by the customary lawyers with a clear conception of communal supremacy. Fortescue, for example, is extremely brief and vague on the source of political authority, and presents the *dominium politicum et regale* more as a matter of royal prudence than as a communal right. Hence he ignores or evades such interesting questions as the right of Parliament to depose a king, to approve appointments of officers, and to meet on a regular and continuous basis in order to supervise affairs, and indeed the over-all import of his *Governance of England* is to suggest that, in a monarchy with properly constituted finances and administration, a king would hardly need to summon Parliament at all.[5] Nor is this surprising in view of the political realities of countries like England in the later Middle Ages, where control of the monarch still depended primarily on the resistance of feudal or quasi-feudal powers, and where the rights of the Estates were rarely a point of major consequence in the conflict of competing interests.

It would appear, therefore, that the only occasion in the Middle Ages where the idea of popular sovereignty is clearly linked to the idea of institutional controls is the conciliar movement of the fourteenth and fifteenth centuries. But constitutionalism in the ecclesiastical domain had yet to be carried over into secular politics. And however much or little weight we wish to give the conciliar movement as a source of constitutionalist conceptions, my present point is that secular constitutionalism is not encountered until the sixteenth century.

The new combination of ideas was a by-product of the political conflicts touched off by the spread of the Reformation throughout northern Europe, and it emerges most clearly and dramatically in France, where the politico-religious crisis was especially protracted and profound. French Protestantism, to begin with, was a social phenomenon not encountered in the Middle Ages—an organized mass movement that cut across class lines to an unprecedented degree, and that was essentially national in scope even though its main centers of strength were in the south. After the St. Bartholomew's Massacre of 1572, the leadership of the movement began to pass from the great nobles to the pastors of the churches, and their tight organization of the party as a federation of local communities already embodies the idea of control of policy by the people or their representatives.

Furthermore, the great power of the Huguenot party, despite its minority status, is largely explained by widespread dissatisfaction not only over ecclesiastical abuses but over the fiscal and administrative burden of a monarchy whose demands had grown considerably as a result of a series of foreign wars and an increasingly expensive court. The crown, which was not competent enough to avoid a conflict with the Huguenots, was also not determined or popular enough to secure the resources required for repression without convoking the Estates. And during the first decade of the civil war, at least, most of the Third Estate and much of the nobility were not only reluctant to encourage civil wars but found religious uniformity a less pressing issue than the avoidance of further contributions. Hence, instead of granting new taxation, they insisted, rather aggressively at times, on more economic management of the royal domain and general reforms of royal and ecclesiastical administration. Moreover, these requests for the elimination of abuses were often accompanied by demands of the Estates for a share in the ordinary conduct of affairs including, among other things, the right to appoint members to the royal council who would ensure that reforms agreed to by the crown would actually be carried out.

Such assertions on the part of the Estates are not unprecedented, for they often appear in the later Middle Ages during those periods when the crown was in serious distress. But they take on particular importance in the sixteenth century because they had special appeal for the great religious parties and were ideologically elaborated in order to defend their interests. The Huguenot party, at least at the beginning, could easily see in the power of the Estates a peaceful means of achieving general reform or at least of assuring effective toleration, for at the Estates of Pontoise in 1560 and at the Estates General of Orléans in 1561 the Third Estate and the nobility clearly favored toleration and, as late as 1576, there was considerable opposition to outright persecution. But even when it came to open civil war, the ideology of constitutionalism enabled the Huguenots to present their resistance to the king as a defense not only of their religious interest but of the liberties of the French nation as a whole.

Finally, the new combination of ideas was strongly promoted by two elements in the intellectual climate of the period. The first of these, curiously enough, was the position of Calvin on the right of resistance. Calvin, who was the leading authority for French Protestantism, absolutely prohibited active resistance to a tyrant-king on the part of ordinary private subjects, restricting this right only to those magistrates or collegial bodies which, where they existed, were specifically charged by the fundamental laws with the duty of controlling the conduct of a ruler. But the unintended consequence of this more severe and restrictive version of the standard medieval viewpoint was to lead the Protestants of France to put the whole doctrine of constitutional resistance on a much deeper and more systematic basis. Faced with the threat of ruthless persecution, the Huguenots were strongly motivated to find some justification for armed defense. And in order to remain in conformity with Calvin's strictures, they had to seek it not outside the constitutional order but within it, and thus to develop a theory of the French constitution on which it could be shown that kings were subject to supervision and control by the people or their representatives according to the ancient fundamental laws. The second element was humanist admiration of the Roman Republic as a model of political wisdom. For here was yet another reason, not uncongenial to their party interest, why Huguenot scholars were inclined to interpret the political examples of the Old Testament and of European antiquities in a republican and constitutional spirit.

In presenting the constitutional ideas of the monarchomachs, I shall impose certain limitations on the materials to be considered. I shall deal only with the French writers, since they seem to be the boldest and most systematic exponents of these principles, although I shall make occasional reference to George Buchanan, whose *De jure regni apud Scotos* had considerable influence on French ideas. Furthermore, among the French monarchomachs I shall consider only Protestant writers, since the Catholic authors are later by about a decade and seem to add relatively little that is new for present purposes. And finally, I shall deal only with the major works, ignoring the pamphlet literature, which does not seem to present any major variations from the doctrines put forward in the more celebrated writings.

The starting point for all the writers here considered is the principle that no legitimate ruler can exercise absolute authority, that the right to royal office is conditioned on observance of the law, and that this is so because all legitimate rulers were originally created by an act of the people as a whole. This derivation of royal power is proven partly from Old Testament examples, but in part also—and with special emphasis in writers more influenced by humanism—from a learned showing that all European monarchies were anciently elective.[6] Hereditary succession is generally regarded as a usurpation of doubtful validity and lawful only insofar as it has been done with the tacit consent of the community. Hence, even an hereditary monarch owes his office to consent, one proof of which is his need to receive the recognition and homage of the people at the time of coronation. He, too, accordingly is obligated

to obey the law, and he takes an oath to that effect in the coronation ceremony.[7]

This historical argument on the ruler's obligation to the law very
readily merges with a more general argument which is quasi-con-
tractual in form. A people, it is claimed, can exist without a king
since they could be governed by their nobles or a popular assembly,
whereas kings quite obviously cannot exist without a people over
which to rule. Kings, accordingly, must have originally been created
by the organized community which, since it is capable of existing
independently, can have no reasonable motive to grant unlimited
power to a single individual who, as experience teaches, would be
very likely to abuse it. It follows, therefore, that all cases of absolute monarchy are either violent usurpations which may rightly be
opposed by violence, or imprudent voluntary gifts which can therefore be revoked on the ground that the right and interest of the
people as the principal are greater than its agent's.[8] All the writers
of the period would seem to agree that power tyrannically usurped
may become legitimate through long acceptance, which implies,
however, the tacit consent of the community and therewith the
obligation of the ruler to observe the law.

This much of the monarchomachs' position does not go very far
beyond the views of their medieval predecessors, although it is now
more clearly and systematically formulated. More novel and remarkable, however, is their general opinion that the activity of the
community is not exhausted by the acts of consent or deposition,
but that there remains within the people or their representatives a
continuing power, ordinary as well as extraordinary, to supervise
and control the conduct of affairs. In this respect the views of Hotman are the clearest and most radical. According to his version of
the ancient constitution, ". . . the Supreme Administration of the
Franco-Gallican kingdom was lodged in the Publick Annual Council of the Nation which in After-Ages was called the Convention of
the Three Estates."[9] And the Supreme Administration is explicitly
defined to include almost all those powers of governance that Bodin,
a few years later, was to list as the rights of a sovereign authority.

> First, [says Hotman] the Creating or abdicating of their kings. Next,
> the declaring of Peace or War; The making of all Publick Laws; The
> conferring of all great Honours, Commands, or Offices belonging to
> the Commonwealth; The assigning of any part of the deceased king's

patrimony to his Children, or giving Portions to his Daughters, which they usually called by the German name Abannagium, that is, pars exclusoria, or Part set out for Younger Children. Lastly, all such matters as in Popular Speech are commonly called affairs of State. Because it was not lawful to determine or debate of anything relating to the Commonwealth but in the General Council of the State.[10]

This idea of the Estates as the center of political decision-making is not a passing piece of rhetoric, but a considered conclusion for which Hotman elaborates a number of institutional guarantees. He is, for example, unwilling to accept the royalist view that the king, although normally required to gain consent for new taxation, could dispense with this requirement in cases of emergency. Such cases are mostly pretexts, Hotman argues, since there is always time enough, and in any event a king gains more from consultation and popular support than he does from an emergency levy.[11] Hotman also refuses to admit that consultation of the Privy Council is a valid alternative to the advice and consent of the Estates, or that the Council is a proper place for the conduct of administrative business. The Privy Council, in strictest law, is but the private council of the king for the conduct of his personal affairs. Its powers, therefore, do not extend to state affairs, the ministers of which, indeed, are officers of the kingdom, not the king, and are appointed by the Estates and not at the discretion of the ruler. And this, he adds, is the most prudent arrangement, since the ruler's personal appointees entrusted with his private business are apt to become counsellors of tyranny if they are charged with public matters also.[12] Hotman, furthermore, regards the claims of the Parlement of Paris to be the final or coordinate authority for the ratification of legislation and appointments as a mere usurpation of the rights of the Estates, an alteration of the ancient constitution introduced by the Capetians in order to transfer the powers of the realm to a small group of "Senators" whom they could name and more easily control.[13] The effect of thus eliminating alternative centers of decision and administration is to ensure that the affairs of government cannot be carried on without frequent meetings and continuing supervision of the Estates-General. And the final guarantee is Hotman's repeated insistence that, according to the ancient constitution, French kings were obliged by fundamental law to convene the general council of the realm each year on the Kalends of March.[14]

The constitutionalism of the *Franco-Gallia* thus goes considerably beyond the medieval idea of royal government which, as long as it remained within the law, needed to gain consent only on exceptional occasions. The representative body is here connected with the power of the whole community, and popular sovereignty is institutionalized in continuing control of government. The king, of course, is a part of the Estates, but he appears within it less as ruler than as presiding magistrate. Hotman, indeed, often refers to the government of France as a mixed constitution and compares it to the mixed constitutions of classical antiquity.[15]

It need hardly be added that the *Franco-Gallia* was intended to be something more than a mere exercise in antiquarianism. The ancient constitution of the French was a better government than the corrupted version of the time and corresponded to the best of ancient prudence. It is a form of government still widely enjoyed in other parts of Europe such as Germany, Aragon, and England. Indeed, constitutional controls are so anciently and widely practiced, and with such beneficial results, that they may be regarded as inherent rights of a community, confirmed by the law of nations, which cannot be understood to have been willingly and knowingly relinquished.[16] Moreover, the corruption of the French constitution is not only not complete but hardly goes back beyond a century, from which one could infer that the good old law could be easily restored.[17] It is therefore clear that the *Franco-Gallia* was intended as a program of reform, and Hotman all but makes the point explicitly in holding that the rights of the Estates are imprescriptible.[18]

Similar programs of reform seem to have been fairly widespread in the period. The *Réveille-Matin des François*, with explicit reference to Hotman, calls for a restoration of the ancient constitution and notes that proposals of this sort were being explored by Protestant convocations.[19] In the opinion of the author of the *Réveille-Matin*, the corruption of the times can be traced largely to the decline of the ancient mixed constitution, which had promoted civic virtue.[20] And on the Catholic side, an extremely radical version of constitutional rights, perhaps indirectly influenced by Hotman's work, was asserted at the League Estates of 1593.

The constitutionalist interpretation of the French monarchy is, moreover, to be found in all monarchomach writings, including works like the *Du droit des magistrats* and the *Vindiciae contra tyrannos*, which in some respects seem more conservative. In these works the emphasis is much more on the powers of magistrates than on the original rights of the Estates. Yet in both of them there is the same idea that the powers of the community were not exhausted by the original creation of the kingship, that the Estates of old had exercised all the prerogatives of sovereignty and continued to do so until some, but surely not all, of these prerogatives were usurped by scheming kings with the connivance of unfaithful magistrates.[21] Indeed, in the *Du droit des magistrats* a comparison is suggested between the Estates-General and the assemblies of Rome and modern Venice, and an analogy is even drawn between the Doge of Venice and a proper king.[22] And in both works it is asserted not only that many rights of the Estates remain in use, and especially the power to depose a tyrant-king, but also that the rest are in some sense imprescriptible.

Furthermore, even though the main emphasis of the *Du droit* and the *Vindiciae* is on the extraordinary powers of the magistrates to resist a tyrant-king, the foundation of magisterial authority is directly connected with the idea of the supremacy of the people or their representatives. The magistrates, first of all, are independent of the king because, unlike servants of the royal household, they are officers of the kingdom, not the king, the proof of which is that they owe their authority not to the king but to the people, by whose representatives they were originally appointed.[23] Hence, although the king as chief magistrate has the right to supervise the conduct of inferior officials, he cannot dismiss them at his pleasure, but only for cause and by judicial proceedings, since they are ultimately responsible not to him but to the people. Second, the right of magistrates to go beyond their ordinary functions and, in cases of emergency, to resist a tyrant-king, is also derived from their position with respect to the Estates. According to the *Du droit* and the *Vindiciae,* the regular magistrates were created by the Estates not only to discharge particular functions but also to serve as protectors of the people. The evidence for this is the oath of office taken by a general magistrate in which he swears to maintain the kingdom as a whole, from which it follows that he is in some sense a colleague of the king and is bound, if the emergency arises, to restrain a tyrant-king in order to fulfill his promise to see that the commonwealth receives no harm.[24]

Finally, according to both of the works we are considering, the right of a magistrate to exercise his ephoral authority is always restricted, in principle at least, by the superior right of the Estates. The ephoral function may not be exercised unless the Estates are prevented from assembling.[25] Particular magistrates, whose jurisdiction is restricted to a town or province, may resist within their territories but may not constrain a tyrant, although in extreme emergencies a right of secession is suggested.[26] General magistrates, who are charged with protection of the kingdom as a whole, may constrain but not depose, for that ultimate power belongs only to the Estates-General. Hence in theory, at least, the rights of agents-particular is restricted by the rights of agents-general, and the rights of agents-general are always inferior to the ultimate control of the Estates. As it is put in the *Du droit des magistrats*, the function of a general magistrate is simply to halt tyrannical behavior and to constrain a tyrant-king until he can be judged by the Estates.[27]

I should like to suggest, therefore, that the apparent differences between the constitutionalism of the *Du droit* and the *Vindiciae* and that of the *Franco-Gallia* and *Réveille-Matin* are matters of immediate political emphasis rather than of underlying principle. The former works are preoccupied with the immediate problem of justifying armed resistance, and if they focus mainly on individual magistrates, it is because under conditions of embittered civil war a permanent center of resistance was required and because the Estates, in any case, could no longer be relied on to come out resolutely and effectively for toleration. There is, however, nothing in the *Du droit* or the *Vindiciae* that precludes or repudiates the constitutional reforms proposed in the *Franco-Gallia* and *Réveille-Matin* and, indeed, the entire doctrine of resistance put forward in the former explicitly depends on the constitutional interpretation expounded in the latter. Conversely, although the *Franco-Gallia* and the *Réveille-Matin* are primarily concerned with constitutional reform, there is nothing in their position which precludes or contradicts an ephoral power of the magistrates in situations of emergency.[28] Indeed, on at least one occasion Hotman describes the rights of the Estates themselves as essentially ephoral in nature, and we have already seen that he regarded the general magistrates as their appointees and their representatives.

But although the political doctrine of the Huguenot monarchomachs was constitutionalist in all its phases, the elaboration, understandably enough, was incomplete in a number of respects. The Estates-General as it was constituted in the early 1560s could not become a viable alternative to royal government without considerable change. Its composition and mode of selection were not yet definitely settled; the power of deputies to bind constituencies was at best uncertain; procedure for arriving at decisions within each estate and among all three was irregular, cumbersome, and often defective; despite sporadic efforts, the Estates had little experience and even less success in enforcing their will upon the crown or its officials; and its constitutional authority was not only unclear but could often be bypassed by an appeal to its provincial counterparts. Hence, at the beginning of the civil wars, the Estates-General had not yet been transformed from an essentially advisory body with certain extraordinary functions into a governing body with a monopoly of legislative power.[29]

Despite appearances, moreover, there was no movement in this period that had the will and the power to effect this transformation. Although almost all segments of French society had reasons to be dissatisfied with royal policy and could sometimes cooperate against the king on specific issues, there were deep divisions among the three estates and within each one of them on all the more far-reaching questions of fiscal and administrative reform. Hence the Huguenot opposition was a coalition of heterogeneous elements held together by religious ties. And it depended largely on the power of nobles and municipalities, whose immediate political concern was the maintenance of local privileges and who were already concerned about the democratic implications that could be drawn from proposals for political reform, although this became a serious issue only in the last stages of the Catholic League. Hence constitutionalism, although loudly demanded at times, and often very sincerely and widely accepted, was for the most part a secondary goal. It remained too a somewhat nebulous idea. And when, in the 1590s, a religious compromise seemed possible, the more thoroughgoing program of reform was rapidly deprived of significant support, and not only on the Protestant but on the Catholic side as well.

Under these conditions, it is not surprising that the Huguenot constitutionalists should leave many matters unelaborated. There is, for example, very little discussion, even in Hotman, of how the Estates should be composed and no examination of either contemporary or ancient methods of selection. Hotman does insist that the presence of the clergy as a separate estate is a corruption of the ancient constitution,[30] and he makes it clear that the presence of the commons as well as of the nobles is required for a valid convocation.[31] But these general ideas are not yet followed up. And Hotman cites for his purposes many examples of a public council, French as well as foreign, which varied greatly in their composition without attempting to define the proper format clearly. Moreover, although the monarchomachs generally insist on the ancient prerogatives of the Estates-General, they are very vague as to the precise procedures by which these prerogatives were or should be exercised and as to the precise jurisdictional relationships between the Estates and other governmental agencies.[32] Many of these questions, furthermore, were not mere matters of detail but raised political issues of considerable moment. Thus it was generally agreed that hereditary succession to the throne and to many of the higher magistracies was an alteration of the ancient constitution, resulting in part from usurpation and in part from the tacit or explicit consent of the Estates. But it was also generally agreed that the rights of the Estates, and of the people whom it represented, could not be prescribed so that, whether consent had taken place or not, the new arrangements could be rightfully revoked. What, then, was to be the status of the crown and of the hereditary magistracies if the full rights of the Estates should be restored? The tactful silence on these and similar questions in the writings we are here considering confirms our previous statement that, at least among the more influential and substantial circles of Huguenot opinion, the goal of restoration was second in importance to the immediate issue of resistance to defend religious interests.

Nevertheless, the limitations of Huguenot constitutionalism are matters of omission or incomplete development that do not affect the basic principle. The broadly based religious parties of this period and the connection of their opposition to the ruler with the assertion of the rights of the Estates are relatively new phenomena without clear precedent in medieval politics. And the response of the Huguenot publicists is similarly unprecedented in that for the first time there is a clear and deliberate connection between the principle of popular sovereignty and the rights of representative institutions which is, as we have seen, the basic formula of modern constitutionalism—the assertion of the right of the people through their representatives to exercise continuous and full control over the ordinary conduct of affairs, and the subjection of all officials, the king himself included, to the supervisory power of the Estates.

Even if we concede that commitment to this idea was often incomplete or superficial, this is not to deny that the monarchomachs have an important place as transitional figures in this history of constitutional thought. The idea of the supremacy of representative bodies among the Protestant monarchomachs, and the broadly similar ideas of their counterparts in the Catholic League, are not mere anticipations of a doctrine that was later to develop independently. They are rather the source of a continuing tradition and they are frequently cited as authorities by writers of the seventeenth century whose more developed and elaborated version of their doctrine corresponds to more favorable political conditions.

[NOTES]

1. Fritz Kern, *Gottesgnadentum und Widerstandsrecht im Früheheren Mittelalter* (Muenster and Köln, 1954), pp. 130, 269–278.
2. *Ibid.*, pp. 146–149.
3. Michael Wilks, *The Problem of Sovereignty in the Later Middle Ages* (Cambridge, 1963), p. 185.
4. Cecil N. Sidney Woolf, *Bartolus of Sassoferrato* (Cambridge, 1913), pp. 36ff.
5. "Fortescue's doctrine of English kingship was the doctrine of a monarchy *limited* though not of a monarchy *controlled;* it was not a doctrine of parliamentary sovereignty." Harold Dexter Hazeltine in Sir John Fortescue, *De laudibus legum angliae*, ed. and trans. by S. B. Chrimes (Cambridge, 1942), General Preface, p. xlvii. For a similar view of the character of constitutional thought in this period as a whole, see S. B. Chrimes, *English Constitutional Ideas in the Fifteenth Century* (Cambridge, 1936), p. 348.
6. Francis Hotman, *Franco-Gallia* (English translation, London, 1738), pp. 38ff; *Le Réveille-Matin des François* (1574), II, 84f. George Buchanan, *De jure regni apud Scotos* (1570, published 1578; English translation, 1721), pp. 159–313, in George Buchanan, *An Appendix to the History of Scotland* (London, 1821), pp. 249ff.
7. Hotman, *op. cit.*, pp. 123f; *Réveille-Matin*, II, 82; Buchanan, *op. cit.*, pp. 255ff; *A Defence of Liberty against Tyrants*, a translation of the *Vindiciae contra tyrannos* by Junius Brutus, 1579, attribution uncertain (London, 1924), pp. 120ff.
8. Buchanan, *op. cit.*, pp. 251, 257ff; Hotman, *op. cit.*, p. 108; *Réveille-Matin*, II, 81f; *Du droit des magistrats sur leurs sujets* (normally attributed to Theodore de Bèze) in *Mémoires de l'estat de France sous Charles Neufiesme*, Simon Goulart, ed. (1576, 1578), II, 497, 508ff; *Vindiciae*, pp. 124, 172, 175ff, 181.
9. Hotman, *op. cit.*, pp. 64–65.

10. *Ibid.*, pp. 77–78.
11. *Ibid.*, p. 123.
12. *Ibid.*, pp. 67–68.
13. *Ibid.*, p. 140. Hotman's bitterness here is explained in part by the general hostility of the Parlements toward toleration and also by his belief, expressed in Chap. XXI, that the expansive ambitions of the Parlements were the cause of excessive complexity in French law.
14. *Ibid.*, pp. 66, 72, 75.
15. *Ibid.*, p. 65.
16. *Ibid.*, pp. 69ff.
17. *Ibid.*, p. 1.
18. *Ibid.*, pp. 71 ff; see also Preface V.
19. *Réveille-Matin*, II, 115ff.
20. *Ibid.*, pp. 119ff.
21. After observing that the French Estates had anciently exercised the power to elect and depose kings, to control taxation, appoint or approve major appointments, and to supervise "other principal affairs," the *Du droit* goes on to lament the partial usurpation of these powers. "Brief que les guerres et les paix se font, les tailles et emprunts s'imposent, les loix tant de l'estat que des affaires particulieres se font et se diffont, les dignitez et offices s'eslisent, se baillent, et s'ostent au plaisir de certaines personnes soyent hommes ou femmes, nobles ou villains, gens du bien ou non, pourveu qu'ils ayent credit à l'endroit de leurs maistres, qui ne voix que par leurs yeux, et n'ouyrent que par leurs oreilles. Sont choses du tout contraires a la maniere de faire de bon Anciens, et droictment repugnantes aux loix posées avec le fondement de la Monarchie Françoise. Sur quoy je laisse à disputer à tous les Iuresconsultes si aucune prescription de long temps au contraire peut avoir lieu par aucun droit divin ni humain" (p. 507). This view of the rights of the Estates is thus essentially the same as Hotman's. It is interesting to note also that in discussing the right of resistance to a tyrant-king, the *Du droit*, referring in passing to the mutual obligations of lord and vassal under feudal law, draws the analogy in such a way that the people are overlord and the king the vassal (p. 512). The *Vindiciae* argues from Biblical and European examples that in all kingdoms there had existed under various names Estates, ". . . in which the principal care is had both for the preventing and reforming either of disorder or detriment in church or commonwealth" (p. 97). Further, in speaking of the power of all magistrates to control a tyrant-king, the *Vindiciae* sees this power as being especially pre-eminent in the Estates ". . . which is nothing else but an epitome, or brief collection of the kingdom to whom all public affairs have special and absolute reference" (p. 97). Among the original powers of the Estates were the right to make peace and war, to depose corrupt kings, to constitute regencies, to levy new taxation, to appoint high officers of kingdom, and to meet at least once a year (pp. 126ff, 133, 135). The *Vindiciae* also holds that the Estates had lawmaking power but is apparently willing to concede that ratification by the Parlement is a valid alternative. ". . . [A]nciently all laws were only made in the assembly of the Estates, or in the ambulatory parliament. But since this parliament has been sedentary the king's edicts are not received as authentical before the parliament has approved them" (p. 151). There are, however, other places —e.g., p. 150—where the *Vindiciae* attributes the power of amending law to the Estates alone. The relationship between Parlement and Estates is

thus left unclear in the *Vindiciae,* but it is apparent that the legislative authority of the Estates is held to be older and in some sense more fundamental.

22. "Les Vénitiens, desquels la République, s'il en faut juger par le seul évènement, est la mieux dressée et conduite qui ait jamais esté au monde quant à la prudence humaine: Elisent un Duc souverain, non comme un phantasme, ainsi que quelques uns peu exercés aux affaires de ce monde, ont osé escrire, mais comme un chef, duquel sans aucun danger de Tyrannie, ils tirent toutes les commodités de la Monarchie" (p. 502). In a somewhat similar tone the *Vindiciae,* referring to the relationship of the king to other magistrates, speaks of the king as being but ". . . president amongst them, and principal only in order and degree" (p. 127).

23. *Du droit,* pp. 493, 494; *Vindiciae,* pp. 128ff, 210.

24. *Du droit,* p. 494; *Vindiciae,* pp. 201, 206.

25. *Du droit,* p. 513; *Vindiciae,* p. 127.

26. *Du droit,* p. 494; *Vindiciae,* pp. 207, 109. The federalist element is more marked in the *Vindiciae.*

27. *Du droit,* p. 495.

28. See, for example, *Réveille-Matin,* II, 90f.

29. See, in general, J. Russell Major, *The Estates General of 1560* (Princeton, 1951), and especially pp. 117, 120.

30. Hotman, *op. cit.,* p. 212; *Réveille-Matin,* p. 87.

31. *Ibid.,* p. 87.

32. There is, however, a passing reference to the requirement of majority rule in *Réveille-Matin,* II, 89.

[6] THEORIES OF TERRORISM AND

THE CLASSICAL TRADITION

Rule by terror, a familiar process in history, has virtually escaped systematic analysis. Despite historic familiarity and the importunate experience of the past three decades, which are punctuated by terroristic outbreaks and burdened by regimes of terror, this form of power remains at the edges of scientific inquiry. Moreover, the idea of a reign of terror is commonly presumed to spring into being during the French Revolution and no one has taken the trouble to explore the intellectual history of the concept or to search the classical tradition of political and social thought for the elements of a comprehensive theory.

Of the several reasons for this neglect, I shall mention two—one intellectual and the other emotional, or, if you prefer, ideological. The former commonly identifies terror with totalitarian systems. According to this way of thinking, terrorism is understood as one feature of an abstract system, and its nature as a distinct process gets lost in a general discussion of totalitarian characteristics. It is true that the study of totalitarianism has been a fruitful source of recent theories of terrorism, but it has led to an incorrect identification of organized terror with systems of total power. To correct this distortion, it is necessary to examine within their historical contexts several typical systems of power in which the process of terror is at home. The second reason for neglect is a difficulty of the kind that Herbert Spencer described as "the political bias." Ever since the

French Revolution, "terrorist" is an epithet to fasten on a political enemy. Burke and his followers would say that if you scratch an ideologue you will find a terrorist. On the other hand, revolutionary radicals would tend to think of terror as a defensive maneuver against counterrevolutionary forces. Still, both ideologies, when it is convenient, tend to disassociate terrorism from acts and threats of violence. Thus, the bourgeois critics of revolutionary movements, when manifest violence diminishes in systems such as the Soviet Union and Communist China, want to redefine terrorism as some processes hidden in the interstices of the system. Similarly, the revolutionary critics of capitalism, when manifest violence is absent, want to identify terrorism with economic intimidation and to find it hidden in the interstices of the system. Under these conditions, the term is vacuous, meaning no more than an epithet for a system one hates.

To avoid confusion with intimidation and other kinds of coercion, terrorism should be defined as a process that includes three elements: the act or threat of violence, the emotional reaction, and the social effects.[1] Even though it does not receive the attention it deserves, the concept of terror has a history that is part of the classic tradition of political and social theory. Sometimes men rely on this tradition to help tell them what they are doing and what is happening to them. Thus, Lenin explains the terror of the Russian Revolution by reference to the French Revolution,[2] and Robespierre and Saint-Just explain their Reign of Terror by a set of ideas that may be found in Cicero, Livy, and Plutarch.[3] Moreover, the classic tradition records, with clarity still unmatched, the phenomenology of terroristic regimes.

Although the concept of terror is familiar to the western literary and historical traditions, theories of terror have not emerged until modern times. In the ancient and medieval worlds, the psychic experience of terror was frequently represented in painting, sculpture, and drama, reported by chroniclers, and described by historians. The men of those times understood the relation between violence and terror and noticed the practice of terrorism in war and civil strife. In the historical writing of Thucydides, the workings of fear and terror constitute a major theme. Probably one of the most lucid descriptions of political terrorism ever recorded may be found in the story of revolution and counterrevolution told by Plutarch in the *Lives* of Marius and Sulla. With intense feeling and great detail, Tacitus describes the paralysis and deterioration of the nobility in terroristic regimes of the Roman Empire. Still, even though the concept of terror was present in the social understanding of historians and philosophers, it was scarcely examined systematically. The classical understanding of tyrannical rule emphasized the presence of fear in the heart of the tyrant and in his relation to the people, but did not examine its functions or explain how the emotion ramified within that system of power. Nevertheless, even though the ancient works provided no explicit theory of terror, implicit theories may be inferred from them, especially if we probe the dimensions of their understanding and examine the ways in which the use of language reveals their comprehension.

Greek Epic

The conceptual and linguistic origin of the term used by English and Romance tongues is the Latin word *terror.* Even German writers, when referring to political terrorism, tend to drop the perfectly good word, *Der Schrecken,* and prefer to use instead, *Der Terror.* In Greek, the equivalents of the noun, *terror,* and the verb, *terreo,* are *phobos* and *phobeo.*

In western literature, the first place to find the idea of terror is at the beginning: in the work of Homer. There, the major terms standing for terror and terrorism are linked to acts or threats of violence, but are used almost exclusively in a military context. The noun, *phobos,* meaning terror, also signifies panic-stricken flight or rout, and the verb, *phobeo,* meaning to terrify, also means to put to flight by means of fear. In *The Odyssey,* the story of a long journey home, full of violent adventures and frightful experiences, these words are used only once each. In *The Iliad,* however, the story of a war, the terms appear often—at least forty times each.

Homer uses a complex of words to indicate extreme fear, although *phobos* stands for terror, and terror implies flight. Nevertheless, terror is not identified with flight, and in *The Iliad,* Homer does use the word, *phudza*—similar to the Latin *fuga*—to mean headlong rout, and he even places the two words together in ways that show they are not identical. Thus, at one point he says the Achaeans were "gripped by rout (*phudza*), the handmaid of icy-cold terror (*phobou*)."[4] He indicates that although terror may stimulate the heat of flight, it may also freeze the blood and have a numbing effect. But the kind of fear that corresponds to the chill feeling of dread is represented by the word *deios* (or *deos*), which is used extensively in both *The Iliad* and *The Odyssey*. "Bleached with fear (*deios*)" is one of Homer's favorite poetic formulas, and in *The Iliad* at one point he describes the Trojans standing by their chariots after flight, "pale with fear (*deious*), terror-stricken (*pephobemenoi*)."[5]

On the battlefield, Phobos, who has the power to scare the staunchest warrior to flight, appears several times as the divine personification of a psychic force: Terror is the spirit son of Ares, who is the god of war.[6] He moves in the company of his brother Deimos, the personification of dread. This frightful pair, Deimos and Phobos —Dread and Terror—work as the companions of their father.[7] They may be accompanied by Eris, or Discord, who is named as the sister and comrade of manslaying Ares.[8] The personifications of Dread and Terror also appear as designs surrounding the Gorgon's head on Agamemnon's shield, looking so terrible as to strike panic in the enemy.[9]

The power to terrify is also exercised by the gods themselves, especially Ares, Apollo, Athena, and Zeus. When Zeus strikes terror, the Poet says, men turn to flight.[10] Still, the highest power to terrify is represented by the divine aegis, fashioned by Hephaistos and designed to put warriors to rout. The god of technology had given it to Zeus, who lends it to Apollo or Athena, coming to the aid of Trojans or Greeks according to his will, or uses it himself.[11] When a god shakes the aegis over an army, the men are plunged into headlong flight by the terrible sound.[12] The fierce sight of it also inspires great fear, for the tasseled aegis includes in its design awful forces such as Discord, Shock, which freezes the blood, the Gorgon's head, and wreathed on it as a crown, Terror (*phobos*).[13] The following passage, taken from the lively translation by Rouse, indicates its effect on the battlefield:

> The Trojans thrust forward in a body, led by Hector in fine form; before them went Phoïbus Apollo with a cloud about his shoulders, holding the aegis-cape, shaggy, conspicuous, terrible, made by Hephaistos for Zeus to carry and confound mankind. Holding this in his hands, Apollo led the advance. . . .
> So long as Apollo held the aegis-cape unmoving, the volleys hit their mark on both sides and the people fell. But when he looked at the Danaäns full in the face and shook it, with a loud and terrible shout, he melted their hearts within them and they forgot their cour-

age. Then like a herd of cattle or a great flock of sheep chased by a couple of wild beasts in the murk of night, with a sudden attack when the keeper is away, so fled the Achaians in panic; for Apollo put fear [*phobos*] into them and gave victory to Hector and his Trojans.[14]

At critical points in the conflict, the aegis appears, borne by a god, stimulating terror, impelling a headlong flight that turns the tide of battle.

Personified spirits, gods, and the divine aegis are not the only sources of terror, for extraordinary fighters, capable of extensive slaughter, are regarded with agitated fear. Hector, greatest killer in the Trojan forces, comes, the Poet says, "bearing terror to the Danaäns."[15] When he refers to some of the most violent warriors, Homer often uses one of his poetic formulas: "mighty masters of terror." Hector, Diomedes, and Patroclus, and even the horses of Aeneas, are called "masters of terror."[16]

As the battle wavers to and fro, however, a most crucial point is reached in the fourteenth book, and the object that inspires the terror which emerges as the tide of battle turns is symbolically very important. This time it is neither god nor spirit nor aegis nor man, but a severed head. The Trojans have been pressing the Argives back to their ships. With Hector placed temporarily *hors de combat,* and with Zeus asleep, they rally, inspired by Poseidon, against the Trojans. At the moment in which the battle turns, Peneleos, a Greek, kills a Trojan and displays his severed head. The moment is captured in Rouse's vivid translation:

> Peneleos stabbed him at the root of the eye, under the brow, and tore out the eyeball; the spear went through the eye and out at the nape of the neck, and the man sank down stretching out both hands. Peneleos drew his sword and cut right through the neck; head and helmet fell to the ground with the spear still sticking in the eye. Then Peneleos held it up for the Trojans to see, like a poppy-head on a long stalk, and cried exulting. . . .
>
> They trembled in every limb . . . and each man looked about to see how he might escape death.
>
> Now the battle had turned and many of the Achaians lifted the blood-spoils of their enemies.[17]

We know from historical experience that severed heads, used to make an emotional impact on the enemy, appear frequently in wars and revolutions, particularly in civil strife, where the feeling is most bitter. Besides the guillotine in the French Revolution, we can think of other conflicts in which heads have been displayed on pikes or on palisades, communicating a message that did not require words. The detached head seems to be more than a symbol of terror, for its universality suggests that it is not bound to a specific set of cultural meanings. Its significance seems to go deeper, to a more primitive level biologically and perhaps even phylogenetically. In a very interesting series of experiments with chimpanzees, the psychologist Hebb has shown that these primates respond with an unlearned, spontaneous "paroxysm of terror at being shown a model of a human or chimpanzee head detached from the body."[18] The evidence indicates that both men and chimpanzees have a similar spontaneous fear, and Hebb's experiments lead one to speculate that the severed head is not merely a symbol but what an ethologist, or social biologist, might call a sign stimulus, which triggers an innate releasing mechanism in the anthropoid nervous system and produces the terror response.

Singularly, despite the enormous differences in our idea of nature, knowledge of physiology, and understanding of psychology, our definitions of the various kinds of fear and the actions they impel have not been refined a great deal since they were described in Epic poetry. Darwin's pioneering study in the expression of the emotions did not alter the ancient descriptions of terror and its typical effects.[19] Similarly, the famous concluding chapter on the "fighting emotions" in Cannon's classic work may be read as a companion to *The Iliad*.[20] The causes of emotion are understood in an entirely different way, but in the twentieth century, our definitions of emotional states, their forms of expression, and our knowledge of typical actions associated with them retain the conceptual framework that may be found in the tale of the Trojan War.

Thucydides

After Homer, the degree of interest in feelings of terror and fear, it goes without saying, varied with the outlook of the writer as well as the mood of the time. When one searches for the presence of these emotions in historical works, one is struck by the contrast between Herodotus and Thucydides—both historians and both writing about vast wars. The terms do not appear often in the former's history of the Persian Wars, but the latter's history of the Peloponnesian War is fraught with words that stand for terror and fear.[21]

After Homer, moreover, the word *phobos* loses its specific asso-

ciation with flight and becomes a more general term. Simultaneously, Deimos and Phobos, the children of War, shedding their
divine life, transmigrate from personified spirits to abstract concepts.
Furthermore, the distinction noticed in *The Iliad* between terror
and dread—*phobos* and *deos*—in the work of Thucydides, as the
French classicist de Romilly has shown, takes on extensive dimensions with far-reaching results, becoming a major factor in Thucydides' analysis of war and politics, not to speak of transcending
the ancient world by influencing his English translator, Thomas
Hobbes.[22]

The distinction between rational and irrational fears must have
been familiar—certainly, it had been stated by the Sophists. Thucydides, by his subtle use of language, separates irrational *phobos*,
which seizes and agitates soul and body, from rational *deos*, the
intellectual apprehension that anticipates the future and makes
plans, calculating ways to avoid or cope with expected evils. When
Thucydides intends to stress affect and the effects of strong feeling,
he uses a *phobos* word; when he is referring to intellectual processes and prevision, he chooses a form of *deos*. Often, he links *deos*
to verbs of thought and to the idea of the future, but connects
phobos to confusion, perturbation, and to the present.[23] Limited to
the present, *phobos* is blind not only to the future, but also to the
past, for "terror drives out memory."[24]

Although they are different mental states, terror and rational
fear may be joined together in the course of historical events. On
the one hand, men through fear may initiate terror. Thus, Athenag-
oras tells the people of Syracuse that men who have private fears
wish to bring terror into the community: They want to throw the
city into consternation so that the common terror will overshadow
their own fears.[25] More often, on the other hand, terror may stimulate a course of action that is subsequently given direction by intellectual fears. In this case, terror provides the foundation for
certain kinds of rational political behavior.

Thucydides stresses the constructive functions of *deos*. It stimulates cautious strategy and prudent policy. It had initiated the
course of Athenian imperialism, which was motivated "principally
by fear, then by honor, and finally by profit,"[26] and it serves as
the most important element in alliances and coalitions. Through
fear, the subject peoples of the Athenian empire—whose defection
Athens always fears—remain submissive. Fear, not friendship, keeps

them from breaking their alliances. As the Mytilenean envoys tell the Peloponnesians gathered in council: "They [the Athenians] courted us in time of war because they feared us, while we did the same to them in time of peace. Trust ordinarily is made secure by good will, but in our case it was made firm by terror (*phobos*), and fear (*deei*) rather than love kept us both in the alliance."[27] Thus, the experience of terror, caused by the threat of destruction, may lay the foundation for a policy that is constructed and maintained by rational fears. At the same time that Thucydides, through his choice of words, carefully distinguishes terror from rational fear, presenting each as a distinct mental state having a specific kind of behavior associated with it, he also shows that the two may be systematically related. As de Romilly suggests, terror indicates the feeling on which everything rests, rational fear the means through which this feeling brings about a certain behavior.[28]

Faced with the terrors of war, men are impelled to construct alliances through the agency of their rational fears. Durable alliances are based on reciprocal fears of equivalent strengths. Although he observes the constructive work of fear in the formation of such associations, Thucydides, in contrast to Hobbes, also recognizes the instability inherent in them. In the world described by Thucydides, any political order shaped by fear is a precarious equilibrium of antagonistic forces.

Roman Social Thought

The argument that rational fear is the basis of social order is also presented by Cicero in his *Republic,* but not as his own position, for it is spoken by Philus, who plays a role similar to that of Thrasymachus in Plato's *Republic.* "When everyone fears (*timet*) everyone else, man fearing man and class fearing class, then, because no one has confidence in himself, a compact, as it were, is made between the people and the powerful."[29] The Latin verb *timeo* and the noun *timor* stand for rational fear, the equivalents of the Greek *deido* and *deos.* Cicero himself believes that trust and mutuality—not fear—are the basis of social order. Earlier in the dialogue, Scipio, the protagonist, declares that political associations are formed not by individual weakness but by a social instinct, and that the commonwealth is a union of men who agree on norms and legal principles and who associate for mutual advantage.[30] Similar to the statement of the Mytileneans in Thucydides' work—that Athenian alliances were not made secure by good will but held firm by terror—Cicero claims that Roman alliances and spheres of control were changing from a rule of law to the rule of force, "so that those who previously obeyed us willingly are held by terror (*terrore teneantur*)." This transformation makes him anxious about the descendants of his generation and for the stability of the commonwealth.[31] Similarly, in his essay *On Duties,* using the most general word for fear—*metus,* which may include the species *terror* as well as *timor*—Cicero declares that fear is a poor keeper of power, and that no amount of force is great enough to enable a regime to endure if its power is weighed down with fear.[32] Therefore, he shares with Thucydides the conviction that an alliance or a social order constructed by fear on a foundation of terror is inherently unstable. That this understanding was not taken for granted, even in legal thought, is indicated by the section on legal definitions in the *Digest* of Roman Law. There, in a mistaken etymology, which is all the more interesting because it is patently inaccurate, "territory" is said to derive from the word "terror." A territory, it is written, is the area of a state within the boundaries of which the magistrate has the right of terrifying the people (*terrendi ius*).[33]

It is no surprise to find that Cicero should think that a stable social order could not be based on a violent emotion. The attitude is consistent with his Stoic conviction that excessive emotions are perturbations of the soul that must be rooted out, for they have no proper place in the virtuous man or, by implication, in the good society. A classical formulation of the idea of emotion as a kind of disorder is also found in Plato's *Phaedrus.* In the myth of the soul as a charioteer drawn by two horses, the emotional component is imagined as an ignoble, unruly steed. James Hillman, a psychologist, has observed in a recent book that the idea of emotion as disorder in the soul "uses a moral and ontological model the foundations of which lie deep in antiquity."[34] Not limited to Stoicism or to Platonism, the idea reaches back to the heroic age.[35] The conduct of the heroes in *The Iliad* is ordinarily cool. When one is overcome by passion as a result of something in his character, the emotion is problematic and his behavior becomes an issue of epic proportions: hence the very theme of the poem is the wrath of Achilles. Otherwise, excessive emotion is not "natural" but inspired through the intervention of a god. In a more philosophical age, the Stoics, inclined to abstractions instead of personifications, identify their concept of Nature with reason and order and consider the strong emotions as fugitive departures from stable mental states and as unnatural kinds of experience. Cicero notes that Zeno, the Greek founder of Stoicism, had defined disorder as an agitation of the soul away from reason, contrary to nature.[36] Still, the Stoics do not minimize the power of the strong emotions, for they recognize that even the ideal man suffers these feelings against his will and that the passions are not subdued by rational methods.[37]

From the literary evidence, the Romans are at least as sensitive as the Greeks to the effects of strong emotions—especially fear—on rational, predictable behavior. "Even the bravest are frightened by sudden terrors," observes Tacitus. "Fear closes the ears of the mind," writes Sallust. "No fear is so ruinous and uncontrollable as panic fear. For other fears are groundless, but this fear is witless," comments Seneca.[38]

In his discourse on the emotions, Cicero follows Zeno, who had defined emotion as an irrational, unnatural movement of the soul or as excessive impulse, and who discussed terror as one of six categories of fear.[39] Cicero's definitions are subtly different from Zeno's: less general and more specifically relevant to political and military contexts. In his eight categories of fear, slothfulness (fear of work) and shame are mentioned first. Then appear six types of fear in the following order.

Terror: paralyzing fear which causes paleness, trembling, and chattering of teeth, just as blushing is caused by shame. *Timor:* fear of approaching evil. *Pavor:* fear unbalancing the mind. *Exanimatio:* fear following after *pavor* like an attendant. *Conturbatio:* fear driving out thought. *Formido:* lasting fear.[40]

Cicero often uses *terror* interchangeably with *timor:* He refers to the "terror of death" as well as "fear of death," mentions "terrors of the soul," and calls the apprehension caused by apparitions and by natural calamities "terror" as well as "fear." In one context, however, he uses the word "terror" regularly; namely, in referring to the fear caused by weapons, by military force, and by the alarms of warfare. Thus, when a tribune is threatened by a sword, he is "constrained by that terror (*hoc terrore coactus*)."[41] And in the opening fragment of *The Republic,* Cicero writes that Rome had been freed from the "terror of Carthage," and later refers to Scipio's role in freeing the city from the "two terrors of Carthage and Numantia."[42]

The historical work of Livy makes even more clear the military context of terrorism, and the historian's use of the term brings into sharp relief the relation between terror and armed violence. Livy is important not only for his authority in the ancient world but also for his influence on modern writers. The case of Machiavelli's *Discourses* is obvious, but Livy also influenced Montesquieu as well as other modern writers, many of whom owed a considerable part of their political education to ancient sources.[43] The triumvirate of Livy, Cicero, and Plutarch shaped the ideas of the generation that participated in the French Revolution—so much so that the Comte de Volney, a conservative historian imprisoned during the period of Jacobin triumph, blamed the excesses of the Terror on the pernicious influence of classical writers. For their Bible, he said, the revolutionary enthusiasts turned to Livy.[44] In our own time, the distinguished historian, Mathiez, claims that Marat's idea of dictatorship was modeled after the ancient Greek tyrannies of Dionysius of Syracuse and others who, in turn, it will be shown below, provided the stereotype for Livy's portrait of Roman tyranny.[45]

In the French Revolution, the concept of *La Terreur* as a form of government emerged for the first time in the modern world, but the word *terreur* had appeared in the fourteenth century—in a French translation of Livy's *Ab Urbe Condita Libri* by Berchorius, a French Benedictine.[46] It has been suggested that Berchorius was the first writer to use the word in a modern language.[47] The translation was the first relatively complete vernacular version of Livy, and it achieved the success of a modern best seller, becoming one of the most read books of the fourteenth and fifteenth centuries.[48] In antiquity, Livy's reputation had been immense. Mommsen observed that "the later Romans derived their views of men and things under the republic entirely from Livy."[49] His idea of terror, therefore, should receive close attention in any effort to explore the intellectual history of the concept.

In giving a name to the extreme fear caused by an attack or by the expectation of a military assault, Livy regularly specifies the "terror" of battle, of cavalry, of the approach of an advancing army, of the fleet, and of other kinds of violence associated with war. Sometimes he includes the violence of nature; for example, the "terrors of weather and waves." In the military context, cities are thrown into "terror and disorder," and on the battlefield, terrified soldiers flee to a camp causing "more terror there than they had

brought with them."⁵⁰ In Spain, all the Illiturgians are butchered
by Roman forces, and by the time Scipio's army appears at Castulo
nearby, "terror and despair had taken possession" of the city.⁵¹ Almost always, terror is a force that occupies or takes possession, and
military leaders seek to "strike terror" into the breasts of the enemy.
In order to fight, soldiers must be "delivered" from terror. In an
early battle with the Sabines, the Romans are beaten back and
Romulus prays to Jupiter, "take away the terror of the Romans
(*deme terrorem Romanis*)," vowing to build a temple to Jupiter
the Stayer.⁵² In early Rome, the psychological forces associated with
extreme fear were personified, and *Pavor* and *Pallor*—Panic and
Pale Dread, equivalents of the Greek *Phobos* and *Deimos*—were
worshiped as deities and had a temple dedicated to them. Livy
records that Tullus Hostilius, the third king of Rome, in a military
crisis vowed to build shrines to *Pallor* and *Pavor*.⁵³

Reserving the term for military action, Livy rarely writes *terror*
when he refers to the fear caused by violence within the city or
by the conflict between political orders or social classes. When a
dictator is appointed—essentially a military office with absolute
power within the city—it is not the Romans who are terrified by the
power of this magistrate, but the enemy. "So great was the terror
of that office (*tantus eius magistratus terror erat*)," Livy writes, that
the enemy withdrew from the walls of Rome.⁵⁴

Usually, the term "terror" is restricted to extreme fear caused by
agencies that are alien to the political community. When civil war
breaks out and the internal antagonist becomes an enemy, then it
is appropriate to name the fear he inspires as *terror*. Otherwise,
when political and social conflict remain within the limits of commonly accepted rules, the fears they generate are given milder
names, such as *timor* and *metus*. In describing the conflict between
the orders, Livy's bias is aristocratic, but his choice of words clearly
indicates that the fear which the senatorial class holds for the political actions of the common people is qualitatively different from—
even though it may sometimes be more intense than—the fear inspired by an external enemy.

In one passage, when Rome is at war with combined Sabine and
Etruscan forces, Livy refers to the foreign terror (*peregrino terrore*)
and describes the political climate within the city. After a night
attack by exiles and slaves in revolt, which had terrified everyone,
the consuls held a meeting of the senate in which it was clear that

the most acute fear was that the tribunes would rouse the people against the ruling class. Yet this feeling—greater in degree than any other fear—is not described as *terror*. Instead, Livy writes, "the consuls were holding a meeting of the senate, where more fear of the tribunes (*tribunis metu*) was displayed than the night attack of the enemy had caused."[55] Earlier in the same passage, Livy explains that fears (*timores*) at the time were many and various, but the one that stood out above the rest was terror of the slaves (*terror servilis*), and so great was this terror that no one had feared the tribunes or the plebs, who were usually considered a milder mischief that popped up when other troubles were quiet, and the apprehension caused by political conflict was lulled by the foreign terror. Yet, when the situation changes and the tribunes are feared above all else, the fear of them is not called *terror*. The case of the slaves is entirely different, for they are always an alien threat—never part of the political community. It is not the degree or intensity of the fear, therefore, which distinguishes *terror* from *timor* and *metus*, but rather the nature of the agency that causes it.

When Livy does use the term *terror* in describing internal political processes, the context is tyranny. In a telling passage in which Tarquinius Superbus, the hated Roman king of Etruscan origin, confronts Turnus, a Latin noble who opposes him, the historian writes that Tarquin looked for some means of destroying Turnus "so that he might inspire in the Latins the same terror with which he had crushed the spirits of his subjects at home."[56] The paradigm for terroristic regimes in Roman history is the legendary reign of this last king, Tarquin the Arrogant, and, according to Livy's account, the violent features of that reign are shared by the tyranny that follows within a few decades—the brief rule of the terroristic *decemviri*, or Commission of Ten, in the early Republic.

The name of the last king and the memory of his reign remain so odious that kingship and tyranny are invariably identified in Roman minds—in contrast to the Greeks, who make a clear distinction between the two concepts. Cicero observes that the Romans use the term "king" to include all rulers who hold absolute and perpetual authority over their people.[57] Hence, Romans react to the word *regnum* as the Greeks respond to *tyrannis*. Historical details about the last Tarquin, when Livy was writing—and by the time of Cicero, before him—had melted in the crucible of Greek political thought, so that the story of Tarquin the Arrogant is an alloy of historical fact and Greek ideas of tyrannical rule. For our purposes, it does not matter if Livy's story of early Rome contains more fancy than fact, for we are interested in the way he uses tradition as a vehicle to express his understanding of how fear is integrated in the type of power system known by the ancients as "tyranny." In a persuasive article in which he argues that the literary tradition—especially as it is transmitted in the works of Livy and Dionysius of Halicarnassus—is still the major guide to the history of early Rome, Momigliano writes: "Men lie about the past because the past is not dead, because they are still struggling with it. Livy and Dionysius still reflect the process whereby the various sections of the Roman people reacted to their past in different centuries. Through the words of Livy and Dionysius the modern historian is in direct contact with what generation after generation of Romans thought about themselves."[58]

In the oldest existing version of the tradition about the Tarquins, appearing in *The Histories* of Polybius and in *The Republic* of Cicero, the facts are irretrievably fused with the Greek stereotype of tyranny. Polybius does not even mention the name of Tarquin, absorbing specific details in a universal theory of constitutional cycles and transforming the facts into a general statement about conditions in which kingship is transformed into tyranny.[59] He indicates that he feels free to take such a liberty because his Roman readers were familiar from childhood with the historical tradition as well as with customs and institutions he is describing.[60] In Cicero's version a few facts appear: Tarquinius Superbus seized power by murdering a good king; he ruled by lawless violence, allowing himself and his kindred to be carried away by lust, so that his son raped the virtuous matron, Lucretia, who then took her own life, and the outrage provoked the revolution which cast out the institution of kingship and inaugurated the republic. These spare facts, however, barely making contact with whatever details the tradition held, are used by Cicero to liven up a didactic statement. Do you see then, he asks, how a king turns into a tyrant and how his failing changes the state from a good to an evil form? For in Tarquin "we see a master of the people such as the Greeks call a tyrant."[61] We are given little information about the tyrant's methods of rule, save for the mention of "lawless violence" and the statement that he "desired to be feared by others," which is at least a recognition of the place of fear in tyrannical controls. Elsewhere, in one of his fulminations against Marcus Antonius, Cicero suggests that perhaps Tarquinius Superbus was not such a bad sort after all, compared to the wicked Antonius. The orator presents us with a remarkable declaration that nothing mean or sordid is attributed to Tarquin, and that no punishments were inflicted by him on Roman citizens—in contrast to Antonius who, in the civil wars, butchered captured Roman citizens.[62] Such statements, linked with the meager facts in the oldest version of the tradition, help to support an argument that the terroristic features of Tarquin's regime, alleged by later writers, are no more than "aristocratic misrepresentations." Ure, who in his economic interpretation of archaic tyranny, prefers to see the tyrants as capitalists rather than as terrorists, argues that "Tarquin's regime was one of sweat and wages but never of blood and iron."[63]

There is no ambiguity, however, in the description of the last Tarquin's reign described in the works of Livy and Dionysius of Halicarnassus, for atrocities, violence, and terror appear in vivid detail. The picture of the tyrant drawn by Dionysius is of an aspect "terrifying rather than genial." He surrounds himself with an armed bodyguard of natives and foreigners, appears in public only rarely and when not expected, makes capricious decisions, and transacts public business alone or in a small circle of intimates.[64] Livy says that just and lawful kingship had perished when Tarquin killed Servius Tullius and seized the throne. The impious tyrant denied Servius, his father-in-law, funeral rites and put to death the senators who, in his belief, were partisans of the old king. To prevent someone else from seizing power by violence, he establishes a bodyguard. Since he has no legitimate right to the throne, and since he could place no trust in the affection of the people, he must safeguard his rule by fear. To inspire fear, he uses the form of trials, with himself as solitary judge, ordering executions without advice or appeal, inflicting death, exile, or confiscation at his will, either to eliminate suspected opponents or to gain plunder.[65] Thus Livy portrays a Roman version of terroristic tyranny, and in later times when Romans had recorded details about the regimes of Marius and Sulla from those who had lived through the terror of the proscriptions, they looked back beyond the facts to the reign of Tarquin as a prototype.

The Greek stereotype was constructed from experience—if not from the archaic period of the seventh and sixth centuries B.C., then certainly from the regimes of later tyrants such as Dionysius of Syracuse in the fourth century. The elements in the stereotype are virtually standard. Insolent pride is one of the tyrant's stock characteristics and the *superbia* of Tarquin is equivalent to the *hybris* of Cambyses described in Herodotus. Moreover, Herodotus has the noble Otanes say that pride and envy constitute all wickedness, and that both lead the ruler to deeds of savage violence.[66] Brutality, lawless violence, and wanton destruction, Polybius explains, seem like the work of a frenzied mind at the height of its fury, but it is the part of a tyrant to do evil in order to make himself the master of men against their will by means of terror.[67] Liquidating political rivals and setting up a bodyguard are other typical actions.[68] Working as a staff of violence, the bodyguard inspires terror in the people and defends the tyrant against his own fear. In Xenophon's dialogue, Hiero, the tyrant, tells Simonides, the poet: "To fear the crowd, yet to fear solitude; to fear being without a guard, and to fear the very men who are guarding; to be unwilling to have unarmed men about me, yet not gladly to see them armed—how could this fail to be a painful condition?"[69] In the advice Simonides gives to make the tyrant's rule benevolent, he suggests that the bodyguard of mercenaries be transformed into a kind of police force, changing its function from a terror staff.[70]

Political liquidation is perhaps the central principle in tyrant-craft. Tarquin taught his son how to control Gabii—by leading the innocent messenger into the garden and without a word striking off the heads of the tallest poppies with his stick. The son understood what the messenger had seen and proceeded to eliminate the chief men of the state.[71] This silent lesson is no more than an adaptation of the same communication between Thrasybulus, the tyrant of Miletus, and Periander, the tyrant of Corinth, with poppies substituted for ears of corn. The story is told by Herodotus and is mentioned again by Aristotle.[72]

Finally, according to the Greek stereotype, the tyrant is driven by inordinate lust. As Plato describes him in the ninth book of *The Republic,* the tyrannical man lives "in a fury of passions and desires." Lust for power and limitless desire for sensual gratification go together, and the tyrannical ruler is goaded by them into committing atrocities, which, added to the more calculated acts of political liquidation, increase the terror of his subjects. Albert Camus presents a classical image of the tyrant in *Caligula,* a modern play about one of the most violent Roman emperors, in which the absence of limits on his will drives the tyrant to madness and to a frenzy of destruction. In Livy's history of Rome, the final atrocity is the rape of Lucretia by the prince, which moves the people to revolution, led by the aristocracy. As Florus summarizes in his *Epitome of Roman History:*

> The Roman people tolerated the pride of this king, as long as lust was not united with it; but this additional oppression they were not able to endure on the part of his sons, one of whom having offered violence to Lucretia, a most excellent matron, she put an end to her dishonour by killing herself. All power was then taken out of the hands of kings.[73]

According to Livy, about a half-century after the kings are expelled and the republic inaugurated, another reign of terror is established. This attempt at tyranny is made by the second decemvirate, an interim board of ten commissioners, who seize control of the state. They had been appointed when the struggle between the orders—the conflict between patricians and plebeians—became acute and the tribunes of the people were demanding codification of the laws to end oppression caused by the manipulation of unwritten law by patricians.

When decemvirs are elected to replace the consuls for a second year, Appius Claudius, a wicked aristocrat, according to Livy's story, throws off the mask he had been wearing and begins to act according to his true tyrannical nature, drawing his colleagues into conspiracy. The first day of their administration is marked by an act of monstrous terror (*ingentis terroris*). Instead of limiting the fasces to one member of the commission, according to the custom, each of the ten appears with his twelve fasces—120 lictors in all—displaying the axes in the rods, which shows that there is no appeal from a death sentence imposed by these magistrates. They seem like ten kings, and they inspire terror in the humblest citizens as well as in leaders of the senate. For a brief period the terror is shared by all, but gradually the full weight falls upon the plebs. Patricians are not molested, but commoners are treated in an arbitrary and cruel manner. A band of young patricians forms a bodyguard and staff, inflicting violence on the plebs and plundering their possessions. Corrupted by such rewards, the young men turn from righteousness and prefer license for themselves to liberty for all. Livy explicitly compares the regime to the regal tyranny that had preceded it a half-century before and even has a senator denounce the decemvirs as "ten Tarquins."[74] Like the tyranny that had preceded it, the regime of the decemvirs is terminated by a sexual crime. Appius Claudius, leader of the decemvirate, devises a trick to debauch Verginia, a plebeian maiden, and her father, to save her honor, stabs her to the heart with his own hand. The outraged multitude set into motion events that eventually remove the decemvirs from power and restore the consulate.[75]

Just as Livy's story of the expulsion of the Tarquins from Rome reflects the expulsion of the Pisistratids from Athens,[76] the tale of Appius Claudius and the wicked decemvirs resembles in many ways the history of Critias and the Thirty Tyrants at Athens.[77] Furthermore, Mommsen has shown that the actions of Appius Claudius in Livy's story "are well-known traits in the picture of the ancient tyrannus,"[78] and it should be clear to us that the terroristic features of the decemvirate are more details deduced from the Greek stereotype. One might pause only to note that, in Livy's mind, the techniques of a terroristic oligarchy are no different from the methods of a solitary tyrant.

Summarizing this cursory analysis of some ancient writers, it is enough to mention a few major points. The idea of terror was familiar to the ancients and may be found in Epic poetry, at the beginning of western literature. In *The Iliad*, the behavior of men impelled by the emotion of extreme fear is no different from the way it is described today. Terror, in the work of Homer, is especially linked to the violence of military conflict. Furthermore, ancient writers understood the difference between terror and rational fears, the distinction becoming an important element in the historical work of Thucydides. Fear is always present to some degree in conflict of all kinds and is expected to be present in some form in political coalitions and military alliances, but it is also understood that structures based on fear or terror are inherently unstable. Finally, terror is a crucial part of the power system called tyranny. Driven by passion rather than reason, the tyrant commits atrocities, but even many of his calculated actions, such as the liquidation of real or imagined opponents, inspire fear. Some of his violence is designed to produce terror in some or all of his subjects. Implicitly, the ancients recognized that the function of political terrorism—deliberate or not—was to inhibit resistance to the tyrant's rule.

Machiavelli and Hobbes

Among modern writers, one naturally turns to Machiavelli and Hobbes as possible sources for a theory of terror—to the former because his works are commonly associated with techniques of violence, and to the latter because fear is a central element in his theory of the state. But Machiavelli warns the prince always to measure fear and violence and to inspire the one and practice the other only when alternatives are absent. It is best to be both loved and feared, he observes; yet if the prince must choose, then he should be feared, because men love at their own free will but they fear at the will of the prince. The wise prince must depend on what is in his power and not on what is in the power of others. Yet the fear he inspires should be kept within limits because he must contrive always to avoid hatred.[79] Sheldon Wolin argues persuasively that Machiavelli works out "an economy of violence" that preserves "the distinguishing line between political creativity and destruction." Every application of violence "had to be considered judiciously, because the indiscriminate exercise of force and the constant revival of fear could provoke the greatest of all dangers for any government, the kind of widespread apprehension and hatred which drove men to desperation."[80]

Machiavelli recommends extensive destructive violence in only two situations. The first is implicit in the ancient principles of tyrantcraft. When a conquering prince organizes anew, he should leave nothing unchanged, destroying old cities and building new ones, leveling social structures, and moving populations. This evil course, using means which "are cruel and destructive of all civilized life," is open to one "who wishes to establish an absolute power, such as ancient writers call a tyranny."[81] The alternative would be to establish a republic or a monarchy—the humane option. A second situation goes beyond the ancient texts and is probably the first statement of a modern theory of terrorism; namely, the recognition that violence and fear may be used to prevent social change. It is true that Machiavelli tends to explain change by an ancient formula —as the corruption of an original principle—but some of his perceptions and descriptions are more modern. He argues, however, that a community often must be brought back to its original foundations by using violence as a kind of shock treatment that purges the forces of change. He writes:

It would be desirable therefore that not more than ten years should elapse between such executions, for in the long course of time men begin to change their customs, and to transgress the laws; and unless some case occurs that recalls the punishment to their memory and revives the fear in their hearts, the delinquents will soon become so numerous that they cannot be punished without danger.[82]

To illustrate this point further, it is significant that Machiavelli shifts from his analysis of Livy's history of Rome to a modern example, the history of Florence:

In relation to this subject it was said by the magistrates who governed Florence from the year 1434 until 1494 that it was necessary every five years to resume the government, and that otherwise it would be difficult to maintain it. By "resuming the government" they meant to strike the people with the same fear and terror as they did when they first assumed the government, and when they had inflicted the extremest punishment upon those who, according to their principles, had conducted themselves badly.[83]

Thus, Machiavelli knows that the civic function of terror is wider than the understanding revealed by Livy or the other ancient texts. Terror is not confined to military conflict or to tyrannies, but may be found in monarchies and republics. It is an intermittent shock that purges the corruption of original principles, restoring a city to its original foundations and preventing social change.

Hobbes too received part of his political education from the ancients, and also draws a conclusion not to be found in their writings. For a master, he had adopted Thucydides, "the most politic historiographer that ever writ," whose lessons through translation he hopes would extend to "all men of good judgment and education."[84] A reader of the great historian, Hobbes feels, could experience the political life of the ancient Greeks as "a beholder of their proceedings, and familiar with the men and business of the time," sympathetically participating "in the assemblies of the people and in the senate, at their debating; in the streets, at their seditions; and in the field, at their battles." From this vicarious experience the reader might "draw out lessons to himself, and of himself be able to trace the drifts and counsels of the actors to their seat."[85] Yet, Hobbes in *Leviathan* draws a lesson that his favorite author never taught; namely, that an entire political system could ultimately rest on a foundation of fear. It is true that one finds statements in the work of Thucydides that fear, along with honor and profit, moved the Athenians to construct their empire as well as an assertion that "fear brings about union,"[86] but fear is at the foundation of such associations in a historical sense. Origins of cities, empires, and alliances may be motivated by fear, but Thucydides did not believe that fear could remain a stable foundation in a structural sense.

For Hobbes, however, human society is not only held up, but also held together by fear. As Raymond Polin observes, Hobbes argues:

. . . through fear of violence, and to guarantee his life and security, man is disposed to submit to a common power and to organize his self defense by sharing a social body in the framework of a society. Men unite in society under the dominion of fear. It is fear which renders man sociable, which humanizes him, and, one could even say, it is fear which renders him human.[87]

Yet this fear is not terror—on the contrary, it is a rational fear that man uses in his flight from terror. Rational fear is a human feeling, quite different from the terror that animals share with men and that fills the state of nature.[88] Hence, social organization, based on fear, escapes from terror, and Hobbes, except for his brief reference to the state of nature, never develops a theory of terror.

Nevertheless, Machiavelli and Hobbes do furnish elements for a modern theory of terror. The former releases the process of terror from its classical restriction to military conflict and to tyranny, and also indicates that terrorism may serve to prevent social change. The latter also detaches the political function of fear from the idea of tyranny, declaring that "tyrant" is merely a name one gives to a ruler he mislikes.[89] Moreover, in contrast to classical writers such as Thucydides and Cicero, Hobbes universalizes fear—understanding, of course, that he means rational fear and not terror—as the fundamental principle of social and political coherence.

Montesquieu

Finally, in Montesquieu we find the writer who draws together concepts provided by ancient and modern sources to organize them in the first systematic theory of terror. He develops a theory of archetypical political forms, each integrated by a constitutive principle, including "despotic governments, whose principle is terror."[90] About the archetypes, Isaiah Berlin observes:

> Montesquieu's concept of types is not empirical; it springs from the ancient doctrine of natural kinds; it is thoroughly metaphysical and Aristotelian. According to him each type of society possesses an inner structure, an inner dynamic principle or force, which makes it function as it does—and this "inner" force differs from type to type. Whatever strengthens the "inner" principle causes the organism to flourish, whatever impairs it causes it to decay. . . . The model is biological, not chemical. The inner spring of these societies is conceived by him as that which causes them to fulfil themselves by moving towards an inner goal, in terms of which alone they can be understood. . . .
>
> [H]is entire philosophy of history is founded upon this central notion: individuals and states decay when they contravene the rules of their particular "inner" constitution.[91]

In the despotic type, terror is the human passion that sets in motion the structure: a single person directing everything by his own will and caprice. In relation to the despot, all the other members of society are slaves. Only in a despotism is terror consistent with the political structure. The purpose of the terror is tranquillity, "but this tranquillity cannot be called a peace; no, it is only the silence of those towns which the enemy is ready to invade."[92] The terror eliminates resistance, prevents disorder, and holds together an expansive area, for it is the natural disposition of a despotic government to organize vast domains. Throughout his description and analysis, Montesquieu draws from history circumstances and events that tend to support or destroy despotic regimes. He thinks of despotism as an inherently "corrupt" form, but corruption is not always unstable. Extrinsic factors such as climate, religion, situation, or genius of the people may lend a despotic government stability at least for a time[93]—and, under those conditions, presumably, the despot "ought" to maintain the terror in order to keep the system intact. Here, similar to Machiavelli, Montesquieu uses a hypothetical imperative, indicating that if you want to get a certain result, then you ought to use a specific technique. Fundamentally, he argues, each government ought to be directed by its principle—"otherwise the government is imperfect."[94] He describes political acts and strategies consistent with each principle.

Montesquieu's immersion in Greek and Latin literature is well known and there is no need for further documentation of his reliance on ancient sources.[95] Yet he stands as a Janus between ancient and modern theory, and what is important about his work is the way he organizes and reinterprets the ancient texts. Raymond Aron has recognized Montesquieu's importance as a transitional writer who links ancient political thought with modern sociological theory, and observes:

> In one sense, Montesquieu was the last of the classical philosophers. He was still a classical philosopher to the extent that he believed a society is essentially defined by its political regime and that his theory culminated in a conception of liberty. But in another sense, one can indeed say he was the first of the sociologists, for he reinterpreted classical political thought in terms of a total conception of society and he sought to explain all aspects of collectivities in a sociological mode.[96]

In the ancient world, the metamorphoses of political regimes occupied attention and presented a central problem for social theory. In contrast, social change was so gradual as to remain virtually undetected. If an object does not move it may escape awareness, and similarly, in the ancient world, patterns of behavior that did change distracted attention from those that did not. Until men experienced the travail of the industrial revolution—an era in which social institutions, particularly ways of life outside the domain of government, were fundamentally transformed—a concept of society and social change as distinct from the state and political change did not emerge.

The historical context of modern theories of terror is fundamental social change accompanying political transformations, beginning with the French Revolution, extending to the Russian Revolution, to the systems of Mussolini, Hitler, Stalin, and to the present ordeal of nations emerging from colonial regimes. A survey of modern theories would include the justifications of the Reign of Terror by Robespierre and Saint-Just, the metaphysical theory of terror developed by Hegel in reaction to the Revolution, the historical reflections of Marx and Engels, the debate between Kautsky and Trotsky on the use of terror in the Russian Revolution, the thoughts of Sorel, the justification of totalitarian terror by Hitler, and the defense of anti-colonial violence by Frantz Fanon. Modern theories of terror, however, are beyond the scope of this essay, which will close with this brief discussion of Montesquieu—the last of the "ancients" and the first of the modern theorists. His passages on despotism make up the first theoretical study of social systems integrated by terror.

In conclusion, I would observe that despite differences in time, space, and culture, terroristic regimes share common features, and that people acting and suffering in those regimes, without learning rules or receiving instructions, when the terror strikes exhibit remarkably uniform behavior. The mechanisms underlying this behavioral uniformity are yet to be explored. At the same time, men have groped for ideas to express what they were doing and what was happening to them. The classical tradition, I have tried to show, is a rich source of concepts and inchoate theories of behavior in conditions of terror, and to help explain the hidden dynamics of terroristic regimes in our own period of history, in the words of Ortega, "We must call the classics before a court of shipwrecked men to answer certain peremptory questions with reference to real life."[97]

To the ancient understanding of terrorism, Machiavelli extended the process to crises of social change. Hobbes added the idea that the emotion of fear—considered by the ancients as an unstable perturbation of the soul—provided a stable foundation for political systems, although he clearly specified rational fear and not terror. In totalitarian systems, of course, terror goes into the foundation along with rational fears.

Theorists have understood that the function of terror is to inhibit resistance. The ancients thought of the process as a means of preventing resistance to the tyrant. Modern theories would add several other categories. One is terroristic disenfranchisement in which specific segments of the population—usually identified by racial characteristics—are prevented from becoming a part of the constitutional system. In this form, the terroristic exclusion of the Bantu from the white South African political system has an ancient counterpart in the Spartan terrorization of the Helots. In another kind of terror, violence is used to prevent behavior that would naturally bring about fundamental social change. Finally, in the totalitarian form, terrorism prevents resistance to extensive social change that is initiated by the government. Explanations of terrorism must be dynamic theories, taking into account what kinds of force are exerted by whom against which potential counterforces and for what purposes. The morphology of terror systems depends on the structure of counterresistance.

[NOTES]

1. I have sketched a conceptual scheme for the study of terrorism in another paper: "Violence and the Process of Terror," *American Sociological Review*, XXIX (1964), 248–257.
2. See E. H. Carr, *The Bolshevik Revolution 1917–1923* (New York, 1951), I, Chap. 7.
3. Cf. Harold T. Parker, *The Cult of Antiquity and the French Revolutionaries* (Chicago, 1937).
4. *Iliad*, 9. 2.
5. *Ibid.,* 15. 4.
6. *Ibid.,* 13. 299.
7. Ibid., 15. 118. The memory of this relationship between Ares and his sons was preserved for the modern world when the astronomer, Asaph Hall, in 1877 discovered the moons that accompany the planet Mars and named them Phobos and Deimos. Upon reflection, it may be more subtle than awkward to give a Latin planet Greek attendants.
8. *Ibid.,* 4. 440.
9. *Ibid.,* 11. 37. The Gorgon may be a later interpolation, but the very ancient origins of Deimos and Phobos are never questioned. See Walter Leaf, *A Companion to the Iliad* (London, 1892), pp. 127, 206.
10. *Iliad,* 14. 522. In the two instances in which *phobeo* and *phobos* are used in *The Odyssey*, the emotion is caused by divine manifestations. Animals feel this terror also.
11. Although the powers of the "tasselled aegis" are revealed, it is not clear just what kind of an object it is. Often it is rendered as a goat-skin cape, although some commentators think it is a shield. The circumstances that it had been wrought by Hephaistos, who typically works in metal, and that it is placed under the body of Hector to protect it when the corpse is being dragged behind the horses of Achilles, lend support to the shield theory. Still, since Athena "flings" it about her shoulders and, on one occasion, throws it around the shoulders of Achilles, it is easier to imagine a cape or mantle.
12. *Iliad,* 15. 230; 17. 591–596. It is commonplace to note that perhaps the sound of the aegis being shaken was associated with the roar of thunder.
13. *Ibid.,* 5. 739.
14. W. H. D. Rouse, *The Story of Achilles* (London, 1938), pp. 290, 291.
15. *Iliad,* 5. 682.
16. Some translations prefer "devisers of rout." The formula is *krateron mestora phoboio*. Cf. *Iliad,* 12. 39; 6. 278; 23. 16.
17. Rouse, *op. cit.,* p. 279.
18. D. O. Hebb, "On the Nature of Fear," *Psychological Review,* LIII (1946), 259–276; *The Organization of Behavior* (New York, 1961), p. 243.
19. Charles Darwin, *The Expression of the Emotions in Man and Animals* (London, 1872).
20. Walter B. Cannon, *Bodily Changes in Pain, Hunger, Fear and Rage,* 2nd ed. (New York, 1929).
21. The following table compares the number of times each word is used by the two historians. See J. Enoch Powell, *A Lexicon to Herodotus,* 2nd ed. (Hildesheim, 1960); M. H. N. Von Essen, *Index Thucydideus* (Berlin, 1887).

	phobos (terror)	*phobeo* (to terrify)	*deos* (fear)	*deido* (to fear)
Herodotus	10	23	4	38
Thucydides	48	105	22	110

22. Jacqueline de Romilly, "La crainte dans l'oeuvre de Thucydide," *Classica et Mediaevalia*, XVII (1956), 119–127.

23. *Ibid.*, p. 120.

24. Thucydides, *History of the Peloponnesian War*, II. 87. 4.

25. *Ibid.*, VI. 36. 2.

26. *Ibid.*, I. 75. 3.

27. *Ibid.*, III. 12. 1.

28. Romilly, *op. cit.*, p. 124, n. 3.

29. *Republic*, III. 13.

30. *Ibid.*, I. 25.

31. *Ibid.*, III. 29.

32. *Duties*, II. vii. 23, 26.

33. *"Territorium" est universitas agrorum intra fines cuiusque civitatis: quod ab eo dictum quidam aiunt, quod magistratus eius loci intra eos fines terrendi, id est summovendi ius habet* (*Digest*, 50. 16. 239. 8). The definition identifies the *"ius terrendi"* with *"summovendi,"* which means removing or clearing away the people, as the lictors clear a path or push back the crowd. A specific number of lictors attended the magistrate, bearing his insignia; namely, the *fasces*, which may be understood as objects inspiring terror. The *fasces*—a bundle of rods (for scourging) that sometimes included an ax—symbolized the power over life and limb. In the Republic, when the magistrates were exercising their civil authority, the ax was removed from the *fasces* and the rods lowered when a magistrate addressed the people, signifying their appellate power. When a dictator was appointed, the lictors attending him displayed the axes. Outside the city, where the military authority of magistrates was not subject to appeal, lictors bore the axes.

The derivation of the word for "territory" is probably not from *terror* but, more likely, from the word *terra* or else from the root which may be found in words such as "tribe" and "tribute" (Greek radical, TRI; Sanskrit, *tri*). This root indicates the number three or division into thirds, suggesting perhaps that the first territorial designations were the boundaries of three original tribes. "Terror," on the other hand, is derived from another root (Greek radical, TRES; Sanskrit, *tras*) which goes into words meaning to tremble or to quake with fear.

34. James Hillman, *Emotion* (London, 1960), p. 209.

35. E. V. Arnold, *Roman Stoicism* (Cambridge, 1911), p. 333.

36. *Tusculan Disputations*, IV. 21.

37. Hillman, *op. cit.*, p. 180.

38. Tacitus, *Annals*, XV. 59; Sallust, *Conspiracy of Catiline*, LVIII. 3; Seneca, *Letters to Lucilius*, XIII. 9.

39. Diogenes Laertius, *Lives of the Philosophers*, VII. 110; 112–113.

40. *Tusculan Disputations*, IV. 8.

41. *Duties*, III. 33.

42. *Republic*, I. 1; I. 46.

43. For an interesting comparison between Livy's approach to history and the

works of Machiavelli and Montesquieu, see Hippolyte A. Taine, *Essai sur Tite Live* (Paris, 1856), Part I, Chap. 6.

44. Parker, *op. cit.*, p. 3.
45. *Ibid.*, p. 6.
46. Petrus Berchorius (Pierre Bersuire), who was the prior of the Abbey of Saint-Eloi in Paris, was commissioned by the king to produce the translation. The exact date on which his *Décades de Titus Livius* first appeared is not known.
47. Jerzy Waciorski, *Le terrorisme politique* (Paris, 1939).
48. K. V. Sinclair, *The Melbourne Livy: A Study of Bersuire's Translation* (Melbourne, 1961), p. 51.
49. Theodor Mommsen, *The History of Rome*, trans. W. P. Dickson (New York, 1891), I, 615. Cf. Curt Wachsmuth, *Einleitung in das Stadium der alten Geschichte* (Leipzig, 1895), p. 591, quoted by B. O. Foster, Introduction to his translation of Livy, I, xxv, in the Loeb Classical Library.
50. Livy, *History of Rome*, 32. 21; 41. 2.
51. *Ibid.*, 28. 20.
52. *Ibid.*, 1. 12.
53. *Ibid.*, 1. 27.
54. *Ibid.*, 6. 28.
55. *Ibid.*, 3. 16.
56. *Ibid.*, 1. 51.
57. *Republic*, II. 27.
58. Arnaldo Momigliano, "An Interim Report on the Origins of Rome," *Journal of Roman Studies*, LIII (1963), 107–108.
59. Polybius, *The Histories*, VI. 7.
60. *Ibid.*, VI. 11.
61. *Republic*, II. 25–26.
62. *Philippics*, III. 4.
63. P. N. Ure, *The Origin of Tyranny* (Cambridge, 1922), p. 226.
64. Dionysius of Halicarnassus, *Roman Antiquities*, IV. 41.
65. Livy, *op. cit.*, I. 49.
66. Herodotus, *History*, III. 80.
67. Polybius, *op. cit.*, V. 11.
68. R. M. Ogilvie, *A Commentary on Livy, Books 1–5* (London, 1965), p. 197.
69. Xenophon, *Hiero*, VI. 4, in Leo Strauss, *On Tyranny* (New York, 1963), p. 11.
70. *Ibid.*, pp. 17–18.
71. Livy, *op. cit.*, I. 54.
72. Herodotus, *op. cit.*, V. 92; Aristotle, *Politics*, V. 1311a.
73. Florus, *Epitome*, I. 7, trans. J. S. Watson in *Sallust, Florus, and Velleius Paterculus* (London, 1852), p. 295.
74. Livy, *op. cit.*, III. 36–39.
75. *Ibid.*, III. 44–55.
76. Ogilvie, *op. cit.*, p. 195.
77. M. Cary, *A History of Rome* (London, 1957), p. 84, n. 12.
78. Mommsen, *op. cit.*, I, 621.
79. Machiavelli, *The Prince*, Chap. XVII. References to this work and to *The Discourses* are from the Modern Library edition (New York, 1940).
80. Sheldon S. Wolin, *Politics and Vision* (Boston, 1960), pp 221–222.
81. *Discourses*, Bk. I, Chaps. XXV–XXVI.
82. *Ibid.*, Bk. III, Chap. I, pp. 399–400.

83. Ibid., p. 400. Cf. Machiavelli, *History of Florence*, Bk. V, Chap. I.
84. *The English Works of Thomas Hobbes*, ed. William Molesworth (London, 1839), vol. VIII, pp. ix, xi.
85. *Ibid.*, p. viii.
86. Thucydides, *op. cit.*, I. 75, 76; VI. 33.
87. Raymond Polin, *Politique et philosophie chez Thomas Hobbes* (Paris, 1953), p. 21 (my translation).
88. *Ibid.*, p. 20.
89. Hobbes, *Leviathan*, Part II, Chap. xix.
90. Montesquieu, *The Spirit of the Laws*, trans. Thomas Nugent (New York, 1949), I, 81.
91. Isaiah Berlin, "Montesquieu," *Proceedings of the British Academy*, XLI (1955), p. 277.
92. Montesquieu, *op. cit.*, I, 59.
93. *Ibid.*, pp. 115–116.
94. *Ibid.*, p. 28.
95. See Lawrence M. Levin, *The Political Doctrine of Montesquieu's Esprit des Lois: Its Classical Background* (New York, 1936).
96. Raymond Aron, *Main Currents in Sociological Thought* (New York, 1965), I, 56.
97. José Ortega y Gasset, "In Search of Goethe from Within," trans. Willard R. Trask, in *The Dehumanization of Art and Other Writings* (New York, 1956), p. 127.

II

ISSUES

[7] CIVIL DISOBEDIENCE:

PREREQUISITE FOR DEMOCRACY

IN MASS SOCIETY

I

During a recent debate on the war in Vietnam an irate member of the audience demanded to know if I was in favor of civil disobedience. My reply was "Yes, on some occasions." He sat down in silence, with a broad grin. Nothing else that I said from then on was worth taking seriously, so far as he was concerned. I might as well have come out in favor of arson. And I am sure many in the audience felt as he did.

This widespread tendency to recoil from the very concept of disobedience, even passive and presumably nonviolent disobedience, in a society priding itself on its liberties, is a measure of the degree of stability, if not immunity to real social change, that has been achieved by the present socioeconomic and political system in the United States.

To the spiritual fathers of the American democracy, most notably John Locke and Thomas Jefferson, it seemed evident that any liberty-loving people should have the right to stage even a bloody revolution against a tyrannical government; by comparison, the remedy of nonviolent civil disobedience would seem a mild brew indeed.

Among the most forceful counter-norms, or norms tending to lead many of us to reject *a priori* the very thought of civil disobedience, is another Lockian principle: the sanctity of the rule of law. Spokesmen for our academic as well as our political and economic establishments are for obvious reasons far happier with this part of Locke's theory of civil government.

Now, the classical writings of our democratic heritage, not unlike the Bible or the classical Marxist literature, can be used to prove the legitimacy of almost anything, and therefore, more critically viewed, of almost nothing. This point should be particularly poignant for those who have followed, during the last decades, developments in research and theory in the field of political behavior. For reasons of convenience and perhaps of habit as well, it has remained orthodox for our colleagues to proclaim their fealty to our democratic way of life (some, indeed, seem to feel that we are entitled to force other nations, too, to be guided by our example); and this fealty has remained unshaken, by and large, by the wealth of data that have come forth to demonstrate the wide and growing gulf between most of the classical ideals of democracy and what goes on in its name in today's mass societies.

Let us return to the part of our democratic heritage of particular concern here: the insistence on the sanctity of the rule of law. Now, a strong case for exalting the law (and indirectly, the lawyer) can be made from my own political ground of commitment to no system but to the sanctity of life, and the freedoms necessary for living,[1] *insofar as* laws (and lawyers) are to operate to protect all human lives, with priority for those most badly in need of protection. But to claim a corresponding sanctity for the laws that we have today, which, as in *every* state to a considerable extent, operate in the service of those who are privileged and influential in our socioeconomic order, seems to me to constitute an outright fraud at the expense of all the political innocents, unless one can claim for oneself, too, the innocence of not knowing any significant part of our modern behavioral literature.

At best a claim can be made that general obedience to the law is a lesser evil than general disobedience, which could well lead to much violence and conceivably even to a return to a Hobbesian state of nature. But this surely is a false issue, for no society has ever known either general obedience or general anarchy. Most of us have become trained, as generations of our ancestors have before us, to obey almost all laws almost by instinct, and certainly by habit if not by conviction. Others have become conditioned to breaking laws, frequently for reasons of stunted growth on account of emotional as well as socioeconomic deprivation.

Democracy has not yet been achieved, at least not in any real sense, as we shall see, in the modern world. If so, then the most familiar justifications demanding obedience to "democratically enacted" laws would seem to have no firm foundation. For the argument that every law represents the will of all, or the will of the majority, is empirically false; so is the argument that all laws aim at serving the common good. So is, as we have seen, the argument that disobedience to *any* law will promote anarchy.

Yet it obviously will not do, either, to assert that all laws can be ignored, or that any particular law can be obeyed or disobeyed as a matter of convenience. Nobody in his right mind will support all disobedience, however "civil," regardless of the issues involved. The question to be tackled, then, is not whether, but when and on what grounds civil disobedience can be justified.

My point of departure is essentially Locke's: Respect for the rule of law, or for the democratic processes that produce our laws, clearly must be contingent on and limited by standards for judging either the caliber of these processes or the purposes they promote; or, more precisely, by standards for judging how well these processes promote the purposes of politics. The *fundamental* purpose of politics, as I see it, is not to perpetuate a given political order but to protect human life and basic human rights. It cannot, if I may rub the point in, be the legitimizing purpose of politics or of government to perpetuate a political order that is democratic in name but in fact serves primarily to bolster privileges, not to equalize rights—as does ours and surely every other political order achieved till now.

The course of my argument in the remainder of this chapter will be as follows: first (II) comes a definition and a discussion of the concept of civil disobedience; next (III) a very brief statement of my own normative position, affirming the value of freedom and, only secondarily, of democracy as an aim; and then (IV) a discussion of the increasing chasm between current realities and the classical aims of democracy. I shall next (V) try to show how an expansion of the role of civil disobedience would, if anything could, turn the trend around, so that we might hope to move toward rather than away from democracy; and, finally (VI), I shall argue how essential civil disobedience is for the liberation of the individual as a political citizen—as a man and as a sharer of the burdens and benefits of politics. Since "real" democracy would require "real" citizens, this argument, too, will support the case for civil disobedience as a prerequisite for achieving something approximating democracy in modern societies.

II

"Civil disobedience" will here refer to any act or process of public defiance of a law or policy enforced by established governmental authorities, insofar as the action is premeditated, understood by the actors(s) to be illegal or of contested legality, carried out and persisted in for limited public ends, and by way of carefully chosen and limited means.

The notion of *disobedience* presupposes the concept of a norm to be disobeyed; typically a legal norm, but in any event a norm which is assumed by *some* people in power to be authoritative in the sense that transgressions would be expected to lead to punishment in one form or another. Disobedience can be active or passive; it can be a matter of doing what is prohibited or of failing to do what is required. But mere noncompliance is not enough; the action or nonaction must be openly insisted on if it is to qualify as civil disobedience, as the concept is interpreted here. For example, failure to vote in a country in which there is a legal obligation to vote does not in itself constitute civil disobedience; one would have to state in public that one does not intend to comply with the particular law; typically but not necessarily, one would publicly encourage others, too, to disobey.

The act of disobedience must be illegal, or at least be deemed illegal by powerful adversaries, and the actor must know this, if it is to be considered an act of civil disobedience.[2] Note the distinction between *conscientious objection* to military service and civil disobedience in countries that permit exemptions from otherwise obligatory service for reasons of conscience. The conscientious objector engages in civil disobedience only if he knowingly and explicitly objects to military service on grounds not recognized by the law, or in a country that makes no exceptions for reasons of conscience.

"Civil" is the more ambiguous of the two terms. At least five different meanings would appear plausible, and in this area it would seem reasonable to cast the net wide and consider each of the following meanings equally legitimate:

1. The reference can be to a recognition of general obligations of citizenship and thus to the legitimacy of the existing legal order as a whole; pains taken to limit defiance to a particular legal clause or policy, and/or to avoid violence, may (but need not) be construed as an affirmation of general citizenship duties.

2. "Civil" can be taken to refer to the opposite of "military," in a broad sense. The customary stress on nonviolence may be construed to signify either (a) a recognition of the state's claim to monopoly with respect to legitimate use of physical violence, or (b) a rejection of all physical violence as illegitimate or morally wrong under all circumstances regardless of purpose.

3. "Civil" can refer to the opposite of "uncivil" or "uncivilized"; acts of civil disobedience may seek to embody ideals of citizenship or morality that will inspire adversaries and/or onlookers, hopefully, toward more civilized behavior, or behavior more in harmony with the ideals that inspire a given campaign of civil disobedience.

4. "Civil" can also be taken to refer to public as distinct from private: as citizens we act in public. Acts of civil disobedience seek not only to affirm a principle in private, but to call public attention to the view that a principle of moral importance is held to be violated by a law or a policy sanctioned by public authorities.

5. "Civil" can suggest that the objective of obedience is to institute changes in the political system, affecting not only one individual's or group's liberties but the liberties of all citizens. A religious sect persisting in outlawed practices of worship (say, the Peyote cult among western American Indians, before the U.S. Supreme Court came to its rescue) may insist only on being left alone, or may at the same time consciously assert a principle to the effect that other sects, too, should enjoy the equivalent rights. Degrees of consciousness about the wider implications of disobedient behavior are not well suited as conceptual demarcation lines, however, and it would seem most practical to include even very parochially motivated acts of disobedience within the scope of the concept of civil disobedience.

The ambiguities of the term "civil" are far from exhausted by this brief list, but the five meanings presented are probably among the more common. The chances are that most of those who practice civil disobedience think of their behavior as "civil" in a sense, whether articulated or not, which embraces more than one of these associations, and perhaps others as well.

Returning now to the definition with which we began, let us note, first, that acts of civil disobedience may be illegal and legal at the same time, in cases of conflict of laws. For example, disobedience campaigns have been conducted against state segregation laws in the American South, in the belief that under the Federal Constitution such acts of disobedience will *eventually* be deemed legal in the Federal courts.

The ends of civil disobedience must be public and limited, it is suggested. The ostensible aim cannot, within the reference proposed, be a private or business advantage; it must have *some* reference to a conception of justice or the common good. (This is not to deny, of course, that individual motives for engaging in civil disobedience at times may be neurotic or narrowly self-seeking, consciously or subconsciously.) The proclaimed ends must be limited, too; they must fall short of seeking the complete abolition of the existing legal system; those who want a "nonviolent revolution" may engage in civil disobedience, but they, too, proclaim specific, limited ends each time. Also, according to the usage recommended here, the proclaimed aims must fall short of intending the physical or moral destruction of adversaries, even if at times a calculable risk of casualties may be tolerated. The ends of civil disobedience must be potentially acceptable to those in the *role* of adversaries even if to current adversaries they may be anathema on psychological grounds.

Above all, the proclaimed ends of civil disobedience, as the concept is understood here, must be formulated with a view to making them appear morally legitimate to onlookers and to the public. Educational objectives prompt most civil disobedience campaigns, and are never wholly absent. If a trade union violates the law to gain equality or justice, in some sense, for their members, we may speak of civil disobedience, but not if a key position in the economic system tempts a union to violate the law for the purpose of extorting unreasonable privileges in return for obeying the law. A civil disobedience campaign can aim at destroying privileges considered unjust, but not at abolishing the right to equal protection of an already underprivileged minority group.

The "carefully chosen and limited means" of civil disobedience are calculated to achieve maximum efficiency in promoting the ends and also maximum economy in seeking to reduce as much as possible the cost of the struggle in terms of suffering and deprivation. True, Gandhi at times stressed the value of bearing or even seeking suffering, but he always wanted to avoid inflicting suffering on his adversaries or on third parties.

"Civil disobedience" should be kept apart from "nonviolent action." The latter concept by definition rules out violent acts while the former does not, as defined here.[3] Among some pacifist believers in civil disobedience it seems to be assumed that a complete commitment to nonviolence, even in the sense of avoiding the provocation of violence on the part of adversaries, is ethically superior to a more pragmatic attitude toward the possible use of violence. No such assumption is made here. "Carefully chosen and limited means" in the definition at the outset refers to choice of means rationally calculated to promote the limited ends. For many reasons it seems plausible that such rational calculation normally will suggest strenuous efforts toward either avoidance or reduction of violence. Civil disobedience activists and social scientists ought to be equally interested in research on the causation and consequences of violence and nonviolence under conditions of social conflict; the expansion of this type of knowledge would seem of crucial importance for achieving increasingly realistic calculations of the most effective and economic means toward the chosen ends of civil disobedience campaigns, and also toward determining when such campaigns are and when they are not likely to be successful.[4]

III

My normative position is essentially a simple one, even if it, like any other normative position, raises complex issues in application. Man and his world are, after all, almost infinitely complex.

The primary purpose of politics and of government, I hold, is to protect human life, and to expand the sphere of freedoms securely enjoyed by the individual—all individuals, mind you, on an equal basis. If all are equally entitled to grow and live in freedom, then those currently most deprived, in every unequal society, must have the highest priority claim on protection by the state.

A different way of stating the same fundamental commitment is to say that governmental coercion—and governments are by their nature coercive—can be justified only to the extent that it in fact serves to reduce coercion; and physical violence and oppressive economic deprivation prior to other, less debilitating restraints.

If I may anticipate for a moment my argument in the next section, no political order achieved so far, and that goes for our western ways of government, too, has been justifiable in these terms, if reasonably strictly construed. Demands on government arising from the lesser pains and frustrations suffered by influentials have generally taken precedence over demands arising, or demands that *should* arise, from the more debilitating indignities suffered by the poor and the inarticulate—whose very deprivation (with its cultural and psychological aspects) in fact prevents them, except in exceedingly rare revolutionary situations, almost unthinkable in the privilege-entrenched North American political order, from playing any political role at all.

According to the classical ideals, democracy should be a commonwealth of political equals, who are free to advance the common good and also their own good by constitutional means—that is, by legislation, brought about by processes designed to make sure that the laws express the well-deliberated desires *and* needs of the people. I feel committed to the aim of achieving democracy in this ideal sense because such a system would, to the extent that it could be brought about, be hospitable to respect for life and for human rights on the basis of equality. It would be easy to obey, presumably, the laws enacted in an ideal democracy. I shall argue, however, that this ideal cannot be realized, or even appreciably advanced, without a much expanded role for civil disobedience, given our present political order.

IV

Many leading political theorists would have us believe that western democracy as we know it in the United States and Britain today comes about as close to perfection as can any political order that fallible human beings can hope to attain. Some would have us dismiss as senseless "extremism" any radical questioning of the merits of our political *status quo*, and have even proclaimed an "end of ideology."

The classical ideals of democracy (excepting, most notably, the rule of law) have been all but abandoned by some of these theorists, or at any rate have been restructured so that their commitment to democracy has become a commitment to uphold what essentially amounts to the *status quo*.[5] Now, Bertrand Russell has remarked somewhere that the ruler of Hobbes's state would be far worse than Hobbes himself imagined if the citizens were to be as meek and submissive as Hobbes wanted. It is a fundamental part of my own thesis that every political order tends to become more tyrannical the more submissive its citizens are. Western democracies probably form no exception to this rule. In fact, as de Tocqueville saw, a peculiar hazard of democracies is that citizens are brought not only to comply with authority edicts but to regard them as binding morally as well, since they claim to represent the people's will.[6]

Democratic governments, like all others, seek to isolate and emasculate radical dissenters. If the domestic methods of democratic governments have been less extreme and less brutal than those of most dictator regimes, this probably reflects the usual stability of established democratic regimes, more so than any real appreciation of the value of dissent and dialogue about political fundamentals. True, the right to dissent is proclaimed as one of the many political virtues of our system, so that radical dissenters must be tolerated to a considerable extent, but there are many safeguards against permitting a fair hearing for their views. States and indeed all large organizations, as numerous studies from Michels'[7] on have shown, tend toward oligarchy and toward becoming instruments in the service of their respective oligarchies, at the expense of rank-and-file members.

The fact that the Anglo-Saxon democracies at most times have been able to dispense with the coarser methods of political repression, which in itself should be valued and indeed welcomed as a major achievement of our species, is at the same time a testimonial to the unlikelihood of any real changes taking place within the framework of established democracies. It is argued in our civics texts that the governing political parties in democracies tend to accept defeat at the polls gracefully because they know they may have a chance to come back to power again another time, if the rules of the democratic game are maintained. A fuller explanation of this willingness to abide by election results surely should include, however, especially in the United States but in most other democracies as well, the fact that not much is really at stake in elections, generally speaking, for the major interests. The tradition of "negative government" prior to Franklin Roosevelt made the United States government unable, even if it had been willing, to reduce the amount of socioeconomic injustice; and even after Roosevelt, though a trend toward "positive government" has been growing, and perhaps culminating with the early years of Lyndon Johnson, the division of powers, the conservatism of the mass media, the enormity of the economic power of the privileged strata, and a host of other circumstances have made it virtually impossible to expect government to become an instrument, even in part, for the interests of the downtrodden, or for the enlargement of human rights at the expense of privileges.

True, there have been proclaimed programs of Square Deal, New Freedom, New Deal, Fair Deal, New Frontier, and more recently, the Great Society. In its affluence America has been able to keep most of its underprivileged from actual starvation and has increased the opportunities for gifted or energetic young people of all classes and races. This has been done perhaps in part with lofty motives but probably also in part to attract votes and also, especially in recent decades, out of concern for America's image abroad; surely also in part as a means to forestall or reduce the incidence of acts of desperation like race riots, industrial violence, and the like.

As Dahl has observed, democratic government, even an ideal democratic government, has no ready way of registering the intensity of feeling about public issues.[8] "One man, one vote" means equal weight for the concerned vote and the indifferent vote; for the intelligent and the foolish vote; for the vote in defense of elemental dignities of life and the vote in pursuit of added privileges for groups already favored. As David Truman has observed, however, in our democracy the potential existence of new groups and new coalitions does put some limits on what a government will do, even if elected by a wide margin.[9] But the trouble is, as most of our civic culture-championing pluralists fail to acknowledge, that the potential groups and coalitions a president or governor or mayor needs to worry about are rarely made up of the underprivileged—except, perhaps, if they are desperate to the point of being riot-prone, or intelligently led to the point of being prone to engage in civil disobedience. Normally, except in countries with strong political labor movements, the underprivileged have been made politically ineffective to the point of emasculation by their circumstances of life; coalitions of influentials and privileged are usually the only effective potential groups, and theirs are the interests that most executives prefer to appease rather than confront. As Murray Edelman puts it, in every conflict of interest between the many and the few, the many tend to be given symbolic gratification by way of democratic rhetoric and nice-sounding laws, while the few are given the tangible benefits, including a way of enforcing or not enforcing the laws that suit them.[10]

As Kolko and others have documented, the structure of economic wealth and power in this country has not been changed at all for the last half-century.[11] For all the slogans, Square Deal to Great Society, political influence remains in the hands of the economically strong while the poor remain inarticulate and largely without influence. Even the trade unions, though in the past they have served the economic interests of some categories of poor, are politically irrelevant today, having become guilds for the protection of their own shrinking number of members only, and uninterested in general issues of social justice, either domestically or internationally.

I am not out to castigate United States democracy as distinct from other democracies. My point is that the realities of western democracies keep stacking the cards in favor of the influentials and the privileged, who are therefore in a position to keep expanding their power and influence, while the underprivileged are becoming less and less able even to *think* and much less to act politically. The United States is merely the society in which this development has come the farthest, perhaps because the accumulation of private wealth has been and is larger than anywhere else. Ironically and significantly, the United States is also the modern nation most explicitly committed to the political principles of democracy, and has been for the longest time.

Democracy as we know it in the West has become, it would seem, an almost foolproof instrumentality to preserve the political and socioeconomic *status quo*. Orderly political change has become impracticable, I submit, except to the extent that citizens free themselves from their prevailing belief that democracy has already been achieved, and that the laws enacted in their society therefore must be obeyed.

Under conditions of democratic pluralism, an uncritical submission to the rule of law means not only the shunning of violence but also, in effect, the abandonment of all intelligent effort to work effectively for changing the system. For it means agreeing in advance to live by rules in fact operating to forestall the development of democracy in any real sense. These are the rules by which the powerful have become more powerful, and the powerless more emasculated, while only the appearances of democracy have been maintained—an ever more challenging task, incidentally, but a task to which our media of communication and indoctrination so far have proved equal. Thus the discrepancies between our rose-colored perceptions of a government "by the people" and the stark realities of poverty and oppression have kept on growing.

Apparently, stability has kept growing, too. But for the human factors of alienation and desperation, this process might continue indefinitely. But social pathologies were bound to grow below the surface. Not only common crimes but also disorderly attacks against "the system" are likely to occur to an increasing extent. They will be destructive of lives and property but will fail to promote more democratic realities. They may well tempt the present and future American governments to engage in increasingly reckless violence abroad, as a means of seeking to recover national unity, to avoid the alternative of reducing the domestic socioeconomic injustice at the root of national disunity.

V

All organizational leaders are troubled by the fact that, as Philip Selznick has put it, human beings can be recalcitrant rather than pliant instruments in their designs.[12] This goes for statesmen and political leaders as well. Dictators may have to rely on secret police and recurrent terror to prevent revolutions and *coups d'état*. Democratic statesmen in some ways have an easier time of it, as we have seen, as they normally can rely on a broad consensus affirming not only a faith in democracy as an ideal but a belief that democracy has been achieved and that all democratically enacted laws must be obeyed, and that whatever is done by democratically elected statesmen is legitimate. If Texas oilmen in effect are subsidized by all consumers of gasoline; if wars are fought to install aggressive satellite regimes on unwilling foreign nations; and so on: To the extent that people believe democracy has been achieved in their country they tend to become pliant rather than recalcitrant; they can be "managed."

Yet degrees of and extent of pliancy vary with issues and with events. Generally speaking, it is greater the less immediately the individual is affected by particular laws and policies—or rather, the less he is aware of being affected. A policy of supplying faraway foreign dictators with napalm and other achievements of American know-how for use against their rebellious compatriots is readily accepted as being in the national interest on the say-so of a president; it is only when sons and brothers and boy friends and husbands are sent off to kill and to risk their own lives far away that a policy may be questioned or even resisted.

On the other hand, these are precisely the situations in which strong feelings about the inherently superior righteousness of the "democratic cause" are most easily developed, and an intelligent dialogue made most difficult.[13] At such times public witness by way of disobedient acts may be the only way to convey to the average citizen even an *awareness* of the existence of strongly felt dissent. In times of hero-worship, resistance to jingo sentiments must perhaps be heroically bold in order to become visible, lest the average citizen either remain unaware of the existence of dissent or else confuse opposition to a war with cowardice.

Ironically, the most striking example of bold and also effective resistance to legislation in recent American history had little to do with heroism. I refer to our experiment with Prohibition during the twenties. Let me stress that this is not an example of civil disobedience as defined in this paper, for the Volstead Act was usually evaded in secret, even if Clarence Darrow is said to have referred to bootleggers as fighters for American liberties and to have predicted the erection of statues to Al Capone in many a public park.[14] My point is simply that our own recent history testifies to the power of popular defiance to change a law.[15] This result is more likely to come about, presumably, the more widespread and determined the defiance, civil or not, of a particular law.

But there is little prospect, alas, that laws and policies supported by far more powerful economic interests—say the Vietnam war, or the continuing inequities in our school systems—can be changed by way of disobedience, civil or not. It takes knowledge, independence of livelihood, and certain skills in interpersonal relations to engage in civil disobedience. True, something has been and more will perhaps be accomplished in race relations, a field in which some acts of disobedience against some southern state laws have become almost respectable elsewhere in the nation, under the impact of a growing concern for America's image abroad in its confrontation with communist nations. But issues of war and peace are beyond the reach of most people, as are even more the underlying issues of an economic system which depends on preparations for war and serves to bolster and expand privileges instead of rights.

Our only hope, as I see it, is in education—that is, education toward intellectual and political independence for the individual. We badly need an education that enables and encourages each young citizen to think for himself about the proper aims of government, or the state, and to judge by his own standards to what extent the government of his own nation pursues those aims. Only to that extent should it have his support. To the extent that his government pursues illegitimate aims, in his judgment, or employs means subversive of and menacing to the values a just government must uphold, civil disobedience may well be the right response if acts of protest within the framework of existing legislation would be ineffective or take too long a time.[16] Or it may be the wrong response. My point is that a man is not educated to the point of political responsibility unless he can and will make this decision for himself.

And the most elementary requirement of political education, thus conceived, is liberation from the prevailing pluralist democratic myth, which claims a reverence for the Majesty of the Law—all laws!—on the ground that they have been democratically enacted. It is about time, I think, that political theorists, at least, free themselves from the stultifying grip of this myth, however convenient it may be as a rationalization for political inaction and, in my terms, political irresponsibility.

VI

In psychological terms, attention to the functions of political opinions for the individual provides an additional ground for arguing that the individual should strive to become sovereign in the choice of his fundamental political commitments.

We are aware today of the wide extent to which government

policies as well as public opinion are the outcome of neurotic anxieties and fears, which are difficult to diagnose with exactitude and are more difficult still to cure. Modern psychologists and political scientists have established in a general way how political opinions are developed to meet personality needs, and how the individual's ability to cope with anxieties at various levels determines his capacity for rationality and a realistic long-term assessment of his own good as well as the common good.[17] Most people are neurotic and conformist as well as rational, in varying mixtures; enlightened, civilized policies are unlikely to emanate from democratic processes except to the extent that influential leaders become capable of far-sighted rationality. Yet democratic competition for office and power almost invariably strengthens the neurotic aspects and lessens the rational aspects of political behavior; most electoral appeals, especially in times of crises when cool rationality is most needed, are directed to anxieties and paranoid sentiments rather than to reason or enlightened hopes.

The conscientious dissenter who cannot opt out of this system has no easy guide available for determining when to obey and when to disobey the law. There is no general solution to his dilemma, except to urge that he insist on protecting his own sanity and powers of reason, the autonomy of his own social conscience, and his own right to grow toward whatever moral stature or humanity he is capable of achieving. The criteria for concrete decisions to obey or disobey must depend on the nature of each situation, anticipating by careful inquiry and reflection the consequences of either obeying or disobeying; but they must also depend on each moral dissenter's personality and beliefs, especially his beliefs concerning priorities among evils or among good causes.

This open-endedness of the modern dilemma of civil disobedience fits well with Albert Camus's theory of rebellion as an individual responsibility: While only an active and pressing social conscience can bring an individual to full life as a human being, his responsibility for action or inaction as a social being is strictly individual and lonesome. What is given, according to Camus, is only the immorality or inhumanity of a life of acquiescence in evil; he goes even further and argues that a commitment never to resist violence with violence amounts to such acquiescence, or "bourgeois nihilism." But he offers no guidelines for concrete political decisions.[18]

It is worth noting that legislation to legitimize certain grounds for conscientious objection to military service has tended to excuse only those who could prove they had no rational, politically articulate basis for objecting to becoming soldiers. In the United States as in other western democracies, only a religious basis for objection was recognized at the outset. To the extent that the courts or subsequent legislation have attempted to liberalize the rules, as has happened in the States and in other western nations, the tendency has been to lower the demand for evidence of church membership or religious orthodoxy of some kind, but to keep insisting that objection is no longer legitimate unless it remains apolitical, and condemns all past and future warfare indiscriminately.

For contrast, take Bertrand Russell's response when he was once chided on a British "Brain Trust" program over the BBC for having gone to jail for resisting World War I as a pacifist, while he had supported World War II, and now once again seemed prepared to object to the point of civil disobedience against preparations for a third world war. He said, "I want to pick my wars." This, in my view, is a simple but profound statement of responsible citizenship. What other human right can be more basic than the right to choose what cause, if any, to kill for and to die for?

Yet this, of course, is precisely the kind of human right that no government, dictatorial or democratic, wishes to grant. Legal recognition of politically motivated conscientious objection would hamper the pursuit of "tough" foreign policies in a way that religiously or pacifistically motivated objection will not. Any government can limit the influence of saints; far more dangerous to established privileges and policies are citizens who combine radical dissent with political know-how, or saintly aims like social justice, freedom, or peace with flexible tactics of protest inside and outside the law.

It seems to me that Camus's theory of rebellion has contributed at least two important thoughts toward a modern theory of civil disobedience. One, which has been touched on already, is his view that a rigid adherence to nonviolent means of protest in some situations may amount to acquiescence in continued violence and oppression. For him as for the orthodox pacifists, violence is always the supreme evil; but to him it is in part an empirical question whether violence in given situations can be overcome or reduced by entirely nonviolent means (or, of course, by any combination of violent and nonviolent means). In my view and in Max Weber's terminology, he argues that an ethics of *a priori* duty must be supplanted by an ethics of responsibility, a responsibility for anticipating as full a range of consequences of alternative means of action as experience and research can establish, if there is time, before deciding on a course of action, nonviolent or in part violent.

It is precisely because the consequences of revolutionary activity are likely to be both violent and to a large extent unpredictable (especially with respect to the extent and duration of acts of violence) that Camus is so strongly in favor of rebellion, in his sense, as an alternative to revolution. His rebel is the piecemeal revolutionary—the politically responsible citizen who is committed to fight violence and oppression by the most *economic* means, i.e., he seeks to avoid the use of violence whenever possible, and above all to avoid the use of remedies that could be worse than the present evil—worse in terms of degrees and extent of violence suffered. With respect to his aims, Camus's rebel is related to the revolutionary in that he will be satisfied with nothing less than complete justice or a complete end to oppression, but he is apt to be less confident that this utopia can ever be fully realized. When it comes to his choice of means, Camus's rebel is identical with the type of responsible citizen extolled in these pages: the person who honors not the Rule of Law so much as the Rule of Justice, and who is prepared to support or commit civil disobedience against oppressive government or legislation.

If Camus has helped draw the demarcation line and develop the rationale for modern civil disobedience, as distinguished from revolutionary activity,[19] he has also, as a second contribution to a modern theory of civil disobedience, been the first to articulate the psychological necessity of being a rebel, or a citizen in principle prepared to commit civil disobedience against oppressive laws and policies, if one is to achieve one's full human stature. Rebellion, as a manifestation of revulsion against injustice, is to Camus an essential dimension of the free man's life; only men who remain too neurotic, too stymied to develop a consciousness of their own humanity, their own solidarity with all men, can remain indifferent and passive when confronted with victims or perpetrators of injustice. In a cruelly competitive society, perhaps most men remain stymied, or in Camus's sense less than fully human; yet at all times there have been rebels, believers in obedience to their own principles as a higher necessity than obedience to the powers that be, or the laws with which these powers guard their interests. I have argued in this chapter that only a good supply of such individuals can help us come closer to the achievement of democracy; Camus argues that only such qualities in a man can help him achieve his own individuality as well as his own humanity.

But in our time, with its unprecedented technology, capable of bureaucratizing acts of murder, and of dehumanizing men who may make decisions about life or death for millions of fellow human beings, the more effective education of an expanding supply of rebels may well be our civilization's last hope of survival. Without thousands of young men able and willing to disobey calls to contribute to moral monstrosities like, for example, American warfare in Vietnam, where is there hope that the bureaucratized, consensus-manufacturing forces of destruction of the modern superpowers—the Leviathans of our time—can be checked before our civilization becomes engulfed in a third world war?

In the name of democracy a new kind of servitude has developed in the West. Witness the hundreds of thousands of men who, educationally unequipped to judge for themselves, have been shipped to a far-off land to kill and perhaps die for what they cheerfully believe is the cause of democracy, or at any rate their own nation's best interests. And witness the many admonitions to dissenters against the war policy that they limit their protests to legal channels, again in the name of democracy, lest its rules of order be violated. Naturally, only harmless, easily manageable forms of protest are desired; violence in contests for power at home is inveighed against with democratic moral fervor by the same leaders who look to violence as almost the only way to engage in contests for power abroad. Advocacy of force and violence at home is condemned, and so is advocacy *against* use of force and violence abroad, for both kinds of advocacy could menace the *status quo*.

Let me conclude by returning to the most fundamental argument of this essay: Governments exist for the purpose of establishing and defending human rights, with the most basic rights, like protection against violence and starvation, taking precedence over less basic rights. The common good, according to this view, hinges on the good of the least favored individuals, taking into account also the prospects for those not yet born.

•This or any similar type of basis for political obligation directed to the ends of politics, which relegates not only democracy but also respect for the law in all its alleged majesty to the status of means, takes the vestiges of the role of subject out of the role of citizen. It substitutes an ethics of individual responsibility for the probable results of one's political behavior, including law-abiding as well as legally obligated behavior, for an ethics of duty to subordinate conscience, knowledge, and individual judgment to existing legal norms, government directives, or a majority vote.

The judgments at Nuremberg and the wide attention given to the Eichmann trial in Jerusalem have increased acceptance for the view that the autonomy of the individual conscience is a vital resource in our modern technological and bureaucratized civilization. The "essence of totalitarian government, and perhaps the nature of every bureaucracy," writes Hannah Arendt, "is to make functionaries and mere cogs in the administrative machinery out of men, and thus to dehumanize them."[20] "Each time we obey an order from higher up, without evaluating and judging it in moral terms, there is the Eichmann within ourselves bending his neck," writes a reviewer of Arendt's book, and further observes: "Eichmann was neither intellectually nor morally worse equipped than most people . . . his fault was that he did not feel personally responsible for what his government did. In this respect he is not unique."[21]

The human race may never fully achieve democracy; no large nation is likely to come very close to this exacting ideal, although I believe it can be approximated in the foreseeable future in university communities and perhaps in some other local communities. What is important, if we value freedom for all on the basis of justice, is that we move toward rather than away from democracy. For this purpose our educational institutions must try to produce, I submit, men and women less like Eichmann, and more like his opposite, more like Camus's rebel. The rebel, or the believer in civil disobedience in the fight against oppression, is to this writer the model of the responsible citizen who wishes to promote democracy. What we don't need, in my view, and what we are now oversupplied with, is the cheerful, loyal, pliable, law-abiding, basically privatist type of citizen extolled not only in our high school civics texts but in our professional civic culture and end of ideology literature as well.

[NOTES]

1. See below, section III. This position is developed at greater length in my *The Structure of Freedom* (New York, 1964, 1958).
2. See Harrop A. Freeman, "Civil Disobedience," in *Civil Disobedience*, Harrop A. Freeman *et al.* (Santa Barbara, 1966).
3. An opposite view is adopted by Hugo A. Bedau, "On Civil Disobedience," *Journal of Philosophy*, LVIII (1961), 653–665; by Carl Cohen, "Essence and Ethics of Civil Disobedience," *The Nation*, CXCVIII (March 16, 1964), 257–262; and by Freeman, *op. cit.*
4. My discussion in section II is adapted from my forthcoming article, "Civil Disobedience," in the *International Encyclopedia of the Social Sciences* (in press).
5. See, most notably, the last chapter in each of the following volumes: Bernard R. Berelson, Paul F. Lazarsfeld, and William N. McPhee, *Voting* (Chicago, 1954); Seymour Martin Lipset, *Political Man* (Garden City, 1960); and Gabriel A. Almond and Sidney Verba, *The Civic Culture* (Princeton, 1963).
6. See Alexis de Tocqueville, *Democracy in America* (New York, 1954), Vintage Books ed., especially Vol. I, Chap. XV.
7. Robert Michels, *Political Parties* (Glencoe, 1949, 1915).
8. Robert A. Dahl, *A Preface to Democratic Theory* (Chicago, 1963), Phoenix Books ed., especially pp. 48–50, 90 ff., and 134–135.
9. David B. Truman, *The Governmental Process* (New York, 1951), *passim*.
10. Murray Edelman, *The Symbolic Uses of Politics* (Urbana, 1964).
11. Gabriel Kolko, *Wealth and Power in America* (New York, 1962).
12. Philip Selznick, *TVA and the Grass Roots* (Berkeley, 1949), pp. 252–253.
13. "The first casualty in every shooting war is common sense, and the second is free and open discussion," wrote James Reston in *The New York Times* of February 12, 1965, five days after the beginning of the United States bombing of North Vietnam.
14. See Harry Elmer Barnes, *Prohibition Versus Civilization* (New York, 1932), pp. 71–72.
15. In fact, Mr. Darrow is quoted as claiming that this "nullification," as he calls it, is a traditional American way of changing the law, *ibid.* See also Clarence Darrow and Victor S. Yerros, *The Prohibition Mania* (New York, 1927).
16. "What I have to do is see, at any rate, that I do not lend myself to the wrong which I condemn. As for adopting the ways which the state has provided for remedying the evil, I know not of such ways. They take too much time, and a man's life will be gone." Henry David Thoreau, "Civil Disobedience," in his *Walden and Other Writings* (New York, 1950), Modern Library ed., pp. 644–645.

17. See especially Daniel Katz, "The Functional Approach to the Study of Attitudes," *Public Opinion Quarterly*, XXIV (1960), 163–204; and M. Brewster Smith, Jerome S. Bruner and Robert W. White, *Opinions and Personality* (New York, 1964). In this section, too, several paragraphs are adapted from my forthcoming article for the *International Encyclopedia*, *op. cit.*

18. Albert Camus, *The Rebel* (New York, 1958), especially Part V.

19. To distinguish the two concepts is not to say that the same person or movement cannot at the same time believe in civil disobedience and in revolution. For example, one may have proximate or short-range aims to be served by civil disobedience and yet believe in eventual revolution; or one may believe in revolution as an ultimate resort if results of civil disobedience are too limited or too slow.

20. *Eichmann in Jerusalem* (New York, 1963), p. 289.

21. Jens Bjorneboe, "Eichmann i vaare hjerter" ("Eichmann in our hearts"), *Orientering*, Oslo (December 18, 1965).

[8] THE OBLIGATION TO DISOBEY

According to liberal political theory, as first formulated by John Locke, any individual citizen, oppressed by the rulers of the state, has a right to disobey their commands, break their laws, even rebel and seek to replace the rulers and change the laws. In fact, however, this is not a right often claimed or acted upon by individuals. Throughout history, when men have disobeyed or rebelled, they have done so, by and large, as members or representatives of groups and they have claimed not merely that they are free to disobey, but that they are obligated to do so. Locke says nothing about such obligations, and despite the fact that Jefferson claimed on behalf of the American colonists that "it is their right, it is their duty, to throw off [despotism]," the idea that men can be obligated to disobey has not played much part in liberal political theory.

"Here I stand; I can do no other"—Luther's bold defiance—is hardly an assertion of freedom or a claim to rights. It is the acknowledgment of a new but undeniable obligation. Nor is this obligation often asserted, as it was by Luther, in the first person singular. In a recent article on civil disobedience, Hugo Bedau has denied the validity of such an assertion, unless it is supplemented by arguments that reach beyond the moral feelings of the individual. "The force of saying, 'I ought to disobey this law' cannot be derived from 'Obeying this law is inconsistent with my moral convictions.'"[1] Perhaps it cannot, and then we must wait upon Luther's further defense before we judge his defiance. But the first sentence is, in practice, rarely derived from the second. Generally it follows from an assertion of a very different sort: "Obeying this law is inconsistent with *our* moral convictions (on behalf of which we have made significant commitments, organized, worked together for so many months or years, etc.)." And it can be argued that having said this, one can then go on, without offering additional reasons, to say, "Therefore I ought to disobey." This, at any rate, is the form that disobedience most often takes in history, even though additional reasons are usually offered. Men rarely break the law by themselves, or if they do they rarely talk about it. Disobedience, when it is not criminally, but morally, religiously, or politically motivated, is almost always a collective act and it is justified by the values of the collectivity and the mutual engagements of its members. In this essay I want first to describe the social processes by which men incur, or come to believe that they have incurred, the obligation to commit such acts. And then I want, very tentatively, to say something about the status of the obligations thus incurred.

I

The process by which obligations are incurred and the process by which they come to be felt are obviously not the same, or not necessarily the same. They are similar, however, in at least one respect: they are both social processes.[2] They occur in groups, and they can both occur simultaneously in different groups of different shapes and sizes. The duty to disobey arises when such processes are more successful (have greater moral and emotional impact) in parties, congregations, sects, movements, unions, or clubs than in states or churches. This happens often in human history, but precisely what is involved when it does needs to be carefully stated.

Obligations can arise in groups of two, between friends, partners, or lovers. But I am chiefly concerned with those that arise in groups of three or more, groups of a more general social, political, or religious nature. These can be obligations to the group as a whole (including oneself), or to the other members, or to the ideal that the group stands for or claims to embody. In practice, none of these occurs in pure form; obligations are generally, perhaps necessarily, admixtures of the three. But they are often described exclusively in terms of the last. Thus men announce that they are bound by God or the higher law, and bound "in conscience," which commonly means as morally sensitive individuals rather than as members. In fact, however, the very word "conscience" implies a shared moral knowledge and it is probably fair to argue not only that the individual's understanding of God or the higher law is always acquired within a group, but also that his obligation to either is at the same time an obligation to the group and to its members. "To be 'true to one's principles,'" Robert Paul Wolff has written, "is either a metaphor or else an elliptical way of describing loyalty to other men who share those principles and are relying upon you to observe them."[3] Perhaps this is exaggerated; clearly people feel that their principles embody what is right and there is nothing odd or metaphorical about saying that one ought to do what is right (though it's not clear whether this "ought" implies an obligation[4]). All I want to suggest is that commitments to principles are simultaneously commitments to other men, from whom or with whom the principles have been learned, and by whom they are enforced.

This becomes clear, I think, if one examines cases in which ideals are renounced or "sold out." For in all such cases it is individuals or groups of individuals who feel, and can plausibly be said to have been, betrayed. To "sell out" is to renounce heretical ideals for the sake of orthodox ones (but actually, it is generally suggested, for the sake of material gain) or it is to desert a small nonconformist group and join or rejoin society at large. Most likely, as the common descriptions of this common phenomenon suggest, it is to do both. "An affront to God and an injury to His congregation"—this is the way one's former colleagues describe a conversion to religious orthodoxy. And if God alone can judge the affront, they can rightly weigh the injury, taking into account the kind of commitment which had been made, the expectations which had been aroused, the ridicule to which they are (or are not) subjected, the possible weakening of their community, and so on.[5] Similarly, but more loosely, an artist who "sells out" by "going commercial" is not merely giving up an ideal; he is giving up an ideal to which others still adhere and those others are his former colleagues. His offense, in their eyes, is not only his betrayal of

Art, but also his betrayal of them. He injures the cause of Art, they would claim, both in its ideal form and in its concrete social manifestation.

The individual involved, of course, may be doing or think he is doing no such thing. He may have changed his mind for good reasons. And he may believe (rightly, I think) that there is or ought to be some due process whereby he can announce this change of mind, explain his reasons, and so escape the charge of betraying his former colleagues. But however far his obligations extend, insofar as he is obligated at all it is to other men as well as to ideals. Indeed, to think of the effect of his actions upon the ideal he once espoused, which is surely a necessary part of any due process of renunciation or withdrawal, is also to think of its effect upon those who still hold fast to that ideal.

Obligation, then, begins with membership, but membership in the broadest sense, for there are a great variety of formal and informal ways of living within a particular circle of action and commitment. Membership itself can begin with birth. Then the sense of obligation is acquired simply through socialization; it is the product and most often the intended product of religious or political education, of incessant and unrelenting communal pressure, of elaborate rites of passage, periodic ceremonial communions, and so on. One does not acquire any real obligations, however, simply by being born or by submitting to socialization within a particular group. These come only when to the fact of membership there is added the fact of willful membership. Different groups, of course, define willfulness in different ways, some in such minimal ways that willful membership becomes nothing more than continued membership after a certain age, some in such maximum ways that even formal adherence by an adult is inadequate without a public profession of the new faith or a period of intensive participation in specified group activities. Sixteenth- and seventeenth-century protests against infant baptism depended upon a maximum definition of individual willfulness, as did Lenin's attack upon the Menshevik view of party membership. And willfulness can be carried even further. Elaborate tests of would-be members, frightening initiation ceremonies, solemn oaths: These mechanisms of the secret society and the revolutionary brotherhood raise to the highest level the individual's sense of having made a choice of enormous personal significance and thereby assumed the most profound obligations.[6]

In general, well-established groups, especially those like the state that claim to be coterminous with society as a whole, are likely to defend the minimum definition, assume the commitment of their members, and punish those who disobey. Radical or nonconformist groups, precisely because they cannot make the assumption or guarantee the punishment, are likely to require that commitments take the form of explicit and public professions or acts. Through such professions and acts men can and do take on obligations to disobey the rules of the more inclusive group and also accept in advance the risks of their disobedience.

There is also a third sort of group, not sufficiently organized to make any precise determinations as to the character of membership. Disobedient citizens sometimes say that they are obligated by their membership in the "human community" or by their "solidarity with the oppressed." These obligations, if they exist at all, must be said to be universal (and men have indeed been punished for "crimes against humanity"). But they are generally cultivated in relatively small groups, often themselves loosely constituted, whose members can plausibly accuse one another, but not everyone else, of selling out when they fail to live up to their commitments. Since the community that is presumably being sold out is not the smaller but the larger group—which does not have any concrete existence and which is only an aspiration—it is difficult to see how or whether anyone else can have made a commitment or what his betrayal would involve.[7] It must be said that efforts to enforce such obligations by individuals against their own states, or by groups of states against individuals, are really efforts to create them. Insofar as these efforts win general support, insofar as an entity like "humanity" acquires some "collective conscience" and some legal and institutional structure, real obligations are in fact incurred by membership. Obviously in such an absolutely inclusive community the willfulness of individuals will play an absolutely minimal part. Humanity can indeed be renounced, but only by becoming a criminal of the very worst sort, by turning oneself into what Locke called a "monster." At the present time, since no group exists that can satisfactorily define crimes against humanity, such "monsters" are necessarily punished *ex post facto*, not for betraying humanity, but in the hope of creating a humanity whose members are capable of recognizing treason.

The state itself can sometimes be imagined as an ideal or potential community, obligating its members to oppose those authorities who act legally, but (it is thought) immorally in its name. Thus those men who disobey the commands of a collaborationist government after military defeat, or of a satellite government after some less formal capitulation, often claim that their state has been betrayed and that they are obligated by their previous membership and driven by their patriotism to resistance. But they cannot claim that all their fellow citizens are similarly obligated. In the aftermath of such struggles, if the resistance is successful, active collaborators may be punished (the legal basis for such punishment is unclear enough), but nothing can be done to those who merely declined to join the fight.[8] They had never incurred any duty to do so. On the other hand, those who did join and subsequently deserted can rightly be said to have broken tangible and morally significant commitments.[9]

To insist that obligations can only derive from willful undertakings is to restate the theory of the social contract. This has very interesting consequences given the rough typology of groups and kinds of membership just outlined. For contract theory clearly applies best to those sects, congregations, parties, movements, unions, and clubs in which individual choices are made explicit, acted out in some public fashion. It is most useful in discussing what are commonly called secondary associations, less useful (though by no means of no use at all) in discussing larger groups like states and established churches or vague and inclusive entities like humanity. Indeed, if the contract is taken at all seriously, it is difficult to avoid the conclusion that groups in which willfulness is heightened and maximized can rightfully impose greater obligations upon their members than can those catholic religious and political associations where membership is, for all practical purposes, inherited. Of course, inherited membership is often seconded by voluntary participation; in such cases the sense of obligation, as well as the obligation itself, is probably strongest of all. But even participation is likely to be more active and willful, and so a more satisfactory token of continuing consent, in nonconformist than in established and socially orthodox groups. Day-to-day procedures will be less conventionalized, the modes of participation and communion less habitual. In short, it is possible to conclude from contract theory, as Rousseau did, that small societies are (generally) morally superior to large ones. For isn't it the case that obligations incurred within some Protestant sect, derived from an explicit covenant and sustained by a continual round of activity, ought to take precedence over obligations incurred in society at large, derived from a largely mythical "tacit" consent and sustained by mere residence or occasional, largely passive, participation? I don't want to attempt an answer to that question immediately; perhaps there are good reasons for the negative answer conventionally given. But I do want to make two points: first, that obligations are in fact incurred within groups of these different sorts; secondly, that the conventionally assigned relative weights of these different obligations are not obviously accurate.

The duty to disobey (as well as the possibility of selling out) arises when obligations incurred in some small group come into conflict with obligations incurred in a larger, more inclusive group, generally, the state. When the small group is called a secondary association, it is being suggested that there is no point at issue here. Secondary associations ought to yield without argument, conflict, or moral tension to primary ones.[10] This is true only of associations clearly secondary, that is, with purposes or ideals that do not bring them into conflict with the larger society. Rotarians can't sell out.[11] But there exist in every society groups that may be called "secondary associations with claims to primacy." Serious conflict begins when groups of this sort are formed and their claims announced. But here a crucial distinction must be made: these claims can be of two very different kinds. Some groups announce what are in effect total claims. Their members are obligated, whenever commanded, to challenge the whole established legal system, to overthrow and replace one government with another, to attack the very existence of the larger society. These are revolutionary groups. There are others, however, that make only partial claims. They demand that the larger society recognize their primacy in some particular area of social or political life and so limit its own. They require of their members disobedience at certain moments, not at every moment; the refusal of particular legal commands, not of every legal command.

It is worth insisting upon the great difference between such groups and between the assertions they make, for defenders of state sovereignty often confuse them, arguing that any challenge to constituted authority is implicitly revolutionary and any group that claims to authorize such challenges is necessarily subversive. They thus assign the labels rebel and subversive to all sorts of people who explicitly reject them. When this is done by officials of the state, the labels often turn out to be accurate, since the men who originally chose not to revolt are eventually forced to do so in self-defense. But there is considerable evidence to suggest that the state can live with, even if it chooses not to accommodate, groups with partial claims against itself. The disobedience of the members of such groups will be intermittent and limited; it is unlikely to be conspiratorial in any sense; it does not involve any overt resistance to whatever acts of law enforcement the public authorities feel to be necessary (unless these are radically disproportionate to the "offense"). Such disobedience does not, in fact, challenge the existence of the larger society, but only its authority in this or that case or type of case, or over persons of this or that sort. It does not seek to replace one sovereign power with another, but only to call into question the precise range and incidence of sovereignty. This is not revolution, but civil disobedience, which can best be understood, I think, as the acting out of a partial claim.

Limited claims against larger societies can themselves be of two kinds. They can involve assertions that the larger society cannot make demands of a certain sort against *anyone,* or they can involve claims for exemptions for the members (and the future members) of the smaller society. When a man refuses to register for military service, without challenging state authority in any other sphere, he may be saying that the state cannot require anyone to fight on its behalf or to fight this or that particular sort of war, or he may be saying that people like himself cannot be so required. The second statement generally accompanies acts of conscientious objection, which represent only one kind of civil disobedience.

The larger society can always recognize the claims of smaller groups and so relieve their members from the burdens and risks of disobedience. Indeed, the historical basis of liberalism is in large part simply a series of such recognitions. Thus, the limited disobedience of religious sectarians was transformed into mere non-conformity when the state decided to tolerate the sects. Tolerance required a limit on the power of the state, a recognition that with regard to religious worship, any church or sect could rightfully claim primacy. Contemporary conscientious objectors are also tolerated nonconformists, but here the tolerance is of a different sort. It is a recognition of the claims of a particular type of person (or of particular groups of people) rather than of the claims of any person (or group) in a particular area. There is no necessary logical restriction on either type of toleration. The state could withdraw all its claims from an infinite number of areas; or it could add to every one of its laws a provision specifying that conscientious disobedience cannot be punished.[12] But few states seem likely to move very far in either of these logically possible directions, doubtless for good reasons.

What is the situation of men who join groups with limited claims to primacy in states where such claims are not recognized? It is a situation that political philosophers have never adequately described—though Rousseau surely understood the possibility of divided allegiance and divided men and bent all his efforts to avoid both. John Locke provides a convenient outline of the possibilities more generally thought to be available: (1) A man can be a *citizen*, which involves a full recognition of the primacy of his society and its government. Certain areas are set beyond the reach of the government, but in such a way as to bar any possible obligations against it. There are only rights and ultimately, so far as action goes, only one right, the right of rebellion. Hence, (2) a man can be a *rebel*, seeking to overthrow and replace a particular government and its laws. These are the only two possibilities available to members of the larger society. But Locke suggests two further options for those persons who do not wish to be members: (3) A man can be an *emigrant*, willfully withdrawing from the larger society and physically leaving its territory. Emigration is the only due process through which social obligations can be renounced, for the rebel is still bound if not to his government, then to society itself. Finally, (4) a man can be an *alien* who, having left the society of his fathers, fails to commit himself to any other and lives here or there at the discretion of the public authorities. An alien, for Locke, has obligations, for he is afforded protection within some particular society and tacitly consents in return to obey its laws. He presumably has rights, at least in theory, since rights are natural. But he does not possess, as citizens do, the practical right to rebel. It is a curious feature of Locke's thought that this appears to be the single most important difference between aliens and citizens.

Now the member of a group with partial claims to primacy falls into none of these categories. His loyalties are divided, so he is not in any simple sense a citizen. He refuses to call himself a rebel, and with good reason, for he seeks no total change in the government, no transformation of state or society (though he would surely claim the right to rebel, in Locke's sense, given the conditions under which Locke permits rebellion). He is not an emigrant, since he doesn't leave, though joining such a group may well constitute a kind of internal emigration. He is not an alien, for while an alien can always leave, he cannot demand to stay on conditions of his own choosing.

Yet the situation of such a man—obligated to obey because of his membership in a larger society, obligated to disobey (sometimes) because of his membership in a smaller one—is, for all its tensions, very common in history and has often been fairly stable over long periods of time. It is the situation of any person who, like Sophocles' Antigone, retains strong tribal or clan loyalties while becoming a member of some (almost any) political order.[13] It is virtually institutionalized in feudal systems.[14] It was lived through with extraordinary intensity by early modern Protestants and has been lived through since with greater or lesser intensity by a considerable variety of religious groups (including Roman Catholics, for Rousseau the visible embodiments of double obligation and moral division)—even in liberal societies, which have recognized some but not all the claims of pious brethren of this or that persuasion. It was the situation of European socialists during the period when their parties and movements had ceased to be revolutionary but had not yet accepted the status of secondary associations. (Otto Kirchheimer describes German Social Democracy as a "loyalty-absorbing counterorganization."[15]) It is often the situation of trade unionists, especially when their country is at war. It is the situation today of all those persons who object to military service on other than the permitted religious grounds. It is, despite considerable confusion, increasingly the situation of many members of the American civil rights movement.

What all these oddly assorted people have in common is this: None of them admits without qualification the political sovereignty or moral supremacy of the larger society of which they are members. None of them absolutely denies that sovereignty or supremacy. They are, then, partial members; they are simultaneously partial emigrants, partial aliens, partial rebels. The very existence of such people, even more, their obvious moral seriousness, ought to call into question the conventional definition of citizenship as involving an absolute commitment (it is sometimes said, "under God") to obey the laws. Surely such a commitment will never be found among every one of those persons who consider themselves, with reason, citizens of the state. For the processes through which men incur obligations are unavoidably pluralistic. Even in a liberal society, which allows considerable room for divergent groups and recognizes many of their claims, what might be called the incidence of obligation is bound to be uneven, the obligations themselves at least sometimes contradictory. Unless the state deliberately inhibits the normal processes of group formation, and does so with greater success than has ever yet been achieved, it will always be confronted by citizens who believe themselves to be, and may actually be, obligated to disobey. According to J. N. Figgis:

> The theory of sovereignty . . . is in reality no more than a venerable superstition. . . . As a fact it is as a series of groups that our social life presents itself, all having some of the qualities of public law and most of them showing clear signs of a life of their own. . . .[16]

I I

Many political philosophers have argued that there exists a *prima facie* obligation to obey the laws of the most inclusive organized society of which one is a member—that is, for most men, the state.[17] This is not unreasonable, so long as the state provides equally to all its members certain essential services. It is not unreasonable even though the state maintains a monopoly of such services and tolerates no competition, for it may be that the monopoly is itself essential to the provision of the services. But the existence of a *prima facie* obligation to obey means no more than that disobedience must always be justified. First explanations are owed to those of one's fellow citizens who do not join in, who remain obedient. I think it can be argued that membership (that is, morally serious membership) in groups with partial claims to primacy is always a possible explanation.

But I want to attempt a stronger argument than this, loosely derived from the preceding discussion of the uneven incidence of obligation in any larger society. I want to suggest that men have a *prima facie* obligation to honor the engagements they have explicitly made, to defend the groups and uphold the ideals to which they have committed themselves, even against the state, so long as their disobedience of laws or legally authorized commands does not threaten the very existence of the larger society or endanger the lives of its citizens. It is obedience to the state, when one has a duty to disobey, that must be justified. First explanations are owed to one's brethren, colleagues, or comrades. Their usual form is an argument that personal security or public health or some other such necessity of the common life—which the smaller groups cannot supply and which is actually supplied by the state—is being threatened or likely to be threatened by particular acts of disobedience, however limited their scope. This, of course, is precisely what is asserted (usually by an official of the state) in every case of disobedience, but it is not necessarily asserted rightly. Indeed, there is very little evidence that suggests that carefully limited, morally serious civil disobedience undermines the legal system or endangers personal security.[18] One can imagine situations in which the acting out of partial claims might encourage or inspire the acting out of total claims. But the two sorts of action remain distinct. It may be necessary for a man contemplating civil disobedience to worry about the possibilities of revolutionary violence, but only if such possibilities actually exist. It is by no means necessary for him to reflect upon the purely theoretical possibility that his action might be universalized, that all men might break the laws or claim exemptions from them. For his action implies nothing more than that those men ought to do so who have acquired obligations to do so. And the acquiring of such obligations is a serious, long-term business which, if undertaken by everybody, would simply obviate the necessity for disobedience: if all men joined the sect, it would become the church; if all men joined the movement, there would be no state to resist; if all men joined different sects and movements, tolerance would not be the claim of this or that group, but a common necessity.

The state can thus be described as a purely external limit on group action, but it must be added that the precise point at which the limit becomes effective cannot be left for state offiicals to decide. For them, the law must be the limit. At the same time, it must be the claim of the disobedient members that the law is over-extended, that its sphere ought to be restricted in some fashion, that this activity or this type of person should be exempted, at this particular moment or for all time. There can be no possible judge of this disagreement. All that can be said is that the moral seriousness of the disobedient members is evidenced in part by their respect for those genuine goods which the state provides not only to themselves, but to everyone. To argue that the state does not provide such goods at all, or that it denies them entirely to particular sections of the population, is to justify unlimited and uncivil disobedience. Revolution always requires (and generally gets) some such special justification.

There are two other ways of describing the state which appear to argue against the claim that disobedience can ever be a *prima facie* obligation. The first is to insist that the state is itself a group, that its members too are willful members who have incurred obligations of the most serious kind. It was the original purpose of social contract theory to uphold just this conception of the state. But there are serious problems here. Since for most men there is no real alternative to state membership, the willfulness of that membership does not seem to have even the most minimal moral significance.[19] A theory like Locke's requires the argument that one can always leave the state; therefore, mere residence can meaningfully be described as a choice. Whatever the value of that description in Locke's time, it has very little today. But there is, I think, another way of describing the willfulness of state membership: this is to take very seriously the possibility of joining secondary associations with limited claims to primacy. Such engagements represent, as has already been suggested, a kind of internal emigration or partial alienation, and so long as the processes of group formation are not controlled or repressed, they offer real alternatives to full state membership. Thus, the possibility of becoming a conscientious objector establishes the possibility of incurring an obligation to military service. One incurs such an obligation by *not* becoming an objector (though perhaps the alternative must bulk somewhat larger in our common life than conscientious objection presently does if it is to have this effect). The obligation is real even if it is incurred for no other reason than that conscientious objection involves penalties, though this is not so if the penalties are unlimited or without proportion or if the state interferes in any way with the groups within which the duty to object is both learned and incurred. The state can only be regarded as a choice, then, if the possible legitimacy of countergroups of a limited sort is admitted.

But the obligations of citizens to the state can be derived in yet another way: not from their willfulness, but from its value. "If all communities aim at some good," wrote Aristotle, "the state or political community, which is the highest of all, and which embraces all the rest aims, and in a greater degree than any other, at the highest good."[20] Obviously, groups that aim at the highest good take priority over groups that seek lower or partial goods. There are two major difficulties, however, with Aristotle's description. First of all, it is not the case that the state necessarily embraces all other communities. A state with an established church and no legal provision for religious toleration obviously excludes a dissenting sect. Groups with universalist or international pretensions, like the Catholic Church or any early twentieth-century socialist party, necessarily exclude themselves. Political or religious communities that oppose war are in no simple sense "embraced" by states that fight wars. It is precisely the nature of secondary associations with claims to primacy that they cannot and do not exist wholly within the established political or legal frame. Secondly, while the state may well provide or seek to provide goods for all its members, it is not clear that these add up to or include the highest good. Perhaps they are goods of the lowest common denominator and only for this reason available to all, for it may be that the highest good can be pursued only in small groups—in pietist sects or utopian settlements, for example, or, as Aristotle himself suggested, in philosophic dialogue. In any case, men do not agree as to the nature of the highest good, and this fact is enormously significant for the processes of group formation. Groups are formed for a great variety of reasons, but one of the chief reasons is to advocate or act out ("without tarrying for the magistrate," as a late sixteenth-century Puritan minister wrote) a new conception of the highest good, a conception at which the state does not aim, and perhaps cannot. To form such a group or to join one is to reject Aristotle's argument and renounce whatever obligation is implied by it. I fail to see any reason why this is not an option available to any morally serious man.

In the argument thus far, a great deal of weight has been attached to the phrase "morally serious." Obviously, the term is not easy to define, nor the quality easy to measure. Yet frivolous or criminal disobedience cannot be justified by membership in a group. There are obligations among thieves, but not *prima facie* obligations against the state. This is true, first of all, because the activities of thieves endanger the security of us all. But it is also true because a robbers' gang does not make claims to primacy. Thieves do not seek to limit the authority of the sovereign state; they seek to evade it. But there is nothing evasive about civil disobedience: a public claim against the state is publicly acted out. This willingness to act in public and to offer explanations to other people suggests also a willingness to reflect upon and worry about the possible consequences of the action for the public as a whole. Neither of these by themselves legitimize the action; but they do signal the moral seriousness of the group commitment that legitimates it.[21]

Frivolous disobedience can also never be a duty, and so groups that do not encourage an awareness in their members of the purposes and actions to which they may become committed cannot commit them. Awareness of this sort would appear to be required by social contract theory; even the notion of tacit consent implies that there exists some knowledge of the duties that are being incurred. Nor, it seems to me, are the requirements of the theory entirely satisfied if such knowledge is but glimpsed at one brief moment in time. Continued awareness, a kind of shared self-consciousness, is necessary before the consent and participation of individuals carries sufficient moral weight to establish obligations— or, at any rate, to establish such obligations as I am trying to defend. A morally serious member of a group with partial claims may, then, be described as follows: he joins the group voluntarily, knowing what membership involves; he devotes time and energy to its inner life, sharing in the making of decisions; he acts publicly in its name or in the name of its ideals. Such a person—not any person—is obligated to act as he does, unless he is given good reasons why he ought not to do so.

III

The problem of civil disobedience needs to be placed squarely in the context of group formation, growth, tension, and conflict. There is a sociology of disobedience, which has greater relevance for philosophy than has generally been thought; it helps establish the proper units of analysis. Now these units doubtlessly have their limits, for it is true that there come moments when individuals must make choices or sustain actions alone—or rather, and this is not at all the same thing, when they must endure the anguish of loneliness. The state always seeks to isolate its disobedient citizens because it is far more likely to bend their wills to its own if it can break the cohesion of the group that initially planned the disobedience and convince its members that they are members no longer. But this only suggests that the men who run prisons are always very much aware of the sociology of disobedience. Surely philosophers should be no less so.

The heroic encounter between sovereign individual and sovereign state, if it ever took place, would be terrifyingly unequal. If disobedience depended upon a conscience really private, it might always be justified and yet never occur. Locke understood this very well, for even while he proclaimed the right of individuals to rebel, he recognized that "the right to do so will not easily engage them in a contest, wherein they are sure to perish. . . ."[22] Rebellion, he thought, is only possible when it engages the "whole body" of the people. But clearly, rebellion and, even more, civil disobedience, is most often the work of groups of much more limited extent. Clearly, too, it is not the mere individual right to rebel, unchanged in groups large or small, which sustains the enterprise, but rather the mutual undertakings of the participants. Without this mutuality, very few men would ever join the "contest"—not because of the fear of being killed, but because of the greater fear of being alone. "This is what is most difficult," wrote Jean Le Meur, the young French army officer who was imprisoned for refusing to fight in Algeria, "being cut off from the fraternity, being locked up in a monologue, being incomprehensible." And then: "Do tell the others that this is not a time to let me down."[23]

All this is not to suggest that there is anything unreal about individual responsibility. But this is always responsibility *to someone else* and it is always learned *with someone else.* An individual whose moral experiences never reached beyond "monologue" would know nothing at all about responsibility and would have none. Such a man might well have rights, including the right to rebel, but his possession of the right to rebel would be purely theoretical; he would never become a rebel. No political theory that does not move beyond rights to duties, beyond monologue to fraternal discussion, debate, and resolution, can ever explain what men actually do when they disobey or rebel, or why they do so. Nor can it help us very much to weigh the rightness or wrongness of what they do.

[NOTES]

1. Hugo Adam Bedau, "On Civil Disobedience," *Journal of Philosophy*, LVII (October 12, 1961), 663.
2. The best description of these processes is probably still Emile Durkheim's *L'Education Morale* (Paris, 1925).
3. Robert Paul Wolff, "An Analysis of the Concept of Political Loyalty," in *Political Man and Social Man*, Wolff, ed. (New York, 1966), p. 224.
4. See Alexander Sesonske, *Value and Obligation* (New York, 1964), pp. 20ff. and *passim*.
5. Where such judgments cannot be made at all, there is no obligation. And this means that obligations are always shared among men, who must judge one another. "The only obligation which I have a right to assume," wrote Thoreau, "is to do at any time what I think right." But when, in jail, he greeted the visiting Emerson with the famous question, "What are you doing out there?" he clearly implied the existence of a common obligation. Common to whom? Common at least to New England philosophers, one of whom was failing to meet it. Emerson believed the same thing when he spoke in his lecture on the Fugitive Slave Law of the "disastrous defection of the men of letters" from the cause of freedom. *The Complete Essays and Other Writings of Ralph Waldo Emerson* (New York, 1940), Modern Library ed., p. 867.
6. Eric Hobsbawm, *Primitive Rebels* (New York, 1963), Chapter 9; for some examples of secret oaths, see Appendix 13.
7. Sesonske, *op. cit.*, p. 107.
8. Henry L. Mason, *The Purge of Dutch Quislings* (The Hague, 1952), Chapter II.
9. See Guillain de Bénouville's defense of capital punishment in the French Resistance: ". . . in the Maquis each man had chosen his own lot, fashioned his destiny with his own hands, picked his own name. Everyone had accepted in advance and without question all possible risks." *The Unknown Warriors* (New York, 1949), p. 220.
10. S. I. Benn and R. S. Peters, *The Principles of Political Thought* (New York, 1965), Chapter 12.
11. People who accuse trade union leaders of selling out are, in effect, accusing them of acting like leaders of secondary associations, the implication of their accusation being that the union (or the labor movement generally) is something more than secondary.
12. Bedau, *op. cit.*, p. 655.
13. The conflict in Sophocles' play is, of course, between primary groups. In general, conflicts between groups of relatives or friends and the state take

forms similar to those described above, especially in modern times when such alliances tend increasingly to be voluntary. E. M. Forster's statement that "If I had to choose between betraying my country and betraying my friend, I hope I should have the guts to betray my country . . ." is roughly analogous to the sorts of assertions sometimes made on behalf of groups. Forster, *Two Cheers for Democracy* (New York, 1951), p. 78. But it is an extreme statement and has reference to exceptional cases. Most often, the choice is between betraying one's friend (or colleagues) and *disobeying the laws* of one's country. Antigone's act is not treason, on any usual interpretation of that tricky term.

14. See Marc Bloch, *Feudal Society* (Chicago, 1961), Chapters IX–XVII.
15. Otto Kirchheimer, *Political Justice* (Princeton, 1961), p. 9.
16. J. N. Figgis, *Churches in the Modern State* (London, 1914), p. 224. See also G. D. H. Cole, "Conflicting Social Obligations" and "Loyalties," in *Proceedings of the Aristotelian Society*, Vols. XV and XXVI (new series).
17. See, for example, W. D. Ross, *The Right and the Good* (Oxford, 1930), pp. 27–28; and discussion in Richard Wasserstrom, "Disobeying the Law," *Journal of Philosophy*, LVII (October 12, 1961), 647.
18. It is often enough said that disobedience even of bad laws undermines the habit of law-abidingness and so endangers that fundamental order upon which civilized life depends. But I have never seen this argued with careful attention to some particular body of evidence. In the absence of such an argument, I would be inclined to agree with David Spitz that there are clearly *some* laws obedience to which is not required for the maintenance of social order. Even more important, perhaps, there are many laws which can be disobeyed by *some men*, without prejudice to social order. Spitz, "Democracy and the Problem of Civil Disobedience," *Essays in the Liberal Idea of Freedom* (Tucson, 1964), pp. 74–75.
19. Wolff, *op. cit.*, pp. 227–228.
20. Aristotle, *Politics*, I, 1; see discussion in Benn and Peters, *op. cit.*, pp. 315ff.
21. Secret societies, if they are not criminal, are implicitly revolutionary; the moral seriousness of their members must be signaled differently.
22. Locke, *Second Treatise of Government*, par. 208.
23. Jean Le Meur, "The Story of a Responsible Act," in Wolff, *op. cit.*, pp. 204, 205.

C. B. MACPHERSON

[9] DEMOCRATIC THEORY:
ONTOLOGY AND TECHNOLOGY

The Race Between Ontology and Technology

The notion of a race between East and West for technological superiority has been familiar since Sputnik. The notion of a competition between eastern and western ways of life, which can be stated as a competition between two sets of ethical values, is, if less precise and less specific, still familiar enough. The notion that the latter competition can be reduced still further to a competition between two ontologies, two views of the essence of man, is less familiar but will repay investigation. I want to suggest that there is now, as between East and West, not only a competition between technologies, and another competition between ontologies, but that these have set up, in the West at least, a fateful race between ontological change and technological change. I shall argue that our western democratic theory—the theory by which we justify and so sustain our western democratic societies—will fail to sustain those societies unless we can revise its ontological base before it is faced with the effects of much more technological progress. My concern, then, is with the race between ontology and technology in western democratic society and theory.

I shall argue that the ontological assumptions of our western democratic theory have been, for something like a hundred years, internally inconsistent, comprising, as they do, two concepts of the human essence that are in the circumstances incompatible. One of these is the liberal, individualist concept of man as essentially a consumer of utilities, an infinite desirer and infinite appropriator. This concept was fitting, even necessary, for the development of the capitalist market society, from the seventeenth century on: It antedates the introduction of democratic principles and institutions, which did not amount to anything before the nineteenth century. The other is the concept of man as an enjoyer and exerter of his uniquely human attributes or capacities, a view that began to challenge the market view in the mid-nineteenth century and soon became an integral part of the justifying theory of liberal-democracy. I shall argue further that changes now clearly discernible in our society, notably the technological revolution, make it possible to move away from this unstable theoretical position, but that this move, far from being an automatic consequence of social change, requires first, among political scientists, a theoretical understanding rooted in the social history of political theory and, concurrently or subsequently (but not much subsequently), a more widespread change in western democratic ideology. I shall suggest, that is to say, that twentieth– (and twenty-first–) century technology will make possible the realization of the more democratic concept of man's essence; but that technological change in our lifetime, if left to operate by itself within the present social structure and guided only by our present ambivalent ontology, without a conscious reformulation of the concept of man's essence appropriate to the new possibilities, is as likely to prevent as to promote the realization of liberal-democratic ends. It is in this sense that I regard the race between ontological and technological change in our society as fateful.

Western Democratic Ontology: The Individualist Base

To demonstrate that the assumptions about the essence of man on which our democratic theory rests are contradictory, we shall have to look at what I have called the social history of political theory in the last century or more, for the two now conflicting sets of assumptions rose at different times in response to different changes in the power relations of our western societies. But we may start from a contemporary point about a distinguishing feature of western democracy.

The first thing that emerges from any examination of contemporary western democratic theory, as distinct from the communist
theory of democracy and the various populist theories prevalent in
much of the third world, is that the western theory puts a high
value on individual freedom of choice, not only as between political parties but also as between different uses of one's income, of
one's capital, and of one's skill and energy. Western democracy is
a market society, through and through; or, if one prefers to confine
the term democracy to a system of government rather than a kind
of society, western democracy is *for* market society.

This observation from the contemporary scene takes on fuller
meaning when the western concept of democracy is traced back a
century and more. It is then seen that the roots of the contemporary
western or liberal-democratic theory are in the liberal market society and the liberal state, which emerged first in England as early
as the seventeenth century, and in the liberal justifying theory,
from (say) Locke to Bentham. As I have shown elsewhere,[1] that
society and state and theory were well established at least half a
century before the franchise became at all democratic and democratic theory became at all respectable or intellectually tenable.
The liberal market postulates were well entrenched before the liberal theory was transformed into liberal-democratic theory. Their
entrenchment meant the entrenchment of a peculiar concept of
man's essence. The predemocratic liberal theory was based on a
concept of man as essentially a consumer of utilities, an infinite
desirer. This concept, clearly dominant in Benthamism, where it is
displayed to perfection in James Mill's essay on *Government,* goes
back through the classical economists, at least as far as Locke.[2]

The liberal theory, in its Benthamite form, specifically made the
criterion of the good society the maximization of individual utilities,
and made the essence of man the desire to maximize his utilities.
Man was essentially a bundle of appetites demanding satisfaction.
Man was a consumer of utilities. The Benthamite analysis was of
course much more refined than to suggest that all the satisfactions
or utilities the individual sought were material consumer goods:
Man's utilities included the pleasures of curiosity, of amity, of reputation, of power, of sympathy, of ease, of skill, of piety, of be-
nevolence, and so on.[3] Nevertheless, when it came to the decisive
question of whether material equality or security for unequal property and profit was the more important, Bentham's answer was

unequivocal: Security for unequal property must outweigh the ethical claims of equality of property, even though he had just demonstrated, by invoking the law of diminishing utility, that equality of property was required in any society where each man was really to count as one in the calculation of aggregate utility. The reason for subordinating the claims of equality was that any regime of equality would destroy incentives to accumulation of capital and hence would prevent all increase of the aggregate of material goods available for the satisfactions of the whole society.[4] Man's good lay in the indefinite increase of the aggregate of material goods. It is clear from this reasoning that Bentham saw man as first and foremost an appropriator and consumer of material utilities.

Indeed, the first two postulates on which Bentham based his case for equality may be considered the bedrock of this whole idea of utility. These are (abstraction having been made "of the particular sensibility of individuals, and of the exterior circumstances in which they may be placed," which abstraction Bentham said was amply justified): "1st. *Each portion of wealth has a corresponding portion of happiness. 2nd. Of two individuals with unequal fortunes, he who has the most wealth has the most happiness.*"[5] The maximization of wealth *is* the maximization of happiness, or at least is the *sine qua non* of maximization of utility. The centrality of the concept of man as consumer is sufficiently evident.

It may be objected that the concept of man as a consumer of utilities does not necessarily carry with it a postulate of *infinite* desire. Logically this may be so. But it can be seen that historically the postulate of infinite desire was required to justify the society of which man the consumer was said to be the center.

The first society that postulated man as an infinitely desirous consumer of utilities was the capitalist market society that emerged in the seventeenth century in England. I do not mean that moral and political philosophers had never before then noticed the appetitive side of man or even postulated the infinitely desirous nature of some men. Many had done so. But they had generally noticed it only to deplore it and to urge its supersession by higher moral values. What I find new, from the seventeenth century on, was the widespread assumption that infinite desire not only was present in man but was also rational and morally allowable.

How may this new assumption be said to have been required by the new society? It was, I think, required in order to justify the change to certain new institutions which were required to realize the great increase of individual and national wealth (and of individual freedom) that was then seen to be possible. Let me try to establish this in two stages: (a) that new institutions, including a new system of incentives to productive labor, were required; (b) that the new assumption about the essence of man was required to justify these institutions.

(a) It will not, I think, be disputed that the system of capitalist enterprise (whether in its mercantilist, laissez-faire, or neo-mercantilist form) requires, by contrast with any previous system, an abandonment of authoritative or customary allocation of work and reward to individuals, and its replacement by freedom of the individual to use his energy, skill, and material resources, through contractual engagements, in the way that seems to him best calculated to bring him the greatest return. Nor will it be disputed that for this system to operate efficiently, everyone in it must base his decisions on the calculation of his maximum return. Only so would the operation of the market produce the socially desirable result of maximizing the wealth of the nation.

The market system, then, requires that men act as maximizers of their utilities. This in itself could be expected to set up a disposition toward a concept of man as essentially a maximizer of his utilities, which implies a postulate of infinite desire. But as we shall see in a moment, another requirement of the market system makes such a concept imperative.

The minimum institutions required for the system of capitalist enterprise are, first, legal contractual freedom to use one's person and property in the most gainful way one can see, and, secondly, a system of markets in which labor-power, capital, and land will continually find prices that will induce their proprietors to enter them in the productive process. These requirements, we should notice, can be met under a mercantilist system of state regulation of trade as well as under the perfectly free market of laissez-faire. A considerable amount of state regulation of trade and prices is quite consistent with the market system, for such regulation simply alters some of the terms of the calculation each individual must make, while leaving as the driving force of the whole system the individual actions based on those calculations.

But while a perfectly free market is not required to get the system going or to make it go, something more is required, by way of incentives, than merely freedom to seek the best return. What is needed, in a society that by definition cannot rely on traditional, patriarchal, or feudal obligations to work, and whose supporters, besides, see prospects of untold wealth under the new market arrangements if only people can be induced to exert themselves, is an institutionalized incentive to continuous exertion. Such an incentive can be, and was, provided by setting up a right of unlimited individual appropriation. The establishment of that right could be expected to move men to continuous effort by giving them the prospect of ever more command over things to satisfy their desires.

Whether this incentive ever did or could operate to induce continuous exertion by the bulk of the employed labor force may well be doubted. The seventeenth-century writers, including Locke, did not think it would. But then they did not think of the propertyless laboring class as fully human, or at least not as full citizens. The right of unlimited individual appropriation would, however, be an effective incentive to continuous exertion and ingenuity on the part of the small and middling independent proprietors as well as the capitalist enterprisers proper. And it was on these that the chief reliance was placed for increasing productivity. The employed work force was expected to continue to be tractable, to work because they had to, on terms set by the market (aided from time to time by the Justices in Quarter Sessions). But the farmers, the manufacturers, and the merchants, the backbone of the new society, would respond to the incentive offered by the prospect of unlimited appropriation.

And it is difficult to see how any incentive short of the right of unlimited appropriation would bring this response. For what limits to the right of individual appropriation could be set? It would obviously have been useless to limit men's acquisition of property to the amounts required to maintain some customary standard of living for members of each traditional rank or class. It would have been equally useless to retain any such limits on the ways one could acquire wealth as were set by the old principle of commutative justice. Nor could the old principle of distributive justice have been retained as a limit on any man's acquisition, for the market system can permit no other criterion of a man's worth than what the market will give him. All these limits had to go, and there was no reason to think up other limits. Indeed, any other limit would presumably have to be justified in terms of some moral principle that would encroach on the market system, whereas the whole point was to get away from moral as well as traditional limits (as Locke did in nullifying the Natural Law limits on individual appropriation).

We conclude, then, that the institutions needed by the capitalist market society included, as an incentive to continuous effort, the right of unlimited individual appropriation.

(b) We have now to show that this in turn required the new assumption about the essence of man.

To justify, that is, to find a moral basis for the right of unlimited individual appropriation (and some justification was needed, for to assert this right was to jettison the hitherto prevalent Natural Law limits on property), it was necessary to derive the right from the supposed very nature or essence of man, just as the previous theories that had limited the right of appropriation had been derived from a supposed nature or essence of man.

The postulate that would most directly supply this derivation is that man is essentially an infinite appropriator—that is, that his nature can only be fully realized in his acquiring ownership of everything. But this postulate is unsuitable, if not untenable. Apart from the difficulty that, on this postulate, no individual could realize his essence while there were other individuals in the same universe, there is another difficulty, less logical but more operational. For what was required was not simply the postulate that men were like that, but that their being so was in accordance with natural law or morality. The postulate that was needed was one that would serve as the basis of a moral justification. It had to be one on which an acceptable moral theory could be built. It would have been too outrageous to postulate that love of wealth was not only natural but also the root of all good.[6]

But if the postulate of man as infinite appropriator was too stark, there was another that appeared more moral and would serve as well. This is the postulate that man is essentially an unlimited desirer of utilities, a creature whose nature is to seek satisfaction of unlimited desires both innate and acquired. The desires could be seen as sensual or rational or both. What mattered was that their satisfaction required a continuous input of things from outside. Man is essentially an infinite consumer.

This does not necessarily make man an infinite appropriator: He need not, in principle, seek ownership of everything in order to expect to consume at an ever-increasing level of satisfactions. And consumer satisfaction could even be represented (as it was by Locke) as a moral reward for honest effort, having nothing in common with *amor sceleratus habendi.*

However, while the postulate of man as infinite consumer does not necessarily make him an infinite appropriator, only a simple additional minor premise is needed to convert him into that. The premise required is merely that land and capital must be privately owned to be productive (a premise which Locke, for instance, explicitly made[7]). Then, to realize his essence as consumer, man must be an appropriator of land and capital. Man the infinite consumer becomes man the infinite appropriator. This conclusion was not usually drawn: The postulate of man as infinite consumer was enough.

A more accurate representation of the essential nature, not of man as such, but of man as shaped by capitalist market society, might have been found but for the fact that the theorists wanted to make statements about man as such, this being the only kind of statement that appeared to provide a secure foundation for a general justificatory theory. Had it not been for this, man might have been described straight away as an infinite appropriator not only of goods for consumption but of revenue-producing capital (which is what capitalist man essentially must be). But it was more fitting to the needs of a general moral theory to describe him, instead, as an infinite desirer of utilities, which could be taken to mean only a desirer of things for consumption. This would entitle him to unlimited appropriation of things for consumption. And by failing to make, or to emphasize, the distinction between property in things for consumption and revenue-producing property, the theory could be taken to justify unlimited appropriation of the latter as well.

I have argued so far that the concept of man as an infinite consumer was not only congruous with the behavior required of men in market society, but was also needed to justify the right of unlimited appropriation, which was needed as an incentive to continuous effort in that society. I do not attempt to deal here with the question of whether this concept was a conscious invention of thinkers who saw clearly that the market society could not be justified without such a concept. I simply propose that the need for such a concept did exist, and that this need was met in the body of liberal theory from Locke to Bentham. The concept is still with us:

It is still needed insofar as our society relies on market incentives to get its main productive work done.

And we should notice one implication of the acceptance of the concept of man as an infinite consumer, an implication whose importance will be evident later in our analysis. If man's desires are infinite, the purpose of man must be an endless attempt to overcome scarcity. This is saying a good deal more than simply that scarcity is the permanent human condition, which was not at all a novel idea. There had always been scarcity, and until the rise of capitalism it had generally been assumed that there always would be. But the precapitalist assumption of the permanence of scarcity did not involve any idea that the rational man's purpose in life was to devote himself to trying to overcome it. On the contrary, it was more apt to result in resignation to scarcity as man's fate (scarcity being thought of as an absolute rather than a relative condition), and in moral theories denigrating a life of acquisition.

The new view of scarcity was quite different. In the new view, scarcity was indeed also thought to be permanent, but not because of any inability of men to increase their productivity, and not in any absolute sense. Scarcity now was seen to be permanent simply because, relative to infinite desire, satisfactions are by definition always scarce. What was new was the assumption of the rationality or morality of infinite desire. And as soon as this assumption is made, the rational purpose of man becomes an endless attempt to overcome scarcity. The attempt is endless by definition, but only by engaging endlessly in it can infinitely desirous man realize his essential nature.

Western Democratic Ontology: The Egalitarian Complement

A second concept of the human essence was introduced at the time when the liberal individualist theory became democratized. The turning point comes in the nineteenth century, made clear in the contrast between John Stuart Mill and Bentham. By the middle of the nineteenth century it was apparent to perceptive observers such as Mill that the market society had produced a working class sufficiently politically conscious that the franchise could not be denied it much longer. At the same time the quality of life in the market society was seen by moralists as different as Mill and Marx, Carlyle and Saint-Simon, Ruskin and Green, the German romantics and the

English Christian Socialists to be little or nothing short of an insult to humanity. Those of the critics of market morality who still hoped to retain some of the values of liberal individualism thus thought it both politically expedient to moralize the clamant democratic forces before they were admitted to a share in political power, and morally right to assert a higher set of values than those of the market.

This meant asserting an equal right of every individual to make the most of himself. And it meant that the concept of man as essentially a consumer of utilities had to yield its pre-eminence, or at least its monopoly position: A concept of man as essentially an exerter and enjoyer of his own powers had to be asserted. Life was to be lived, not to be devoted to acquiring utilities. The end or purpose of man was to use and develop his uniquely human attributes. A life so directed might be thought of as a life of reason or a life of sensibilities, but it was not a life of acquisition. If we wished to express this concept of man's essence in terms of maximization, we could say that man's essence is not maximization of his utilities but maximization of his human powers. Or we could say that man is neither an infinite consumer nor an infinite appropriator but an infinite developer of his human attributes.

The liberal-democratic thinkers who took this view—J. S. Mill and Green most notably—were of course going back to a much older tradition than the Locke-to-Bentham theory of man. They were, in a sense, exposing Locke-to-Bentham as a deviation from the western humanist and Christian traditions that go back to the Greeks and to medieval Natural Law. They were reasserting the old values, and on a new and more democratic plane.

It might seem that this concept of man's essence as exerter and enjoyer of his own powers, and the assertion of the equal right of every individual to make the most of himself, would be a sufficient basis for a viable liberal-democratic theory. It could be claimed that a liberal individualist society, redeemed by these principles (the latter of which would be enforced by the sanction of the democratic franchise), would have the best of both worlds—the individual freedom of the liberal society plus the equality of a democratic society. This is, in effect, the claim made by Mill and Green and subsequent liberal-democratic theorists.

The claim has never been made good. The reason is that it has been impossible to jettison the Locke-to-Bentham concept of man, and impossible to combine it with the other concept of man.

The reason it has been impossible to jettison the concept of man as infinite consumer or infinite appropriator has already been suggested: That concept is needed to provide the incentives and justify the power relations of a capitalist market society. The western liberal-democracies are still capitalist market societies. We still demand, as an essential freedom, the individual's freedom to choose how he will use his natural and acquired capacities and his acquired material resources (if any) with a view to maximizing his material utilities (including capital as well as utilities directly for consumption). And we still rely on the capitalist market incentive of a right of appropriation, no longer quite unlimited (for our tax structures generally set an upper limit) but with a limit so high as to be far beyond the reach of most men, and so, for them, virtually unlimited. So long as we rely on this incentive, we cannot dispense with the concept of man as infinite desirer, nor deny the rationality of infinite desire.

The proposition that our society is based on the assumption of infinite desirousness may seem to be controverted by the phenomenon of modern advertising. The purpose of mass advertising of consumer goods, its critics assert, is to create demand, that is, to create desires which otherwise would not exist. If the system has to create new desires by this stimulus from outside the individual, the system does not seem to be based on the assumption of infinite natural desire.

There is some substance in this objection, though not as much as first appears. We may grant that the purpose of advertising is to create a desire for a certain commodity (X's detergent) or, in the case of institutional advertising, for a certain category of goods or services (beer is best, wine is smart, worship in the church of your choice). The purpose is to create a desire that did not exist, or to increase the amount of desire that did exist, for these specific things. But this may be no more than an attempt to divert part of a given mass of desirousness from one product to another. If it is more than this, it appears to be an attempt to increase the mass of desirousness by artificial creation of desires for new things or for more things. This would not seem to be consistent with the assumption of innate infinite desire.

Yet on closer analysis it may be thought to be not only consistent with that assumption but actually based on that assumption. For what else are the advertisers assuming than what economic theory commonly assumes; namely, that every want satisfied creates a still further want, which is to assume that desire does automatically increase without limit, although by stages? The assumption is that the mass of desire is naturally ever increasing: The purpose of the advertiser is to capture some of the increment and make it a demand for his product. The assumption, after all, is that man is infinitely desirous.

Any discussion of this sort soon runs into the vexing question of the relative importance of innate and socially acquired desires. It is sometimes said that civilization consists in the acquisition and satisfaction of new desires. If it is assumed that it is man's nature to civilize himself (and some such theory of progress generally goes with that view of civilization), then infinite desire is not only good but is innate. The acquisition of new desires becomes an innate need. The line between innate and acquired desire disappears. So does any moral criterion for choosing between different patterns of desire.

Much of this difficulty comes from the way the question is put. If you start from the assumption that there is a permanent unchanging nature of man, then you are forced to subsume all changes, such as increase of desires, under his innate nature. If you drop that assumption, and assume instead that man changes his nature by changing his relation to other men and the material environment, the difficulty disappears. It can then be seen that man can in principle choose and impose what moral rules he wishes, and can change them as circumstances seem to him to call for. This is what men in different societies commonly have done. In the market society they created an image of man as infinite desirer and infinite appropriator, and set the moral rules accordingly. In reaction against the results of this, theorists began in the nineteenth century to try to replace this image with another one, and to propose a revised set of moral rules. The new image and morality have as good a claim as the market image and morality, or a better claim, since they go back to a longer humanist tradition. Neither one can be judged by the principles of the other. And it is difficult to see how they can both be held simultaneously.

My apparent digression on advertising and ethics has brought me back to the point that had next to be considered. I have said enough, I hope, to show that, and why, it has been impossible to jettison the market concept of man as essentially an infinite consumer. I have still to show that it is now impossible to hold this concept simultaneously with the more morally pleasing and now politically necessary concept of man as an exerter and enjoyer of his human capacities.

Let me say at once that the two concepts are not, in the abstract, logically contradictory or even logically incompatible. For it can be held that the maximization of utilities is a means to, rather than being opposed to, the maximization of human powers. What is incompatible about the two concepts may be put in either of two ways. First, what is opposed to the maximization of individual human powers is not the maximization of utilities as such, but a certain way of maximizing utilities; namely, a system of market incentives and market morality including the right of unlimited individual appropriation. For in such a market society, inequality of strength and skill (if nothing else) is bound to lead to greatly unequal holdings of property that effectively deny the equal right of each individual to make the best of himself. It is indeed a requirement of the capitalist system of production that capital be amassed in relatively few hands and that those left without any should pay for access to it by making over some of their powers to the owners. Thus in the capitalist market society the arrangements made to promote the maximizing of utilities necessarily prevent an effective equal right of individuals to exert, enjoy, and develop their powers.

Or we may put the point in a second way. What is incompatible with the concept of man as exerter, enjoyer, and developer of his powers is not the concept of man as infinite desirer of utilities, but the concept of man as infinite appropriator. For if man, to realize his essence, must be allowed to appropriate without limit, he must be allowed to appropriate land and capital as well as goods for consumption. The same result as we saw a moment ago then follows: All the land and capital is appropriated by some men, leaving the rest unable to use their powers without paying part of them for access to the resources without access to which they cannot use any of their powers. This is necessarily the position in a capitalist market society. And indeed, as I suggested earlier, the real meaning of the postulate that man is essentially an infinite consumer was, historically, that he is essentially an infinite appropriator. What was needed was a postulate that would justify a right of unlimited individual appropriation. The postulate that man was essentially an infinite appropriator would have been simpler but would have been too stark a repudiation of Natural Law. It is presumably for this reason that it was not consciously entertained by most theorists or, if entertained, rejected. The less obnoxious postulate—man as infinite consumer of utilities—seemed to provide the justification that was needed, but we can see it now as a surrogate for man as infinite appropriator.

I have suggested two ways in which the concept of man as maximizer of utilities or infinite consumer and the concept of man as maximizer of individual human powers or as exerter, enjoyer, and developer of his human capacities can be seen to be incompatible. And I have argued that both concepts are contained in our western democratic theory and that both have been needed by it, the first because we are still capitalist market societies, the second because our thinkers were (and are) morally revolted and our leaders were (and would be) politically endangered by the society that shaped and was shaped by the first concept alone.

Because western democratic theory contains these inconsistent postulates, its condition is internally precarious. This might not matter, for we have made do with the theory in that condition for something like a century now, except that western democracy from now on will have to face increasingly strong competition from the communist nations (which are sustained by a different notion of democracy), and even, on a moral plane at least, from the underdeveloped nations of the third world (which have a still different idea of democracy).

Moreover, we have to expect in the next few decades a technological change in the productive base of our society that will change our problem. I want now to argue that foreseeable technological change both requires and makes possible a change in our theory; that if the technological change is left to operate by itself in our present society it will aggravate our weakness, but that there is a possibility of utilizing it to cure the weakness of our society and our theory.

Technology, Scarcity, and Democracy

The most fundamental change in the political theory and, hopefully, in the ideology, of western democracy that I believe to be both required and made possible by technological change is the rejection of the concept of man as essentially an infinite consumer and infinite appropriator (which I shall refer to, for brevity, as the market concept of man's essence). That change was, in an obvious sense already indicated, needed many decades ago, if only for theoretical tidiness. But the change has become more urgent now, because of the conjuncture of two changes in our society; namely, the increasingly democratic temper of the world as a whole, and the technological revolution of our time. The two changes are not unrelated.

The rejection of the market concept of man's essence is increasingly needed now because, as I have argued, that concept, as it is entrenched in our present society, is incompatible with the equality of individual right to make the most of oneself which is now being demanded by the increasingly democratic temper of the world as a whole. Given that change in temper, and given the competition for world influence and power between western and non-western systems, it is probable that the continuance of western societies combining individual liberties and democratic rights depends on those societies providing to their members an equal right to realize their essence as exerters, enjoyers, and developers of their individual human capacities. For this is the concept of man's essence avowed in the theory and ideology of both the communist and third worlds. If the realization of this concept in the non-western worlds were to remain only a millenarian hope for their people, the matter would have no immediate implications for the West. But it is here that the technological revolution of our time makes a difference.

By the technological revolution I mean the discovery and application of new sources of energy, and new methods of control of the application of energy and of communication in the widest sense: cybernation and all that. This revolution is not confined to the West. It is shared by the most advanced of the non-western nations. And it can be expected to bring them up to a level of productivity where they can begin to realize the Marxian vision of man freed for the first time in history from compulsive labor.

Thus, for the non-western nations, the technological revolution brings closer the realization of their concept of the human essence. For them, technology assists ontology.

What of the western nations? Here too the technological revolution *could* provide the means of realizing the democratic concept of the human essence (which is fundamentally the same as the

Marxian concept). It could, that is to say, by releasing more and more time and energy from compulsive labor, allow men to think and act as enjoyers and developers of their human capacities rather than devoting themselves to labor as a necessary means of acquiring commodities. At the same time the technological revolution could enable men to discard the concept of themselves as essentially acquirers and appropriators. For as we have seen, that concept was needed as an incentive to continual exertion of human productive energy and continual accumulation of capital. These incentives will no longer be needed. The problem will not be to enlist men's energies in the material productive process, but to provide alternative outlets for those energies; not to accumulate ever more capital, but to find socially profitable uses for future accumulation at anything like the rate to which we have become accustomed.

The technological revolution in the West thus offers the possibility of our discarding the market concept of the essence of man, and replacing it by a morally preferable concept, in a way that was not possible when previous generations of liberal-democratic thinkers, from John Stuart Mill on, attempted it. But the technological revolution by itself cannot be relied on to do this. Its immediate effect is likely rather to impede this. Before we consider why this is so, we should look at one logical objection that may be made about the possibility of discarding the market concept of the essence of man.

Can we just play about with these postulates of the essence of man, rejecting one because it does not suit our moral values and setting up another because it does? Do we not have to demonstrate the truth or falsity of the postulates, and have we done so? I think we do not have to, and certainly we have not done so. All we have demonstrated is that the postulate of man as essentially consumer and appropriator was brought into western theory and ideology at a certain historical period and that it did fill a certain need (in that it provided a justification of capitalist market relations). This does not in itself demonstrate either the truth or the falsity of the postulate.

But the truth or falsity of the postulate is not in question. For it is not entirely a factual postulate, however much it may be presented as such. It is an ontological postulate, and as such, a value postulate. Its basic assertion is not that man *does* behave in a certain way (although it may make this assertion), but that his *essence* can only be realized by that behavior. An assertion about man's essence is surely a value assertion. One can agree that man as shaped by market society does behave in a certain way, and even that man in market society necessarily behaves in a certain way, but this tells us nothing about the behavior of man as such and nothing about man's essence.

Since postulates about essence are value postulates, they may properly be discarded when they are seen to be at odds with new value judgments about newly possible human goals. The discarding, now, of the postulate of man's essence as infinite consumer, infinite appropriator, infinite antagonist of scarcity, comes within the category of allowable discards. The rejection of the market concept of man's essence is thus logically possible as well as now technically possible.

But there is one great difficulty. The technological revolution in western nations, if left to develop within the present market structure and the present ideology, would have the immediate effect of strengthening the image of man as infinite consumer by making consumption more attractive. As technology multiplies productivity, profitable production will require the creation of new desires and new amounts of desire. (What will be required may properly be described as *creation* of new desire, in spite of what I said above about advertising not creating new desire, if we reject, as I have argued we should reject, the factual accuracy of the postulate that man as such is naturally infinitely desirous.) Since profits will increasingly depend on creating ever more desire, the tendency will be for the directors of the productive system to do everything in their power to confirm western man's image of himself as an infinite desirer. Efforts in that direction are evident enough in the mass media now. Thus in the West the immediate effect of the technological revolution will be to impede the change in our ontology which it otherwise makes possible and which I have argued is needed if we are to retain any of the values of liberal-democracy.

What, then, should we do? I hope that as political theorists we may widen and deepen the sort of analysis here sketched. If it stands up, we shall have done something to demolish the time-bound and now unnecessary and deleterious image of man as an infinite consumer and infinite appropriator, as a being whose rational purpose in life is to devote himself to an endless attempt to overcome scarcity. Scarcity was for millennia the general human condition; three centuries ago it became a contrived but useful goad; now it is dispensable, though we are in danger of having it riveted on us in a newer and more artificial form. We should say so. If we do not, the liberal-democratic heritage of western society has a poor chance of survival.

[NOTES]

1. See my *The Real World of Democracy* (Oxford, 1966).
2. On Locke's view, see my *Political Theory of Possessive Individualism* (Oxford, 1962), Chap. V, sec. 3, ii (a). Hobbes, while holding that man was not by nature infinitely desirous, did hold that man in market society was necessarily so (*ibid.*, Chap. II, pp. 41–45).
3. Jeremy Bentham, *Introduction to the Principles of Morals and Legislation* (London, 1823 ed.), Chap. V, Chap. X, sec. 3.
4. Bentham, *The Theory of Legislation,* ed. by C. K. Ogden (New York, 1931), p. 120.
5. *Ibid.,* p. 103. Italics in the original.
6. Hobbes, who came nearest to postulating man as an infinite appropriator (though he did not quite do so), got a bad press for it. Not until the late eighteenth century had market morality become so respectable that Burke could refer to "the love of lucre" as "this natural, this reasonable, this powerful, this prolific principle. . . ." *Third Letter on Regicide Peace, Works* (Oxford), World Classics ed., VI, 270.
7. John Locke, *Second Treatise of Government,* Sects. 35, 37.

[10] SOCIAL ORDER AND HUMAN ENDS: SOME CENTRAL ISSUES IN THE MODERN PROBLEM

This essay examines the basis, achievement, and values of social order, with central reference to some problems arising out of the modern situation.

We inquire into the relation between politics and the ordering of human affairs, stressing the challenges that are raised in the modern context; note and criticize the alternative responses and develop principles of order that take account of the criticisms; turn to the attitudes and institutions that impede achievement of the democratic nonrepressive world social order; and finally advert to the question of ends and means.

Politics and the Social Order: The General Issue
and the Modern Dimension

In terms of an ideal typology, we may suggest three ways in which collective human affairs might be ordered.[1]

In the first, the customary and prepolitical, division of labor is at a low point, man's material wants are relatively few, and the whole of both collective and individual existence is guided in considerable detail by folkways and mores that have arisen unconsciously. It is a state of life in which the phenomena associated with "individuality" have yet to arise. Using modern jargon, it is a condition of "undifferentiated" consciousness where group and individual are seen as one. Religion, law, and way of life are virtually interchangeable terms, are unquestioned, and are seen as divine.

A second type arises when this community is disrupted and the dynamic forces inherent in what we have come to call individuality are released. Man sees himself as "differentiated." With increasing division of labor, his wants increase, his social violence is accentuated, and his technological capacity is expanded. But he no longer has the sure guidance afforded him by long-standing and unconsciously developed custom. The ordering of affairs appears to be, to borrow Plato's vivid language, through "legislation by accident."[2] Life is at the mercy of impersonal Social Forces; for no sooner do customs appropriate to a new stage develop than they are overturned by yet other dynamisms. While the accidental is not, of course, political, it has gone beyond ordering by detailed habit and opens the way for the political.

In the third stage, man increasingly becomes aware of the possibilities for deliberate or "political" ordering. Division of labor is stimulated yet more. The city becomes central and with it a whole cluster of characteristics, including impiety, skepticism, and a growing awareness of the secular as against the rapidly shrinking sacred dimension of life. Man's enlarged consciousness of the accidental leads him to ask whether his life need be ruled by fortuitous concatenations of the forces that have been released through the breakdown of the customary and prepolitical.

Under the first two kinds of ordering, man does not even ask how collective matters should be arranged. Initially, he cannot ask because he has not yet differentiated his individuality from the group. In the second type, he does not ask, for he is still in a state of puzzlement or he hopes that the gods will somehow restore the sure guidance of the folkways.[3] Only in the third does he hesitantly begin to envision the possibility of deliberate creation of the social order. Partially freed now from the demands of custom and the shock of the gods' retreat, he very reluctantly becomes political.

Obviously, ideal types are never reflected in pure form on the plane of history. There has probably never been a society in which deliberation did not play some role, and the same has been true of what we have called accident and custom. Nevertheless, there are some societies that approach the first form more nearly than the other two; and others in which either the second or third become more notable than the first.

Although traditional accounts of primitive societies are no doubt often colored by ideological considerations, we may instance ancient Israel down to the foundation of the monarchy as a society where the deliberative, while surely present, played a much smaller role than after the establishment of kings.[4] In the evolution of Greek society, there came a point where commerce and piracy, together with a gigantic population explosion, broke up the society of wont and forced the Hellenes to move into a state in which the deliberative became a much larger element than heretofore. With the decline of the Roman Empire, the political withers and governance by custom once more assumes a much larger place. On the other hand, the revival of the city and the growth of commerce in early modern times forced men out of the order of wont and once more into accidental and then political ordering.

Universally, as the political type struggles with the accidental, endeavoring through deliberation and intelligence to discover substitutes for prepolitical arrangements, certain issues of social ordering become ubiquitous. They are both the root and the fruit of the political: the root, in that they accompany the decline of the prepolitical; the fruit, in that the very process of deliberation and therefore of political ordering will seem to accentuate them.

The first problem is that of division of labor, which from Plato's classical account on down has been seen as a key to the breakdown of the sacred society. Division of labor stimulates a differentiated consciousness and tends to pull human beings apart from one another—through radically distinguished outlooks on life and in formation of social classes—even while it forces them to become interdependent for material production. Man's economic activities come to be in tension with his social inclinations; and political ordering is called upon to heal the breach through deliberation.

Related to the division of labor are problems of land and technology. Natural resources are essential if technology is to do its work; and the question of control of land and tools becomes a key one in the interpretation of political history. Technology, moreover, together with the social arrangements entailed by its particular forms, has a way of imposing its own imperatives on its creators and thus shaping their choices.

Thirdly, the coordination involved in bringing together the labor that has been divided gives rise to a series of issues. Deliberate coordination, of course, is political. What will be its effect? To repress or enhance man's newly found individuality? Coordination involves discipline and some restraint on natural impulses. But the tendency is for the coordinators or ruling classes to go beyond their functions and to use their strategic position to restrain beyond functional needs. Man no sooner escapes the stifling rigidities of ordering by custom than he finds himself in danger of repression and enslavement by rulers. Like technology, rulership tends to develop a life of its own and to become an end in itself rather than a means.

Finally, political ordering is in some measure both rooted in and itself the stimulator of imperialism and war. As Plato suggests,[5] the breakdown of the prepolitical order is in a sense due to man's aggressive tendencies: He presses for knowledge, for more material goods, and for domination. The myth of the Fall of Man offers a similar hypothesis: Man's aggressive curiosity opens up possibilities for knowledge, which may be used both to build and to destroy.[6] Man's wants tend to be insatiable and lead him to take a slice of his neighbor's land in order to satisfy them. His growing powers of deliberation and hence politicizing enable him to carry on organized and imaginative slaughter.

The existence of these four closely interrelated problems poses a whole host of issues: alienation of men from one another, from their community, and from their work, and the best way to overcome this alienation; the ethical nihilism of economic forces and the degree to which men can limit it; bureaucracy in all of its manifestations; the way to make rulers accountable and responsible; how to distinguish between restraints that are "functional" and those that become repressive; and questions of political obligation. War is an example of the more general phenomenon of social conflict, whose control involves such varied questions as the alleged lust for power and the psychology of subordination.

In the modern world, the underlying issues and the problems of political ordering to which they give rise are enormously magnified. As ordering by custom becomes more and more fragile with the rapidity of social change, the question centers increasingly on the possibilities of reducing the role of the accidental and correspondingly increasing that of legislation by design.

The key factor in the modern situation is, of course, industrialism, which implies an even more minute specialization, an abundance of material goods hitherto thought impossible, and an incomparably great increase in supposed knowledge. Basically, the origins of industrialism did not lie in any acts of collective deliberation but rather in the same kind of curiosity symbolized by the story of Adam and Eve. Thus the Pandora's box of ultimately political problems posed by the process of industrialization roots in the hit-and-miss developments of invention and discovery. Industrialism set the pace and men were dominated by its demands, even though they were never consulted about whether they wished it in the first place.

Division of labor is vastly accentuated within industrialized societies and with it the problem of relating man in his economic function to the whole man of citizenship. The possibilities of alienation are substantially enhanced, particularly where the transition is sudden, as when, in Asia and Africa, for example, an industrialist culture disrupts more primitive customary governance.

The factor of complex technology is almost immeasurably greater than in previous epochs. For the vast mass of mankind who exist far below the poverty line, the machine is seen as a kind of salvation that promises to overcome for the first time the age-long curse of poverty. For those residing in already industrialized societies, machinery and the accompanying division of labor have already revolutionized whole ways of life, with legislation by accident usually playing the predominant role. At the dawn of the age of automation, moreover, society is likely to be shaken up still more as automative equipment makes obsolete many established skills, imposes new educational demands, and steps up the pace of human migration.

The sheer amount of energy released by division of labor and technology under industrialism dwarfs anything known before and poses the problem of whether the energy can be controlled for deliberately formulated ends of the human race as a whole. Up to now, mankind has not done so. We have not advanced much beyond the chaos described by Henry Adams more than a generation ago: "Forces grasped his [man's] wrists and flung him about as though he had hold of a live wire or a runaway automobile. . . ."[7]

The complacent and fatalist attitudes to it that have accompanied introduction of complex technology make difficult any over-all deliberate direction. By and large, after initial flurries of dissent, accelerated mechanization has been implicitly accepted either as an act of God beyond human control or as a symbol of beneficent progress in every realm. Its benefits have been lauded and, relatively speaking, its social costs have hardly been considered. Rather thoughtlessly, mechanical progress has been equated with the general good, and men have rarely if ever asked whether the inevitable disruptions in family life, the shaking up of traditional social structures, the exploitation of labor (under both western "capitalism" and Soviet "communism") were not too large a price to pay for its admitted benefits. To be sure, voices like those of Mary Shelley,[8] Samuel Butler,[9] William Morris,[10] and A. T. Wright[11] have argued that the "logic" of complex technology bids fair to make the machine the master and the creator of the machine the slave. But for the most part, objectors of this stamp have been laughed out of court. An over-all unprejudiced political assessment of complex technology has never taken place.

The problem of coordination has, of course, been profoundly affected by all the phenomena connected with industrialism. As Lewis Mumford has remarked, the machine is a "communist"[12] in the sense that large pools of capital and "collectivized" institutions are essential to utilize it. The corporation collectivizes capital and deliberately plans its own internal life: In this respect it becomes political, even though the complicated results of corporate practices, in the absence of any over-all planning, may add up to legislation by accident. But whether the collectivizing takes the form of the private government of the corporation or of a "public" government, the general problems of coordination—the rise of bureaucratic mentalities, the stimulus to oligarchy, and difficulties involving accountability and responsibility—are magnified almost endlessly.

A significant accompaniment of these tendencies has been the idea of "democracy." As material production has increased and, in one way or another, industry has become collectivized, the notion that the whole community should share in political decisions has become at least the slogan of a large part of the world. To be sure, variations in the understanding of the idea are enormous. But it is significant that industrialist culture everywhere should be associated with it. At a time when the imperatives of the machine and division of labor seem in many (even if not in all) respects to make the achievement of democracy less and less possible, its arguments have been pressed most vociferously.

Finally, the ancient mythologies (such as the Fall of Man) which saw knowledge and technique as cutting both ways—providing enormous potentialities for constructive effort but equally gigantic possibilities for utter destruction—are no more dramatically confirmed than in the phenomena connected with modern war. The annalist of the future will be astonished by the degree to which men were willing in our age to commit their best human and natural resources to the cause of devastation. He will be amazed by the sheer scope of destruction involved in the most developed instruments of war and he might see here an outlet for that enormous energy which Henry Adams said the machine released but which man either would not or could not direct deliberately for other than death-dealing purposes. With R. H. Tawney, he might say: "Mankind, it seems, hates nothing so much as its own prosperity," allowing its rulers "to drain away each new accession of superfluous wealth" by war.[13]

If we view industrialism politically, accept the arguments for democracy, and see the whole against the background of the three types of ordering, two underlying questions emerge.

The first is whether we should de-industrialize or, on the other hand, continue to expand the culture of industrialism and, if so, to what degree. Is complex division of labor like that attained under highly industrialized conditions the situation most conducive, on the whole, to the moral, aesthetic, and political development of human beings? Granted that industrialism has brought enormous benefits in its train, do they always entail a price that is too high to pay? In general, what should be the balance between Nature and Civilization in the ordering of human life?

The second question, assuming that a measure of industrialism is to be retained, turns on the issue of how, if at all, it can be controlled for deliberately and collectively formulated ends. What should be left to accidental ordering? How can the organizations and attitudes of control, so largely inherited from a pre-industrial age and weighted with repressive conceptions of governance, be made adequate? How ought economic power to be allocated? How should complex technology be introduced? Assuming the idea of democracy, in what measure can planning on a large scale be made compatible with it? Where does the nation-state fit into an over-all scheme of political ordering?

These are only a few of the queries that will be raised by a politically conscious individual in an age when legislation by design struggles against legislation by accident and ordering by folkways—however nostalgically men may regard it—seems increasingly impossible.

The Responses and the Nature of an Ideal Type Social Order

In examining the actual implicit responses to questions of this order, we might take the Soviet Union and the United States as representatives of somewhat contrasting views within areas of high industrialization. We shall then refer to the responses of the under-developed areas. Finally, we criticize the responses and, in light of the criticisms, suggest certain principles of an ideal-type ordering of human affairs.

The Soviet Union is governed ostensibly under an ideology that has had but little sympathy for rural ways of life and has accepted uncritically virtually all the imperatives of industrialism.[14] Thus movement from country to city has been deliberately stimulated by planners, who act in part under Marxist ideology and to some degree under the general hypnotic power associated everywhere with the ideology of mechanization. Although decisions are made by the general planning organs and thus are positive political decisions, the ideas under which planning agencies operate are ones committed to the notion of universal industrialization. While there is much discussion about details, the basic decisions are made by relatively small bodies not effectively controllable by the general community. In essence, the citizen is told, for example, that he must accept increasing industrialization and adjust his personal way of life to it: In the long run, it is said, he will be freed. He may have to sacrifice in the short run, through the belt-tightening process necessary to accumulate capital, but he is assured that he or his children will have both an abundance of material goods and control of his or their own destiny. Very few, if any, have asked why it is legitimate to require sacrifices of the contemporary generation that would benefit the remote future, if at all.

The general allocation of resources is, of course, publicly debated, but only rather nominally. Since the decisions are made by a relatively few individuals, the "democratic" element is low; and if we do indeed say that deliberate or political decisions shape the destiny of the country, it is only with this enormous qualification. Moreover, the governors are limited in the kinds of decisions they are likely to make by certain rigid and uncriticized stereotypes that ill comport with fully political decisions.

The kinds of decisions made are also limited severely by the way in which economic power is allocated. Although reliable figures are not easy to obtain, it is probable that the disparity between lowest and highest personal incomes is at least as great as (and possibly greater than) in the United States, where the upper 10 percent of income recipients receive, after taxes, approximately 28 percent of the income and the lower 10 percent only 1 percent, and where the basic distribution continues to show virtually the same distortions as two generations ago.[15]

In the United States, the active decision-makers are somewhat more numerous and the conditions for debate about decisions more open. Hence the "democratic" element, while still very much limited, is greater than in the Soviet Union. On the other hand, the ideological stereotypes are as rigid as in the Soviet Union, even if different. There are two types of government—the "public" so-called official rulers, on the one hand, and the "private" political organizations such as industrial and finance corporations, on the other. The ideology creates a split between the two. Public government responds to changes in the economy through social legislation and helping the victims of industrial upheaval; but the basic technological changes that create the need for social legislation and that produce the victims are introduced into the economy under the motivation of private profit and by individual private governments. Where public government does take the initiative in technological innovation, as in the development of atomic energy, it is frequently under conditions of secrecy that belie the term "public" and frustrate the principle of accountability. The general ideology of the split still holds. Most political scientists, curiously enough, appear to accept it, confining their studies largely to the "public"—and often least important—side of politics. The over-all result of the division between the two realms is, of course, to emphasize legislation by accident.

When the private governments act, their aim is to maximize their profits, and the social impact of, for example, extended automation, is of no concern to them. Thus automative equipment will be introduced by one corporation to increase its material gains, another will follow it in order to compete, and soon an additional slice of the economy will be automated. Although we said that the "democratic" element was somewhat greater in the United States than in the Soviet Union, this statement must now be heavily qualified. About all we can venture is that a somewhat more democratic formal structure of public government, which acts under very rigid ideological considerations, has implicitly accepted the view that the actions of private groups in key matters affecting large masses of the people cannot be questioned. In introducing new automatic equipment, those most directly concerned—the workers who will be profoundly affected in their economic and social life—are not required to be consulted in the United States any more than in the Soviet Union.

American law frequently requires a vote of the taxpayers before new school bonds are issued; but in the far more important and revolutionary question of whether new automation should be introduced, neither the workers nor the general citizenry—whose way of life will be affected more profoundly than by anything Communists propose to do—are asked to pass judgment. The general effect of individual corporate decisions is to be left to the exigencies of accident. Thus there has never been an over-all political decision on how to transport the American people most comfortably and conveniently. At best, there have been debates about segments of transportation; but the relation of the segments to one another, to value structures, and to general objectives, has never been discussed. Meanwhile, private governments have introduced the automobile, which, once on its way, began to clutter up streets and impose burdens that in some instances made it of doubtful value to the whole. Generally speaking, we may say that in the United States only the secondary issues are subject to general political discussion and decision. The first-level factors, such as the always revolutionary introduction of new technology—the factors that determine the nature of the second- and third-rate issues—are largely within the domain of accident. We do indeed, as Michael Harrington has observed, live in the "accidental century."[16]

As for so-called underdeveloped areas of the world, the pressure of need is so great that it is not surprising to find them accepting the ideology of industrialism rather uncritically. In so doing, of course, they sometimes fail to see that in their particular circumstances an uncritical adoption of the industrial way of life may not only run counter to noneconomic values they hold, but may even be deceptive from the viewpoint of providing adequate material subsistence. India, for example, appears to have slighted the possibilities of the agricultural sector in favor of complex industrial machinery, despite the warnings of Gandhi who on many grounds questioned the value of extreme industrialization. Whether underdeveloped regions can develop a measure of industrialization without paying a disproportionate price in terms of cherished values depends on the degree to which they can emancipate themselves from rigid industrialist dogmas and the extent to which they can be made a part of some wider deliberate ordering of affairs.

All responses to the modern challenge have been strongly conditioned, of course, by the fact that the "state" historically has emerged, in considerable measure, as an instrument for war-making (whether civil or foreign) and has been so influenced by the wars of the past four hundred years that its organization and spirit have been military to a high degree. Its tendencies to extreme centralization of authority and to exaltation of the Executive,[17] for example, while undoubtedly affected by the nature of industrialism itself, are probably even more shaped by the exigencies of war. The ceremonial paraphernalia associated with the modern State—gun salutes, guards of honor, and military symbolism of all kinds—are largely those appropriate for ideologies of deliberate mass killing. Where states have attempted to plan the processes of industrialism, it has often been so that the resources would be more nearly available for war.[18] While much is heard in twentieth-century political discussion about the "welfare" state, the fact remains that as far as large states are concerned, "warfare" state would be a better designation.

In sum, the challenge to political development of social order has met responses that are mixed and diverse and certainly inadequate if the goal be a democratic control by mankind of the major factors affecting its collective life. Despite the prevalence of "democratic" ideas during the very period when industrialism became central, most systems in practice have remained highly undemocratic. Although some seek to reduce the element of legislation by accident, this takes place within grossly undemocratic contexts and under dogmas that are frequently not questioned. In other systems, private governments are allowed to diminish the accidental within their own limited purviews; but the ideology does not permit an over-all ordering, thus leaving the forces set in motion by private governments to clash and struggle among themselves; and general political debate is confined largely to secondary and tertiary issues. The vast majority of mankind find themselves in a kind of halfway position between prepolitical governance and accident, on the one hand, and semipolitical undemocratic ordering, on the other. For a vast proportion of the human race, changes in the material culture, like the weather, are givens, to which the majority of men must simply "adjust" and cannot collectively control. Wars occupy a similar status. When we have thus characterized the modern age, we have indicated both the enormous political challenge and some of the dimensions of man's failure to respond.

Having touched on and criticized the actual responses, we return to the two questions: Ought mankind to adopt industrialism politically? And secondly, assuming a measure of industrialism, what would be the general characteristics of a deliberately shaped order within the premises of democracy?

With respect to the first question, there are powerful arguments for attempting to reverse industrialization, at least in a measure. The mere fact that it can produce an abundance of material goods is not in itself definitive, in view of the other tendencies we have noted elsewhere. If the goal be democratic ordering, both in ends and in means, some of the past accompaniments of the industrial way of life are either of doubtful assistance or are positively detrimental. And it is by no means certain that such phenomena as bureaucracy, alienation, impersonalism, and oligarchical organization can be effectively counteracted by all our devices. There may be "natural" limits beyond which industrialism cannot be combined with even a measure of democracy. Certainly no highly industrialized society can be regarded as more than rather faintly democratic.

On the other hand, to reverse the process in any considerable degree would probably be too costly. Not only would the material benefits be lost—and a certain minimum material standard of life would seem to be a necessary even if not a sufficient condition for

any genuine democracy—but de-industrialization itself would require a degree of planning similar to that entailed by much industrialism. How, moreover, could the present population of the world
be supported?

In view of these considerations, a political decision about industrialism would probably conclude, albeit with many doubts, that
de-industrialization is on the whole not desirable. At the same time,
such a decision would emphasize the necessity for a deliberate ordering that would positively control industrialism, with genuine
options both for checking mechanization and for encouraging its
development.

What, then, would be the general characteristics of such an
order?

The vindication of its democracy would rest on the proposition
that a democratic ordering is the one which most nearly does justice
both to man's desire to be free and his need to belong. Human
personality is both horizontal—the group is a necessary though not
a sufficient condition to account for its full development—and vertical—it has ends of its own and is not merely a product of the
group. A truly democratic social order will thus repose on methods
for gathering consensus that do not rely primarily on such mechanical devices as voting and do not leave minorities to be coerced.
Although any actual order may fall below this goal, to the extent
that it does it is less than democratic. In a democratic ordering,
spontaneity and planning blend together and supplement each
other; functional differentiations do not overwhelm the things that
human beings have in common; the integrity of personality is a
central value; social equality is the rule, with class constraints abolished; and the economy is subordinate as a means, never taking
precedence over noneconomic values. In such an order, distinctions
between active and passive citizenship will have been destroyed;
for a "democracy" that is not "participatory" has the wrong label
attached.

The institution of such an order would attempt deliberately to
provide as its basic unit the neighborhood group of possibly three
to five hundred people. Through physical arrangements in the re-
ordering of cities, each of these groups would not only live in sur-
roundings that could make for community, but would also carry on
cooperatively many functions of collective life—establish nursery

schools, for example, manage a community hall and recreation facilities, provide for child care, and constitute itself the fundamental consensus-gathering division.

Because members could know one another in face-to-face relations and would be cooperating in so many essentials, underlying political decisions—which would be transmitted to higher coordinating levels—could actually be made through discussion. Voting and "majority rule," which are at best mere expediencies and ought never to be considered as principles of democracy, would decline as decision-making by consensus developed. Generally speaking, political parties—particularly of a rigid kind—would be regarded as antagonistic to the making of democratic decisions, inasmuch as they tend to reduce the decision-making role of genuine discussion and debate in general public organs: Thus a party system like that of Great Britain would hardly be compatible with the order envisioned here.

It would be an order which, while recognizing that change is inseparable from life, also builds into its structure the notion that there are probably limits to the changes which man can endure and remain man; limits imposed by his physiological, psychic, moral, and spiritual nature.[19] Change is not a good in itself. The mere fact that the technological capabilities exist is not a sufficient justification, to cite only one example, for increasing the speed of vehicles indefinitely. Decision-making bodies might well limit social and technological change, as well as encourage it, depending on circumstances.

The architects of the order would fully understand that legislation by accident can do terrible things to human personality and hence would assign a large role to legislation by design—a role that seems, moreover, to be called for by the enlargement of the "public" sphere which has inevitably accompanied greater economic interdependence. At the same time, however, it would be recognized that legislation by design must be confined primarily to those matters where accident is likely to be arbitrary and enslaving—largely the realm of scarce goods and technology. The whole of the spiritual domain—written and oral expression and religion—would naturally remain free, as would such matters as dress, sex relations (except in the event of violence), and marriage and divorce (except where children are involved).

The communal pole of man's experience would no longer be in

sharp conflict with the dimension of individuality. The individual would be coerced neither by the majority rule so exalted by contemporary liberal democratic theory nor by the minorities associated with aristocratic, timocratic, oligarchical, and monarchical doctrines.

Land and natural resources would, of course, be regarded as belonging to the human race as a whole, with administration to be carried out under terms fixed by public deliberative organs. The whole technological problem would be the subject of general political debate and no new complex tool could be introduced without approval of a public deliberative body under conditions that would exclude purely private profit. Men would no longer be told that they must "adjust" to revolutionary changes wrought by a technology about whose introduction they had not even been consulted. Obviously, of course, the decision would often be in favor of the new technology, for most men might conclude that its benefits would outweigh its social and psychological costs; but the alternatives would at least be assessed as a whole.

The value system of such an order would not be obsessed with the desirability of a machine-produced "leisure." Under conditions of industrialism, much such "leisure" is specious in any event, as Sebastian de Grazia has shown.[20] What is gained in shorter hours of work is partly lost again through, for example, the necessity of commuting. Although arrangements in the future might conceivably reduce this lost "free time," it would not be assumed that increased free time is necessarily a good in itself.

The center of the political and administrative processes would be positive direction rather than repression. It would be prevention rather than correction of social ills. Police could and would be unarmed: Indeed, this condition already exists in some parts of the world, including Britain. Prisons, which most studies show do little to deter men from crime and almost nothing to reform the criminal, would be abolished; and in their place would stand well-developed probation systems. Even today this might be possible: The writer was once told by an able prison warden that 90 percent of his charges might have been discharged had a satisfactory probation and parole scheme been established.

Accent would be on shaping of the economy and the commanding heights of the society to ends deliberately arrived at politically. The molding of the material order through deliberation would, of course, help provide the context for activities of human beings; but direct control of the latter would decline as over-all control of scarce goods increased. Purely economic action is "blind," as a modern philosopher has pointed out.[21] Democratic political deliberation, like the activity of Plato's demiurgos in the cosmos,[22] has as its purpose the imposing of forms on what is essentially the partial, the unseeing, the formless. As the introduction and utilization of tools are increasingly subjected to the over-all deliberative process and as all men can share in that process, the feeling of alienation or apartness from the community might be overcome. As the emphasis on positive control of things rather than negative restraint of people increases, human beings might be liberated from many of their anxieties and frustrations and emancipated for the spontaneous activity that would be one of the prime values of the order.

Throughout the structure of an ordering of this type would run the theme of the primacy of the whole man, with his multidimensional values, rather than the half-man—the economic or technological man—with his reduction of life to the material dimension. Political man refuses to accept automatically any finally authoritative character in Social Forces or the Major Trends of History or the Necessities of Economic Efficiency. He decides what he values as a whole and then, while fully recognizing his limitations and the contingencies involved, proceeds to implement those values collectively. Instead of simply responding to social change, which is initiated from outside the process of general deliberation, he decides what social changes ought to take place and then adjusts economy and technology accordingly.

It would be an order in which a substantial proportion of all goods and services would be distributed on a "free" basis. Already this is true to some degree, but it could conceivably be vastly extended, as many anarchists have long ago suggested. As the material order is brought more completely under the conscious and deliberate direction of the human race and desirable technological potentialities become actualities, the list of free goods and services could be expanded. With free goods could come free men, or at least freer men. The spirit of a democratic socialist society would require that goods and services not on the free list would be distributed on the basis of approximate equality of income. Only on some such principles could the distortions in economic power, which today are a large factor in making "democracy" farcical, be over-come.

It is obvious that such an order must be cosmopolitical, for any-thing less would deny the unity of the human race and the moral as well as the material and physical interdependence of mankind. This means more than an internationalist order in the usual sense of that term; for internationalism implies that every person is re-lated primarily to his national state and then, through his national state, to the world. By contrast, a cosmopolitical order means that every man and woman is related both to his many groups and to the human race as a whole. And he is not connected with the human race merely as a member of his nation but also directly. Implicit in the original spirit of socialism was cosmopolitanism. Unfortunately, much modern so-called socialism has deserted this ideal and has given hostages to the national state. Only if socialism returns to the ideal will it once more become a truly revolutionary force in the modern world. The notion of the human race as a unity deliberately acting to shape the material basis of the social order is perhaps the most exciting of all twentieth-century possibilities. Indeed, it must be an essential aspect of any order worth striving for.

Impediments, Dilemmas, and Possibilities

We may note at least three types of impediments to the achieve-ment of such an order. First of all, and perhaps most basic, man is puzzled about his own nature and particularly its political poten-tialities. Secondly, certain inherited and often uncriticized concepts restrict his actions. Thirdly, there are institutional impediments. In the course of discussing these, we can suggest some of the structures and practices essential for the order projected.

Man sees himself as called to political life—the life of delibera-tion, of control of his own collective destiny, of rationality, of free-dom—yet there is a side of his being that rebels against this call. Placed on this isthmus of the middle state, to cite the poet,[23] the human being cannot make up his mind whether he is a god or beast. He has an element of divinity and obviously of beast-hood. Yet he appears to be neither the one nor the other. He comes forth like the flower, according to the Bible, and is cut down;[24] but also, according to the same Scriptures, he is only a little lower than the angels.[25] At times, he tries to escape his uneasy status by imagining himself as only a god; at other points, he refuses to distinguish himself from the beast. He seems to be unwilling to accept his middle position. His ambivalence affects his judgment of political affairs and, indeed, his very evaluation of the political process. At times, he denies his political nature; at other times he affirms it. He is challenged to form social order deliberately, yet he doubts his capacity to do so. He is asked to shape the formless, yet he is sufficiently torn within himself to wonder whether he can have any great measure of success.

His uncertainty about political ordering is quite easy to understand, too, when we recall the brevity of human experience with the political, relative to the total span of human existence on earth. After all, generously speaking, men have not lived in societies that have even aspired to the political for more than about eight thousand of the tens of thousands of years during which human beings have existed on earth. And experience with the political thus far has been mixed, to say the least. Certainly when one looks at the modern state with its wars and massacres, its institutionalized hypocrisies, and its prevarications, one can legitimately doubt whether it has been a greater benefit than hindrance to what some would call human progress.

Dubiety about the political in general is closely connected with the quest for security, for the political is associated with the uncertainties of deliberation, the difficulties of prediction, and the ease with which rationality can be confused with rationalization. Man attempts to reject all this. Even when he has reached a conclusion by deliberation, he often wishes to enshrine it as part of the sacred, thus removing it from future deliberation. Men have yearned to restore legislation by custom and thus to escape from freedom and to find security. Even legislation by accident has had its appeal, since one can always plead that it is the will of the gods, or of History, or of Social Forces. Compulsive subordination to a leader, too, can afford a kind of specious security, which, however, contributes to tyranny and hence to a negation of political and particularly of democratic ordering.

In addition to this uncertainty about his own nature and his efforts to seek a security incompatible with the political condition, there are important conceptual bars to the achievement of a cosmopolitical order in the twentieth century.

The Augustinian notion of political institutions as essentially holding actions against wicked men still lingers; and the idea of planning the material order and only indirectly controlling the lives of men still struggles to be born. To be sure, there is an element of validity in the Augustinian view: Men are indeed apparently obdurate and willful. But it is doubtful whether the way to overcome this obduracy and this willfulness is through the repressive mechanisms so often associated with the thought of men like Augustine and Luther.

A second kind of conceptual impediment, rather contrary to the first, is inherited from overly optimistic early socialist theorists. They were often amazingly naïve about bureaucracy and the tendency to oligarchy in all human organization and they were uncritical with respect to complex technology and its social imperatives. The deliberate development of an order such as we have suggested can hardly be accomplished without a certain toughness and sophistication about these matters. No possible combination of devices designed to counteract oligarchical and bureaucratic tendencies can probably succeed completely.

Certain other stereotypes inherited from the past also act as inhibitors. We have referred to the implicit belief that all technological change is valuable as one example. Equally important is the work ethic that has played so overwhelming a role, particularly in certain parts of the world. If all technological progress is not necessarily to be identified with moral and social progress, it is also true that not all idleness is wicked. Although in an order such as we have envisioned, men may choose at points to work longer hours with more primitive techniques, they must also be prepared to consider other options in a world where men's options to work or not to work may be vastly enlarged. One can imagine a situation in which human beings need to work no more than an hour a day or even less. But today we are ill-equipped morally, economically, and politically for such a world.

Closely related is the view, frequently associated with certain nineteenth-century socialist and liberal perspectives, that with every increase of free time there will almost automatically be a heightened level of political activity on the part of the many, thus making complete "participatory democracy" not only possible but, in a sense, inevitable. It would, of course, make the achievement of the order much less difficult if such an optimistic prognosis could be sustained. Unfortunately, however, it must be questioned. Despite a considerable increase in free or "leisure" time since the beginning of industrialism, the proportion of men and women active in civic concerns does not appear to have increased appreciably, although exact measurements are, of course, difficult. We can also ask whether the average level of political consciousness, in its broadest sense, has been enlarged during the past century. What are the devices by which men overcome their very profound tendencies to remain at a sub-political level? Whatever they may be—and it is presumably one of the tasks of the emerging order to discover them if they can be found—experience seems to show, at least in some measure, that while increased free time may be a necessary condition for full participation, it is by no means a sufficient one. Insofar as hope for a democratic and nonrepressive social order depends on the belief that men will inevitably participate when released from grinding toil, it is an uncertain hope indeed. And unless we can discover the key to this riddle, any would-be democratic, politically shaped social order will fall far short of the goal.

Finally, the view continues to persist, despite the classical arguments of Madison and Hamilton and our historical experience, that a world order can be built on the principle of military coercion of states. This conception is reflected in the charter of the United Nations and appears to linger in the minds of many who cherish the idea of a world at peace. But human experience seems to indicate that any ordering of human affairs grounded on the notion of military coercion of states as such creates greater perils than it corrects. One builds into the structure the making of war in the name of peace and attempts the impossible task of reconciling the militant sovereign national state with the idea of world order. The notions of national "aggression" (a word almost impossible to define) and its restraint assume that states retain their own armies and that some kind of world army keeps them in awe. But this will not do. If the utilization of physical force becomes as central as the idea of coercion of states implies, it means defeat for world order from the very outset. A world order, like all order, is the product not of imposition by force but rather of subtle understandings and multiple arrangements for cooperation. Force can be constructive, if at all, only when marginal, limited, and discriminate as between and among individuals. The war that conceivably could arise through coercion of large states could not meet these criteria.

In what ways are present institutions inadequate for the tasks which we have envisioned?

Any democratic world order must entail certain institutions of a planning nature and these exist today, if at all, only in embryo—in, for example, the so-called functional agencies of the United Nations. If we begin, as we must, with the assumption that the resources of the globe belong to the whole of the human race, then organizations must be developed to allocate those resources in accordance with some deliberately arrived at scheme of values. Such central organizations need to have world-wide jurisdiction over the basic utilization of land and natural resources. At the same time, they ought not to control the economy in detail, lest essential flexibility and adaptability to local conditions and the diversity of human beings be impaired. The principle should be integration in a few fundamental decisions, with decentralization and local and functional autonomy in details. In the present world, we are only dimly beginning to be aware of the human race as a self-conscious political entity seeking in major matters to limit the scope of legislation by accident. Contemporary institutions tend to encourage each nation-state to be a kind of pressure group seeking to wrest what it can from mankind as a whole. The so-called public interest is all too frequently not public at all; rather is it the particular interest of a segment of the human race in seizing a disproportionate share of the world's resources.

Within the context of world institutions having general planning responsibilities, the area of the nation-state would often be too large for adequate and effective coordination of details. Today, because of the pressures of war and an often obdurate industrialism allied with national military power, extreme centralization frequently characterizes many of the nation-states. This would have to be broken down in some measure, in favor of smaller-scale regional and local institutions, cooperative societies, and producers' and consumers' guilds. Regional, local, cooperative, and guild organizations could deal with one another directly—or horizontally—as well as vertically with higher coordinating bodies. Much can be learned from communist anarchist and guild socialist theory in these matters. Too great a thrust to centralization can dry up human energies, make the task of administration hopeless, undermine possibilities of democratic control, and prevent that practical and small-scale training in public affairs which J. S. Mill rightly thought of as essential for the development of man.[26]

Nor is there anything particularly startling in the proposition that the movement must be simultaneously toward greater world integration and centralization, on the one hand, and to a vast decentralization, on the other. If we can imagine a somewhat rational world order in which the central value is the development and enrichment of human personalities, the nation as a cultural entity might persist, but the "state" of the past four hundred years would disintegrate. Movements for nation-states in Asia and Africa are from this point of view already anachronistic; and while they may in some sense be inevitable, they cannot, any more than the older nation-state structures, be fitted into the order that the development of political man requires. One of the reasons men feel so hopeless in politics today is that the units within which they have to act are often so irrelevant for what the world obviously needs: There are few ways in which they can act at a world level except through the war-making national state whose purposes are generally antagonistic to world order and which, like a god, is enormously jealous of its prerogatives; and when they wish to act at local and regional levels, they often find that effective autonomy has been stifled by a combination of the nation-state, highly centralized industry, and a proliferation of legislation by accident.

The great pre-World War II debate about rational allocation of resources in a planned socialized society seems to have settled that in principle this is possible with at least as wide a latitude of consumers' choice as men possess today.[27] The Planning Board, guided by over-all judgments of a democratic assembly as to allocation of resources during a given planning period, would adjust prices in accordance with the rise and fall of consumer demand. The adjustment could take place more quickly than in an oligopolistic capitalist society, thus providing a stabilizing effect. This scheme would apply, of course, only to that segment of goods and services distributed through the pricing mechanism. In the ordering we are envisioning, always assuming deliberate collective choice of a considerable measure of mechanization, the segment in which goods and services were distributed on a free basis would be considerably broadened.

Since World War II, the debate about economic planning and freedom has turned on such issues as the relation of planning to "totalitarianism" and to such phenomena as bureaucracy and oligarchy.[28] It has been argued that once a given level or segment of a society is planned, the inevitable tendency is to expand planning into every area, including sectors that by almost any definition can only be regarded as nonpublic. Planning *per se* is "totalitarian," if one accepts this contention. But even if it is not totalitarian, some critics go on, it simply accentuates those tendencies to bureaucracy and oligarchy that arise with complex division of labor and advanced technology.

Is it true that any planning tends to become all-encompassing? Is "totalitarianism" implicit in all efforts to liberate human beings from legislation by accident through legislation by design? Are the only choices arbitrary and capricious dictation by accident, on the one hand, and equally arbitrary and capricious direction by design, on the other? The answers are not easy and our experience under industrialism is relatively brief. Much would seem to turn on the character of the planning itself, in terms both of means and of ends. Something depends on the particular form of institutions and on whether the principle of law is valued highly. Even more would appear to be related to the spirit of the community—whether it consists of active or of passive citizens, for example. But the fatalism implicit in the critics' argument would seem to be unwarranted, on the whole. At any rate the alternative to over-all legislation by design—assuming an option in favor of considerable industrialism—is not absence of planning but rather legislation by design on the part of self-interested segments of the community, like nation-states and corporations, with the over-all results left to the caprice of legislation by accident. Surely there is a better alternative than this.[29]

Any organization of complex nature does indeed tend to become an end in itself and to devolve authority on a few. Any would-be democratic politicized social order must face these facts. We have yet to discover ways of fully counteracting the tendency. But certain principles may be suggested. The notion of centralization in only a few fundamentals and a wide degree of decentralized autonomy in specifics would appear to offer possibilities not only of much-needed flexibility but also of a check on bureaucratic and oligarchic tendencies. The principle of vertical and horizontal rotation in administrative structures might also be a valuable one: An individual would remain in a high position for only a limited period of time and would then revert to a subordinate status. Since incomes would be approximately equal, this would involve only a shift in "status." Similarly, he would move frequently from position to position at the same level. These notions would run counter to many cherished ideas and practices and might, indeed, lower the level of "efficiency" to some degree. But here again efficiency would have to be weighed against other equally or more important values.

There is no simple answer to the questions that the critics raise. But unless we opt for a fundamental reversal of the industrialization process, these are problems that will be perennial. Ultimately they raise the question, so emphasized by Rousseau, as to whether democracy is at all compatible with any economy and society that exceed a very limited division of labor and a relatively primitive technology.[30] Earlier we suggested that man is trapped by the imperatives of past industrialism, whether for good or for ill, and that the best he can hope for from the future is the development through design of a social order in which industrialism can be made somewhat subordinate to democratic values. We should be under no illusions, however; the task is an enormous one.

An order such as we are suggesting would also confront, no doubt, an issue much emphasized in British socialist thought since World War II: how to combine a measure of business autonomy with genuine accountability and responsibility to the community as a whole.[31] That day-to-day decisions in an enterprise ought to be made by those immediately on the spot is a proposition with which few would dissent. Equally clear, however, is the principle that a business cannot be isolated from the whole: It must be related to other segments of the economy and must answer to the community for such questions as how it treats its employees, its relations to the general consuming public, and whether its activities fit into the over-all scheme of production and distribution of which the general community is presumably the guardian. Just as professional groups cannot be allowed complete autonomy, since their decisions may vitally affect a wider circle, so business establishments must in some sense be accountable to laymen. The wider issue of the relation of the "generalist" to the "specialist" is in fact posed and we return to one of the seeming contradictions involved in any society of complex division of labor: On the one hand, its overwhelming tendency is to put a premium on the production of specialists and to discount the value of generalists; on the other hand, it cannot be held together without far more coordination than in lower-level division of labor, and this coordination calls for men who transcend their own particular specialties.

The generalists we need are figures who presumably resemble Plato's philosopher-kings; yet in a social order that aspires to democracy, it is the intense specialists who are required suddenly to change functions and collectively take on the generalist role.

The over-all scheme of values to be implemented must be fixed by man acting in his capacity as a generalist: the role of a political assembly vis-à-vis a business establishment or profession. It is easy enough, following this, to say that the specialist carries out the values in specifics. But this is too easy an answer, for ends and means are so entangled that the means selected by the specialist will themselves affect the end; and the goals postulated by the generalist will limit the types of means permissible. It would seem that any division between business or professional autonomy, on the one hand, and general accountability and responsibility, on the other, must take the form of only provisional demarcations; and institutional forms and practices may have to vary depending on experience and the particular kind of business or profession involved.

As the movement from Nature to Civilization proceeds, certain values are both lost and acquired. Those lost can never be completely regained, which accounts, perhaps, for the nostalgia with which man looks back to the primitive. Nevertheless, there is ground for maintaining that the human being cannot be completely himself without at least a minimum of access to the Nature which used to dominate so much of his life. Tolstoy was undoubtedly right when he argued that without the possibility of an intimate relationship to Nature, along with development in something like a family context, man tends to disintegrate.[32] The institutions appropriate to an order such as we are envisaging must attempt to make provision for this access. As the principle of the City is exalted, the possibility of communion with Nature becomes increasingly a matter of politics and can no longer be taken for granted. One of the functions of world institutions would be to reserve possibly a quarter of the surface of the globe as a wilderness area in which only sketchy reminders of civilization would be permitted.

The size of cities would also be restricted—possibly to not more than a quarter of a million each—with provision for ample unoccupied ground between them. The sprawl and congestion of modern cities are excellent reflections of legislation by accident and defeat the goals of that high civilization which historically has been so intimately connected with the life of the City.

But issues involving access to Nature and the size of cities cannot be sharply separated from those of population and technology. To-day we hardly regard either as matters of politics, despite the evident fact that they have perhaps a greater impact on the future of the human race than almost any other phenomena. At best, they are subject to only limited and segmental political cognizance.

Because population directly involves human personality and choices about children are legitimately regarded as partly within the private domain—even though admittedly also public—controls would have to depend on provision for free access to contraceptive devices and a growing consciousness, through adequate education, of the issue. Today our institutional framework and beliefs do not encourage any over-all assessment of this question.

The question of introducing new complex machinery would be within the jurisdiction of the several assemblies. Simple tools could be freely introduced. More complex ones, however, could be adopted only after positive public decisions preceded by debate. Discussion would no doubt consider not only the probable impact of the proposed technology on human beings in general but also its bearing on geographical and regional disparities and conditions.

Legislation by consensus would be abetted by the economic principles implicit in an ordering of this kind. With land owned and administered by the community, with industry socialized in the broadest sense of that term, with an enlargement of free goods and services, and with the control and administrative notions suggested, the class basis of politics could decline. No doubt divisions grounded to some extent on status and personal animosities would always be incipient, but even they might play a smaller role than they do today. Freed in some measure from class biases—both in general organs and in the workers' control bodies of industrial, professional, educational, and other work units—political discussion could more easily lead to general agreement; and the need for a given policy could be made so nearly obvious that implementation and compliance could become voluntary to a degree not attained in the past.

It is not easy to visualize the details. All we can suggest is that the institutions would not be simply a projection onto the world

scene of forms made familiar to us in the nation-state. In considerable measure, the specific institutions of the nation-state, having
been in no small degree shaped by war and ideologies of repression,
might be discarded. Certainly the image of the political order as a
"monopoly of force"—so cultivated still by the textbooks that idealize
the nation-state—would fade. Accent would be on politics as general
coordination of life reposing on an ultimate and active consensus
developed in the small neighborhood groups, which would be deliberately arranged in moderate-sized cities.

The general thrust of institutions would be toward a decline in
the direct government of men and a vast extension of the notion
that policy ought to be concerned primarily with the direction and
administration of things. Obviously the administration of things
affects the conduct of men; but the relationship would be a much
more indirect one than that involved in the repressive activities so
often connected with states and cultures of the past. Active democratic direction of things could have the effect of liberating men
from the arbitrary and capricious rule of Nature, of custom, of
accident, and of other men. Obviously, of course, this remains only
a hope, subject to all the contingencies and doubts that have been
expressed in previous pages.

Ends, Means, and the Social Order

Both John Dewey and Aldous Huxley[33] have done much to make us
increasingly aware of the organic relationship between means and
ends in politics. Yet this consciousness never seems to be sufficiently
clear and deep for us to act on it, except intermittently. Thus we
"protect" a country by devastating it. We make war in the name
of peace. We manipulate men to "free" them.

An order such as we have envisioned is not one where conflict
has been abolished—for to do that would be to destroy individuality itself, which we have assumed to be a high-order value—but
rather one where its level, as suggested by the French sociologist
Jacques Novicow,[34] has been transformed. Intellectual and spiritual
conflict remain; and they continue to help enlarge human consciousness. But the brutal physical violence, so ubiquitous in the pages of
history, disappears.

But if this is the end, the means must not contradict it sharply.
A philosophy of means which keeps this and previously suggested

ends in mind will doubt that war or violent revolution ever advance the cause of either justice or freedom; for war and violent revolution set up ends of their own that tend to escape any limits which the will of man may attempt to impose. If liberty was advanced in French revolutionary days, it was despite the violence of the Revolution and not because of it.[35] A doctrine of means will be suspicious of the claims of those liberals and socialists who, accepting these propositions in the abstract, seem to waive them in the concrete, as when they cease to be highly critical of the violence of a Castro.[36] In some considerable degree, as a matter of fact, the significant issue in modern politics is between those, on the one hand, who have only a slight consciousness of the means-end question and those, on the other, who make it the center of their attention.[37]

We still find torture and killing justified in Vietnam—all in the name of protection and democracy. As a notable liberal weekly suggested in 1965, the United States seems to insist on bombing Vietnam and creating a million refugees in the name of protecting the Vietnamese people from the Chinese.[38] We need to kill, in other words, in order to keep others from killing. Such a principle must be rejected by those seeking deliberately to create a nonrepressive social order.

A deliberately developed social order requires us to assess a wide variety of potentialities in the world, some of which need to be encouraged and others to be restricted. To be sure, not everything is possible: The tensions at work in human personality, the multifarious factors that go to make up history, and the level of awareness attained at any given time limit possibilities as well as open the way to achievement. In the struggle between those who would understand human affairs biologically and psychologically and those, on the other hand, who adopt a social and cultural interpretation, we must insist on a measure of validity in each perspective and on an interpenetration of the two.[39] A key to the problem would appear to lie in factors that make for an enlargement of human consciousness and hence render possible the shaping of the world in the direction of a reordered scheme. Whether the historical process be conceived in terms of cultural and national conflicts or thought of as a struggle of classes, formal education, important as it is, would seem to be no substitute in developing consciousness for such emotional shocks as war, hunger, or unemployment.

Some conceptions of change seem to assume that once consciousness is enlarged men will, rather inevitably, act rationally on the new awareness. But views of this kind would seem to fail to take full account of the irrationalist tendencies that Freud and others have taught us to associate with the human condition. Socially and politically, as well as personally, there is justification for St. Paul's statement that "The things I would do, those I do not, the things that I would not do, those I do. What a wretched man am I!"[40] Thus today there seems to be a widespread consciousness of the nature of a future war, yet most seem to be as ready as ever to submit to the dictates of war machines, given very minimal rationalizations. It would appear that Freud was in some measure justified in his pessimism when he engaged in his famous colloquy with Einstein.[41]

Yet there have not been wanting evidences both of a new consciousness and of a will to act on it. The wave of revolts following the death of Stalin in 1953; the statements of leaders showing at least a superficial awareness of the nature of a future war; the development of nonviolent resistance in the American civil rights movement; the decline of naïve *laissez-faire* ideologies; growing comprehension of the political and social as well as of the economic ramifications of population growth; the unpopularity of such ventures as the war in Vietnam; American students' broadened political awareness; critical approaches by many Soviet and Chinese young people; the burgeoning world scientific community with its debate on the social responsibility of the scientist;[42] and the partial breakup of rigid international alliances—all these phenomena must surely raise doubts about an unmitigated pessimism, at least in small degree.

What is needed is a consciousness which, because it recognizes the violence and exploitation that help distort frequently professed objectives of contemporary orders, rejects violence as a means and develops forms of nonviolent power both to undermine the distortions of existing systems and to help sustain a remolded order. Orthodox political activity may, of course, constitute a form of nonviolent power in the partially democratic communities of the present. But most men do not live in even semidemocratic societies today; and even where the formal structure exists, inertia, public complacency, legislation by accident, and covert oligarchy serve to perpetuate gross injustice and to limit effectiveness of political action within the prescribed channels. It is at this point that the various forms of "direct action" made familiar to us through the Gandhi and civil rights movements become significant, not only in the building of a nonrepressive order but also in its maintenance.

Nonviolent direct action is both the product of increased political consciousness and an important method for its enlargement. Demonstrations, marches, various forms of noncooperation, and, on occasion, civil disobedience, dramatize issues, help construct an edifice of social power, and enable men to confront even the violence of the *status quo*. The late H. G. Wells used to speak longingly of an "open conspiracy" under which men and women, linking hands across national boundaries, would simply refuse to obey the orders of war-making states. Although no technique can give assurance of "success"—and violence is notably uncertain—nonviolent direct action, properly disciplined, shows more promise than other would-be revolutionary devices. While our experience with it is relatively limited, already it has shown its effectiveness—whether against Nazi rulers of Norway during the first two years of the German occupation or in the context of the brutal power structure in the American South. Further experimentation with it will enlarge our understanding of its weaknesses and strengths and possibly suggest novel situations in which it might be employed.

As a form of nonviolent power, direct action can help break the idols of the past and keep a more rational and just social order from disintegrating. The readiness of segments of the population on occasion to carry on nonviolent strikes helps give full recognition to the fact that living social orders must depend on consent and that consent is of individuals taken not only separately but also as members of social groups. Direct action of many types provides a vehicle for expression of approbation as well as of disapprobation. It can counteract the tendency present in all societies to make citizenship merely passive.

It is also one among many methods for checking those tendencies to bureaucratic formalism and oligarchy which, as we have suggested, characterize all efforts to overcome legislation by accident. The formal political structure, to be sure, can build in all manner of safeguards and checks. But this will never be enough, even assuming a provisional attainment of what appears to be a democratic cosmopolitical order. Without a population ready at times to utilize the nonviolent power implicit in direct action, the tendencies for structures to develop their own ends and to become essentially suppressive are always emerging. And direct action can serve positive as well as negative functions in this respect. It was the direct action of the Freedom Riders, for example, that spurred administrative officials to implement already existing law.[43]

Thus direct action is more than a device for bringing about a different ordering—a means that can then be discarded once the outlines of the order are established. On the contrary, the informal and varied methods associated with nonviolent resistance must be seen as persisting, at least potentially, into any decentralized socialist and cosmopolitan order; for such an order, once approximated, must not be conceived as being immune to the possibilities of disintegration. Direct action must be seen to be an integral part of the political process, broadly understood. Its existence reminds us of the perils of institutionalization, the precariousness and fragility of any deliberate ordering of affairs, and the enormous dangers of violence to man's aspirations.

An Overview

In sum, we have suggested that:

1. The problems of political ordering—always present in any society of involved division of labor—are extraordinarily challenging in the modern world as ordering by wont tends to become vestigial and legislation by accident continues to shape so much of life. Is it possible to direct the industrialism created so largely by accident to goals that will make it the servant of man? Is it possible, moreover, to do so democratically? Thus far, we have in practice been largely unable to answer either question in the affirmative.

2. An order in which these queries might conceivably be answered positively would imply a dissolution of the national state; institutions that at the center would provide a framework for such basic decisions as allocation of resources; a decentralization in control and administration of details, which would be both general and "functional"; cities strictly limited in size and divided into small neighborhood groups that would constitute fundamental units for cooperation and decision-making; the principles of socialism and cosmopolitanism; introduction of all complex technology through acts of public deliberation only; approximately equal distribution of those goods and services not allocated on a free basis; and a

public value system in which economic, social, political, aesthetic, and other considerations are all taken into account.

3. The "democracy" implicit in such an ordering would be closer to the anarchist pole of thought than most contemporary democratic ideas would permit. Democracy would not be identified with majority rule, which is at best an unsatisfactory expedient, but with a consensus arrived at through discussion in deliberately planned small groups—a consensus passed on to higher coordinating centers, which would then act according to similar principles. Coercion by a majority is still coercion. Most so-called democracies today are oligarchies or plutocracies. Political parties and particularly rigidly disciplined political parties are incompatible with democracy. The achievement of a truly democratic ordering is filled with obstacles and often men might have to choose between purely economic and technological goods, on the one hand, and democracy, on the other.

The outlines of institutions cannot be too specific. But they would surely not be simple projections of the organizations characteristic of the repressive and war-making national state. Negatively, however, we would have to expect a drastic decline in executive prerogatives; elimination of all military ceremonial; and the abolition of prisons and an armed police.

4. Potentialities for such an ordering exist but in no sense can the order be called inevitable: Industrialism can provide an indispensable material base but it also sets up impediments. The enlargement of political consciousness is vital; but even growing awareness does not assure action. Finally, a full understanding of the means-ends issue in politics is of prime significance; and one of the most important tasks for the future is that of developing forms of nonviolent power.

[NOTES]

1. The types are suggested by Plato, in the *Republic* and the *Laws*. But ancient Greek political literature as a whole appears to imply them. Thus Hesiod's *Works and Days* is concerned with what the poet conceives to be an unfortunate decline in ordering by custom.
2. Plato, *Laws*, Bk. IV. Among the accidents suggested are disease and war. The gods are said, however, to preside over accident.
3. In part, the significance of such men as Solon and the half-mythical Lycur-

gus lies in their reflection of the growing consciousness that if men did not wish accident to legislate, they must make their own social orders; and they must dispense with the aid of the gods.

4. I and II Samuel may be said to reflect the breakup of the Hebrew tribal society and the rise of the political—a situation similar to that taking place in many parts of Africa today. Resistance to political ordering is reflected in Samuel's famous speech predicting the consequences of rule by kings.

5. *Republic*, Bk. II.

6. Man's "fall," in other words, makes for "freedom" as well as "knowledge." And both are extraordinarily perilous.

7. *The Education of Henry Adams* (New York, 1918), p. 494.

8. In *Frankenstein*.

9. In *Erewhon*. "The Book of the Machines" avers: "Machines will serve only on condition of being served, and that too upon their own terms; and the moment their terms are not complied with, they jib, and either smash both themselves and all whom they reach, or turn churlish and refuse to work at all. How many men at this hour are living in a state of bondage to the machines? How many spend their whole lives, from the cradle to the grave, in tending them by night and day? Is it not plain that the machines are gaining ground upon us . . . ?"

10. In *News From Nowhere*.

11. In his great anti-industrialist and decentralist novel *Islandia* (1940).

12. *Technics and Civilization* (New York, 1934), p. 354.

13. *Religion and the Rise of Capitalism* (New York, 1960), Mentor ed., pp. 69, 70.

14. Marx had a genuine prejudice against rural ways of life and an equally strong predisposition to think of industrialism as primarily a "liberator."

15. For an elaboration, see Gabriel Kolko, *Wealth and Power in America* (New York, 1962). The distribution has not changed substantially since at least the pre-World War I period, despite New Deal, Fair Deal, and Great Society.

16. Michael Harrington, *The Accidental Century* (New York, 1965).

17. Robert Maynard Hutchins truly observes that the overwhelming power of the President of the United States in foreign affairs is a "vestige . . . of the royal prerogative." Yet it has been greatly strengthened by the exigencies of twentieth-century life and its potential for sheer destruction of human life is almost infinitely greater than in the eighteenth and nineteenth centuries. See Hutchins' column, "The Decline and Fall of the U.S.," *St. Paul Pioneer Press* (July 10, 1966), p. 3.

18. See Fred Cook, *The Warfare State* (New York, 1962). It is noteworthy that in order to obtain many vital educational appropriations in the United States, the plea had to be made that they served the cause of military "defense."

19. "Liberal" culture is so impressed by the ubiquity of social change that it seems at times to make change a desirable end in itself. But it can be plausibly argued that the pace of change, other things being equal, is a large contributing factor to such phenomena as mental disintegration. George Soule persuasively contends that while humanity appears to be "almost infinitely plastic in the long run . . . , not all individuals can adapt to rapid change in the course of a single lifetime." *What Automation Does to Human Beings* (London, 1956), p. 85. One is immediately reminded of Lord Keynes' "In the long run, we are all dead." We may even

question Soule's assertion about the "infinite" plasticity of human beings in the long run.

20. Sebastian de Grazia, *Of Time, Work, and Leisure* (New York, 1962). De Grazia also makes an important and necessary distinction between "free time" (time not actually spent at work) and leisure, which, as he points out, classically meant activity pursued as an end in itself rather than for goals outside itself.

21. C. E. M. Joad, *Guide to the Philosophy of Morals and Politics* (New York, 1937), p. 773.

22. In the *Timaeus.*

23. Alexander Pope, *Essay on Man.*

24. Job, XIV, 2.

25. Psalms, VIII, 5.

26. J. S. Mill, *Representative Government.*

27. See *On the Economic Theory of Socialism*, ed. by Benjamin Lippincott (Minneapolis, 1938), where the views of two well-known economists, Fred Taylor and Oskar Lange, are stated at length.

28. This would seem to be among the central themes in such works as Ludwig von Mises, *Omnipotent Government* (New Haven, 1944) and Friedrich von Hayek, *The Road to Serfdom* (Chicago, 1944). And Karl Popper, *The Open Society and Its Enemies*, 3d ed. (New York, 1957), in his criticism of Plato, adverts to similar arguments.

29. The older works dealing with the subject—for example, Barbara Wootton, *Freedom Under Planning* (London, 1945) and Herman Finer, *The Road to Reaction* (Boston, 1945)—are still worth reading.

30. And not only Rousseau. Both Plato and Aristotle, as is shown in their semidemocratic projections, doubted whether any measure of popular control could be reconciled with complex commercialism or with societies containing more than extremely small populations. Although Rousseau sought to reconcile the principle of small-scale decision-making units with the social need for larger scale integration by means of the notion of confederation, he remained vague as to how this could be done.

31. *The Political Quarterly* (Winter, 1950) contains an interesting early discussion of the problem that has continued to trouble British socialist theoreticians ever since.

32. Leo Tolstoy, *My Religion,* trans. by Huntington Smith (New York, 1885).

33. Aldous Huxley, *Ends and Means* (New York, 1937). See also his *Grey Eminence* (New York, 1941).

34. Jacques Novicow, *Les Luttes entre Societes humaines et leurs Phases successives* (Paris, 1893).

35. D. W. Brogan in *The Price of Revolution* (New York, 1951) emphasizes that while some may contend that violent revolutions have achieved certain desirable ends, they did so, even assuming the correctness of the thesis, at costs that make one ask whether the attainments justified the enormous price.

36. Just as, we might observe, many liberals remained uncritical of the violence of the Bolsheviks, being so impressed by the professed ends of the communists that they rationalized their means.

37. Curiously enough, from this point of view, pacifists and Fascists are in the same camp, both having an appreciation of the ends-means issue.

38. *Manchester Guardian Weekly,* October 7, 1965.

39. Freud by some is accounted as one who neglects social and cultural fac-

tors. But Herbert Marcuse points out that the "revisionists," who accused Freud of overemphasizing the biological, misread him. The "internal" and the "external" are both included within the dynamic of Freud's concept. See *Eros and Civilization: A Philosophical Inquiry into Freud* (New York, 1961), Vintage ed., particularly pp. 225–251.

40. Romans, VII.

41. Albert Einstein and Sigmund Freud, *Why War?* (Paris, 1933).

42. This is particularly true of the natural scientists. But, curiously enough, this world consciousness seems to be at a much lower level among social scientists. Natural scientists constituted the overwhelming majority of those participating in the so-called Pugwash conferences; and it was natural scientists who initiated the Society for Social Responsibility in Science. Yet the fruits of social science are as likely as those of natural science to be used for particular interests and for the destruction of the human race.

43. The segregation of railroad and bus waiting-rooms was clearly illegal before the Freedom Rides began. The Riders developed the social and moral pressure that led to the promulgation of rules implementing the law. For a general discussion of the relation of direct action to the struggle for racial integration in the United States, see Mulford Q. Sibley, "Direct Action and the Struggle for Integration," *Hastings Law Journal*, XVI (1965), 351–400.

[11] CORPORATE AUTHORITY AND DEMOCRATIC THEORY

I

The policy decisions of huge corporations have an impact on the general community at large, well beyond their own boundaries. An investment decision of the magnitude of several billion dollars by a single corporation may well influence the values and lives of a significantly large portion of society. The corporate giant not only exercises an influence on the character of the business cycle and on the tastes and habits of the people, but it also exercises considerable authority,[1] along with the Congress and the Pentagon, in deciding which communities will decay and which communities will prosper.[2] It is not an exaggeration to say, therefore, that the large corporation performs a governmental function by sharing with governmental institutions in "authoritatively allocat[ing] values for society."[3] Its authority is reflected by the adherence, with few exceptions, of both the public and the government to its decisions, whether it is to close a plant—with all of its potentially devastating human effects—or to increase the rate and extent of automation, or to make a major capital expenditure in a foreign country. The fact that its decisions have been challenged by government, although infrequently and not always successfully, attests to its political nature. That the corporate leviathan sometimes directly exercises authority over only a segment of the public does not diminish its political nature. Government agencies are also limited in this respect, but surely this does not make them any less political.

To argue that the giant corporation is not public because it is not officially designated as such is to place an undue reliance on form at the expense of function. Established political theory is simply not adequate to accommodate this empirical understanding; we know that over a wide scope there has been a fusion of public and private interests and that the more powerful "private governments" are in effect public. In theory, however, we make a clear separation between the two, placing all groups under the private label that do not have an official government label. By placing giant corporations in the category of "private governments," the political scientist has created a political fiction that rivals its counterpart in law—that the corporation is a "person" within the meaning of the Fourteenth Amendment.

Considered as private institutions, one is at a loss to justify the tremendous authority that the large corporation is capable of exercising; indeed, there is no theory of legitimacy which warrants a "self-perpetuating oligarchy"[4] making decisions that affect the lives and well-being of tens of thousands of people both within and outside the corporate constituency. It is amazing that the public regards these oligarchies as legitimate. This is so largely on the strength of the hackneyed myth that directors are somehow responsible and accountable to stockholders. On a more sophisticated basis, to argue that corporate leaders are responsible to their various constituencies—such as employees, suppliers, customers, and the public—is to avoid a difficult question: By what means or machinery can these groups enforce accountability? Within a limited area the union has recourse against what it considers to be irresponsible corporate action; and the government is able to call the giants to account, on an *ad hoc* basis, when it finds sufficient sanctions and deems it politically propitious. But this leaves a vast area of discretion in which corporate leaders are responsible primarily to themselves. Moreover, we can no longer assume, as Grant McConnell makes vividly clear, that an irresponsible decision by one leviathan will be countered by an opposing force, or that, so opposed, the conflict will produce policies in keeping with the public interest.[5] Nor is there much force in the argument that the only solution to the control of corporate power and authority is government regulation. At this late date we still seem to be burdened with the Roosevelt-Wilson dilemma: If a concentration of corporate power is not dissipated at the outset, it will eventually take over the government agency set up to regulate it. But to attempt to break up the corporate structure into competitive units is to defy an irreversible technological trend. We are left, as Edward Mason put it, with "this powerful corporate machine, which . . . seems to be running without discernible controls. The young lad mastering the technique of his bicycle may legitimately shout with pride, 'Look, Ma, no hands,' but is this the appropriate motto for a corporate society?"[6]

I suspect that among the reasons for our plight is the fact that we lack not only a theory of legitimacy of the giant corporation, but also a viable theory of private power. In my view, the core of the difficulty is an inadequate theory of democracy. Its inadequacy is revealed by the inability of scholars to utilize it in a meaningful way in their analyses of the corporate problem. Moreover, despite the growing complaint that the corporate way of life and values has sapped the political vitality of the middle class[7] and has markedly contributed to the alienation of the faceless masses who man the factories and offices,[8] democratic theory has remained aloof and unchanged. I do not mean to imply that the problem has not been analyzed in the light of democratic values, but rather that it has not been regarded as an integral problem of democratic theory. This distinction is of considerable importance. It is the difference between regarding it as an ordinary problem, to be solved in due course in accord with the democratic process, or as a problem of the democratic process itself. More dramatically put, it is the difference between viewing it as a corporate crisis or as a democratic crisis.

Several writers, including Scott Buchanan, W. H. Ferry, and Earl Latham, have argued that the corporation should be democratized. But none has argued that within the context of democratic theory it is imperative that this reform be carried out. Latham, for example, has expressed concern that the dominance of corporate power and values has had debilitating effect on American democracy.[9] He argues that since the corporation has all the internal characteristics of a political body and has pre-empted its constituent power from the state, the Federal Government, by means of a compulsory Federal incorporation statute, should impose constitutional limitations upon all corporations. In effect, he wants to apply to corporations "the whole pattern of controls laid upon the states when the Federal Republic was created under the constitution of 1787."[10]

In constitutionalizing the corporation, the present "make-believe democracy" would be replaced by one in which management would be accountable to stockholders and to the state. Aside from the merit of Latham's proposal, it is clearly designed to safeguard the on-going democratic system rather than to meet the requirements of democratic theory. It is one thing to argue that the giant corporation should be held more accountable to the state and another to hold that the democratic system itself is defective if corporate structure remains oligarchic and not accountable to the public.

Grant McConnell's recent and perceptive study, *Private Power and American Democracy*, comes closest to relating democratic theory to corporate power. He recognizes that the larger corporations exercise a great amount of power and authority directly and indirectly over various segments of government and society; that they have no legitimate claim to their power; and that because of the great fragmentation of American government and politics, corporate power has not been effectively curbed. What is most interesting about McConnell's analysis is that he rejects, on democratic grounds, the thesis that champions the democracy of the small political unit. Throughout the book he tells us that the small constituency is not the "natural home of democracy," as is traditionally supposed, but, being small and homogeneous, is ideally suited to that kind of oligarchy in which elites are able to silence and dominate the majority.[11] It follows from McConnell's argument that proposals involving the devolution of corporate decision-making leading to greater participation in policy determination are ruled out. He concedes that small constituent units may "offer qualities of life that modern man craves—face-to-face human contact, a sense of place within a comprehensible world, warmth and abiding certainty."[12] However, he argues, the cost to liberty and equality for the relatively powerless is too great. It is in the larger constituency that their liberty and equality are able to flourish. For it is here that the majority has the best chance to be heard and for its interests to prevail, and it is here that the political leader can generate sufficient power to keep private governments, including corporations, within bounds. Translated into institutional terms, McConnell looks to the presidency and to what he considers to be the core of a centralized party system to control corporations in the public interest.[13] He is silent, however, on the key question of how these institutions are expected to marshal sufficient power to continually police these authority-power centers.

But this point aside, his otherwise excellent study is marred by his failure to explore the implications of his interpretation of the relationships between democracy and individual freedom. Although he neither defines nor discusses what he means by democracy, it is clear from his argument that he regards its central attribute to be the accountability of political leaders to the led, and that its contribution to liberty and equality is measured by the degree to which the interests of the people are served. On the basis of this set of premises, he has little difficulty driving home his argument that it is the large, not the small constituency which is conducive to democracy. The difficulty with the argument is that man's political interests are not one-dimensional. Of course, his interests are served by a responsive and responsible government. But does not his interest—indeed, his self-esteem—also include an opportunity to participate in making decisions that affect him? Without the sense of responsibility and challenge gained by shared experience in solving or attempting to solve communal problems, how can we expect the common man to be other than apathetic and uninformed? It is understandable that, brushing aside these questions, McConnell is saying that the key to the restraint of private power is centralized governmental power. Perhaps he is right, but will the millions of men and women who will continue to live under corporate oligarchies be freer simply because they know that their corporate masters are somewhat restrained by presidential power? This question is central, I believe, to an analysis of corporate control from the standpoint of democratic theory. And it cannot be disposed of by posing an option between small constituencies that are dominated by elites and large constituencies which facilitate the control of private power by a higher, more encompassing power.

II

The insular and narrow conception of democracy adhered to by most social scientists today is the primary reason, in my view, why a major problem, such as that posed by the giant corporations, has not been analyzed within the context of democratic theory. While it is true that there are many theories of democracy,[14] there is consensus among political scientists regarding the validity of certain key concepts of the theory. One of these concepts is that democracy is a political method for arriving at political decisions, and, as Schumpeter emphasized, it is a political method "incapable of being an end in itself, irrespective of what decisions it will produce under given historical conditions."[15] Not being committed to an overriding objective—such as enhancing the self-esteem and development of the individual—democratic theory is free of the charge that democratic means have failed to achieve democratic ends. It must only be self-perpetuating as method, and thus able to secure the open society through time.[16] In focusing upon openness *qua* openness—avoiding the question of openness for whom—the contemporary democratic theorist is in a position to show that the system is in good health while acknowledging at the same time the possibility that a large number of people are alienated from social and political life around them.[17] For, given this position, the standard for judging democracy is not, in the first instance, the well-being of the individual, but rather the degree to which the political process conforms to the basic principles of the democratic method: political equality, freedom of discussion, majority rule, free periodic elections, and the like. Thus the charge of William Whyte, Andrew Hacker, Erich Fromm, and others, that the combination of corporate welfarism and corporate authoritarian rule stifles man's moral and intellectual development, cannot be construed as a deficiency of the democratic system. As long, it can be argued, as unfree men within the corporation are free outside of it to voice their complaints and to be heard within the political realm, the democratic commitment has been met.

Of course, the democratic theorist is concerned with man's dignity, freedom, and development, but these ends are viewed as a product likely to be forthcoming from the democratic process rather than a prescription for it. Instead of asking, "How should and can democracy be revised and expanded to enhance man's freedom and his development?" he asks, "How does the democratic system work? and, at most, "To what extent does it operate in accord with established democratic principles?" It is my contention that this restrictive view of democratic theory is a formidable bar against using the theory productively in the analysis of practical problems.

The contrast in recent years between the development in the field of democratic theory and the field of constitutional law is, I believe, instructive. While the political theorist has been largely absorbed in clarifying the meaning of various concepts and in the defense of the existing political system, legal scholars and jurists have been intent upon expanding the reach of the Constitution in a wide variety of areas affecting man's liberty and rights. In constitutional adjudication on matters touching the Bill of Rights, considerations of history, logic, and precedent are increasingly being set aside when they conflict with the abiding purpose of safeguarding the rights of the individual.[18]

I suggest that it is time that democratic theorists emulate the spirit of their judicial brethren. Essentially this would involve a shift in emphasis from explanatory to prescriptive democratic theory —a shift from a self-restraint to an activist philosophy toward democracy. Of course, explanatory theory is important to an understanding of democratic politics. However, by scrupulously avoiding the question of whether the society being described can be changed for the better, it supports the tendency to accept as unalterable the configuration of society as shaped by impersonal forces. To submit to those forces which threaten to emasculate democracy, to eagerly adjust values to facts as the latter turn against us, is not the attitude of the scientist but of the defeatist.[19]

Stripped of normative ends, political theory, including democratic theory, cannot perform the crucial function of providing direction to man's actions. To argue that we must be content to struggle modestly forward by combating social evils as they arise is to assume that a series of incremental moves to combat various evils will inevitably add up over time to progress. That is not necessarily the case. In any event, the fundamental issue is not whether democracy should or should not have an overriding objective; it is rather whether its objective should be dedicated implicitly to the stability of the existing system or explicitly toward creating the conditions necessary for furthering the self-development of the individual. Following the basic supposition underlying traditional democratic theory, I believe one basic requisite necessary to man's growth and development as a functioning and responsive individual in a free society is an opportunity to participate actively in decisions that significantly affect him. The giant corporation, I will argue, could be a medium for achieving this objective.

III

The unduly restrictive and unrealistic concept of "political," held by many political scientists, constitutes another bar to the proper relating of democratic theory to the problem of corporate authority. From the standpoint of their internal structure, various organizations, including corporations, trade unions, universities, and religious orders, are generally considered political in nature. These groups are also considered political institutions when the focus of inquiry is upon the impact of their authority and power upon government. However, although it has been recognized that the largest of these institutions directly influence society, they are not considered political for purposes of defining or delineating the boundaries of the political system as a whole. Thus the scope of "political," in which democratic rules and norms apply, comprises those rules and methods for making public policy in the form of laws, proclamations, and orders that are related to and enforced by *government*.[20] Political scientists, in other words, tend to accept two conflicting concepts of "political": one, functionally oriented, emphasizes power relations, while the other, structural and traditional, focuses on state, government, and law.

Harold Lasswell's treatment of elites, for example, employs both the functional and structural use of the term. He defines the political elite as those who comprise "the power holders of a body politic."[21] In elaborating on this definition, he states that "those who are called officials do not always make severely sanctioned choices, and the severely sanctioned choices are not necessarily made by persons called officials." Among the political elites, he includes "the monopolist who is in a position to impose severe deprivations."[22] If, in Lasswell's terms, political elites comprise the "power holders" —both inside and outside government—does this not mean that in existing democracies there is a likelihood that there are a significant number of institutional leaders who make "severely sanctioned choices" affecting the entire society, but who are not, either directly or indirectly, held accountable to the electorate?

He dodges this question. When he speaks of accountability, he relates it to the structural meaning of political—that which pertains to government—and when he discusses the functional concept of political elites he is silent on the problem of accountability. For example, he states that "government is always government by the few, whether in the name of the few, the one, or the many. But this fact does not settle the question of the degree of democracy . . . since a society may be democratic and express itself through a small leadership. The key question turns on accountability."[23] Here clearly, accountability is limited to government leaders. However, as we have seen, when he discusses the political elite in power terms, he observes that other institutions than government make "severely sanctioned choices."

Robert Dahl also vacillates between a functional and structural meaning of political. In his general treatise on political science, he broadly defines the political system as "any persistent pattern of human relationship that involves, to a significant extent, power, rule, or authority."[24] However, in other works, he reverts to its traditional meaning—that which is related to governmental decisions. For example, in his paper on "Power, Pluralism and Democracy," presented at a meeting of the American Political Science Association in 1964, his analysis of the meaning and role of the concept "equality of power" was confined within this narrower scope.[25] In his now classic study of New Haven[26] he does not rule out the possibility that corporate heads or "Economic Notables," to use his term, could also be members of a political elite. But for them to qualify, he argues that it must be shown that they exercise a preponderant influence on concrete "key political decisions," and here "political" is contextually confined to include either decisions relating to the control of political parties or to governmental decisions on such issues as urban redevelopment, public education, taxation, expenditures, and the like.[27] In short, he does not consider the possibility that the more powerful among the "Economic Notables" persistently and *directly* exercised power or authority to a significant extent over the citizens of New Haven. If they did, under Dahl's functional definition of political, they must be considered political elites—irrespective of their influence on government—and a part of the political system.

David Easton also defines the political system broadly and then shies away from its implications. In boldly conceptualizing the political system as centering on the "authoritative allocation of values for society," he implicitly raises the question of whether certain nongovernmental institutions also engage in this type of decision-making for society and thus should be considered a part of the political system. Theoretically he recognizes that it is possible: "If the scope of the claims to obedience by such groups or organizations extends beyond their own membership to the whole of a society with respect to the major problems of a shared existence, either they will come into conflict with the existing governing structure, or they must become identical with that structure."[28] But, practically, he assumes that the allocation of values by a parapolitical system—a private government—is not authoritative beyond the membership of the group. Thus he does not consider, for example, whether the decisions involved in the expenditure of several billion dollars over a short period of time by a parapolitical system could not in fact constitute an authoritative allocation of values on major problems affecting the entire society. Nor does he consider whether the sheer existence of a large corporation through its size, power, ubiquity, and public acceptance does not make it a participant in the shaping of societal values, whether its leaders choose this role or not. The reaction of the United States Steel Corporation to racial strife in Birmingham in 1963 is a case in point. Under pressure, it declared its neutrality in regard to the civil rights issue raised in the dispute and thus was forced to admit implicitly to itself and to the Nation that its actions are political in nature. In effect, its directors said to the public: "We realize that owing to the magnitude of our business operations in Birmingham, we are in a position to exercise a considerable amount of authority and power, that, if actually exercised, would have profound effects not only on race relations in Birmingham, but upon the attitudes and values of businessmen and citizens generally throughout the nation. But we believe that it is not proper for a corporation to intervene in politics."[29] But in deciding not to act in support of the integration cause, the U.S. Steel decision favored the *status quo*. And it was authoritative since the public generally regarded it as a decision that was rightly theirs to make.

An interesting parallel can be drawn between the dilemma faced by the United States Steel Corporation in Birmingham and the problem confronted by President Kennedy about that time as to whether or not he should, to the extent that it was legally permissible, cut off the flow of Federal funds to the State of Mississippi. Both the President and the leaders of the Steel Corporation were capable of exercising power and authority of sufficient degree to alter radically their respective situations; both decided not to act; and both, by not acting, engaged authoritatively in allocating values for the society. The parallel breaks down of course on the key question of accountability: the President was accountable to the electorate, the leaders of the corporation only to themselves.

Obviously, United States Steel is not the United States Government. There are important distinctions between them, one of the more important of which is that the Federal Government possesses the exclusive and legitimate right to exercise force. However, there is a basic similarity between the two institutions: They both authoritatively allocate values for society. It is on the basis of this similarity that United States Steel and other giant corporations should be considered a part of the political sector in which democratic objectives and principles apply.

I V

If the large corporations are to be recognized for what they are—political institutions that participate in an important political function—it is a democratic imperative that they be held publicly accountable. To the extent that this principle is not embraced, the democratic process is defective. Moreover, in regarding democracy as a political method dedicated to the self-development of the individual, it is also an imperative that these leviathans become radically transformed to afford a significant expansion in participation in decision-making among members within their constituencies. Again, to the extent that they are not democratized, the democratic process is defective.

Casting the corporate problem within the context of democratic theory not only provides criteria for the redistribution and legitimation of corporate authority; it is likely also to have a significant effect on the nature of public response toward corporate reform. No longer can it be assumed—given this perspective—that corporate privilege could maintain its present political immunity from serious attack. For, as the proponents of the free-enterprise myth must be very much aware, changing the frame in which an institution is regarded can radically alter its capacity to exercise authority.

By the process of substituting constitutional and democratic procedures for oligarchic rule within the corporate structure and by the devolution of its decision-making process to various divisions, plants, departments, sub-departments, and committees, it is not improbable that a reasonable degree of internal accountability could be obtained together with a significant expansion in sharing in the determination of policy by members of the corporate constituency. By a diffusion of power among its diversified constituency—including various categories of employees, customers (among whom would be the Federal Government), and representatives of the general consumer[30]—it is less likely that the corporation would be able to dominate a governmental agency assigned to keep it within the bounds of presidential policy.

It might be objected that I place an unwarranted importance upon broadening the base for participation in decision-making in the corporate sector. Does not my argument erroneously assume that ordinary men and women actually desire a greater share in shaping policies that affect them? If this were the case, one would think that the people would have already exploited to the fullest every opportunity to engage in politics within existing political institutions. Yet one study after another has shown that a comparatively large portion of the public is indifferent to politics; they abstain from voting, they are virtually ignorant of public affairs, and they lack a strong commitment to the democratic process. Would not this same pattern of indifference exist within a broadened political area?

If the newly recognized political sector were the factory, the office, the enterprise, I do not believe this would be the case. For many individuals issues of social policy and elections of public officials appear either trivial or remote and beyond the reach of their influence. Of a different magnitude are issues that directly affect them in their place of work, issues that are comparatively trivial, yet are overlaid with tensions and emotions which often infuriate and try men's souls. It is here, despite the legitimatizing effects of bureaucratic forms, that the ugliness of man's domination of man is fully revealed, and it is here, consequently, that democracy must become established and put to use. I am not suggesting that the average worker, for example, if given the opportunity to share in the making of factory decisions, would be magically transformed—in the fashion of Rousseau's common man—from an unimaginative, parochial, selfish human being to a broad-minded, intelligent, public-spirited citizen. I am saying that political education is most effective on a level which challenges the individual to engage cooperatively in the solution of concrete problems affecting himself and his immediate community.

There is no denying the force of McConnell's thesis that small units conducive to popular participation are also vulnerable to elite manipulation and domination. However, this danger can be avoided, at least to a considerable degree, if the membership of the small unit is not also homogeneous and thus congenial to elite control. Since the constituencies of the larger corporations are composed of a wide range of interests, there should not be great difficulty in establishing along functional lines decision-making units that are reasonably small to facilitate rank-and-file participation, and yet are sufficiently heterogeneous to prevent pressure of conformity from overwhelming those sharing in the decision-making process.

It would be ludicrous to argue that the highly complex, mammoth, industrial corporate structure should or could be organized with the sole objective of conforming to democratic norms. It would be equally ludicrous to contend that economic efficiency should be the sole criterion by which to judge the performance of a politico-economic institution. But even accepting efficiency as a major criterion does not necessarily preclude reorganizing the giant corporation in line with democratic objectives and principles. Admittedly at this stage it is a matter of conjecture whether such an undertaking is workable from a political and economic standpoint. However, in my view, it borders on dogmatism to reject this challenge out of hand by asserting, for example, that accountability and decentralization in the corporate decision-making process are irreconcilable, or that the devolution of decision-making must result in serious loss of productive efficiency.[31]

We cannot, with any degree of confidence, extrapolate a democratic scheme for modern industry from on-going oligarchic institutions. Nor can we conclude from the observation of oligarchic practices that such a democratic scheme, if put into practice, would be doomed to failure. If democracy is to be taken seriously, we cannot remain on dead center on this issue. What is called for, at minimum, is discussion, debate, and experimentation with the view toward expanding democracy to meet the needs of modern man in this important area of his life.

[NOTES]

1. For purposes of this essay, authority is regarded as a relational concept in which a command or a decision is obeyed because it is regarded as reasonable or legitimate within the context of the value frame of those who obey. When compliance to a decision or existing rules, rituals, traditions, etc., is forthcoming in order to avoid severe sanctions, power has been exercised. See Peter Bachrach and Morton S. Baratz, "Decisions and Nondecisions: An Analytical Framework," *American Political Science Review*, LVII (1963), 632–642.

   The distinction between these concepts is, I believe, important in an analysis of the role of the giant corporation in a democratic society. For the corporation's capacity to exercise authority—rather than power—is the key to an understanding of its present role in American society and perhaps its radical transformation in the future.

2. *The Corporation Take-Over*, ed. Andrew Hacker (Garden City, N.Y., 1965), p. 9. For a discussion of the public nature of large corporations, see also Grant McConnell, *Private Power and American Democracy* (New York, 1966), pp. 246–298; Michael Reagon, *The Managed Economy* (New York, 1963), pp. 73–120; Morton S. Baratz, "Corporate Giants and the Power Structure," *Western Political Quarterly*, IX (1956), 405–415; Robert Enger, *The Politics of Oil* (New York, 1961), pp. 132–150; and *The Corporation in Modern Society*, ed. Edward S. Mason (Cambridge, Mass., 1960), especially Mason's "Introduction," and Earl Latham, in *ibid.*, "The Body Politic of the Corporation."

3. The phrase is David's Easton's, *The Political System* (New York, 1953), p. 135. I attempt to defend this point in some detail in Section III, below. A giant corporation, as distinguished from smaller corporations, is one which, to a significant extent, shares authoritatively in allocating values for society.

4. A. A. Berle, "Economic Power and the Free Society," in Hacker, *op. cit.*, p. 91.

5. *Op. cit.*, p. 362.

6. *Op. cit.*, p. 4.

7. Andrew Hacker, "Politics and the Corporation," in *op. cit.*, pp. 239–261.

8. Of the growing literature in this area, see especially, Otto Kirchheimer's perceptive study, "Private Man and Society," *Political Science Quarterly*, LXXXI (1966), 1–25; and Lewis Lipsitz, "Work Life and Political Attitudes: A Study of Manual Workers," *American Political Science Review*, LVIII (1964), 951–963. On the impact of corporate bureaucracy on middle management, see Robert Presthus, *The Organizational Society* (New York, 1962); William Whyte, *Organization Man* (New York, 1956); and Alan Harrington, *Life in the Crystal Palace* (New York, 1956).

9. His thesis is primarily presented in "The Body Politic of the Corporation," in Mason, *op. cit.*, but also see his "Commonwealth of the Corporation," *Northwestern University Law Review*, LV (1960), 25–38; and "Anthropomorphic Corporations, Elites, and Monopoly Power," *American Economic Review*, XLVII (1957), 303–310.

10. "Commonwealth of the Corporation," *op. cit.*, p. 35.

11. *Op. cit.*, pp. 91–118.

12. *Ibid.*, p. 361.

13. *Ibid.*, pp. 336–368.

14. Robert Dahl, *A Preface to Democratic Theory* (Chicago, 1951), p. 1.

15. *Capitalism, Socialism and Democracy* (London, 1961), p. 242.

16. See, for example, H. B. Mayo, *An Introduction to Democratic Theory* (New York, 1960), and his "How Can We Justify Democracy?" *American Political Science Review*, LVI (1962), 555–566; Thomas Thorson, *The Logic of Democracy* (New York, 1962); and Daniel Boorstin, *The Genius of American Politics* (Chicago, 1964).

17. See, for example, William Kornhauser, *The Politics of Mass Society* (New York, 1959), and Bernard Berleson *et al.*, *Voting* (Chicago, 1954).

18. The expansion of the concept of "state action" by the Supreme Court, which has had a significant effect in constitutionalizing private governments, is a case in point. See, for example, *Marshall v. Alabama*, 326 U.S. 501 (1946); *Terry v. Adams*, 345 U.S. 461 (1953); *Burton v. Wilmington Parking Authority*, 325 U.S. 705 (1961); *Lombard v. Louisiana*, 373 U.S. 267 (1963); and Evans v. Newton 382 U.S. 296, decided January 17, 1966. Also see Arthur Miller, *Private Governments and the Constitution* (Santa Barbara, 1959); and Wolfgang G. Friedmann, "Corporate Power, Government by Private Groups, and the Law," *Columbia Law Review*, XLVII (1957), 155–186.

19. Some of the ideas of this essay, including this one, are drawn from the concluding chapter of my book, *The Theory of Democratic Elitism: A Critique* (Boston, 1967).

20. H. B. Mayo, "How Can We Justify Democracy?" *op. cit.*, p. 555.

21. *Comparative Studies of Elites*, with Daniel Lerner, *et al.* (Stanford, 1952), p. 13.

22. *Ibid.*, p. 16.

23. *Ibid.*, p. 7.

24. *Modern Political Analysis* (Englewood Cliffs, 1964), p. 6.

25. "Power, Pluralism and Democracy: A Modest Proposal," a paper delivered at the 1964 Annual Meeting of the American Political Science Association, Chicago, September 9–13, 1964. Here Dahl is primarily concerned with the problem as to what extent equality of power can be realized in large pluralistic democracies. His analysis, however, is limited by his conceptionalization of equality as "equality of power among adult citizens with respect to key governmental decisions," p. 10.

26. *Who Governs?* (New Haven, 1961).

27. *Ibid.*, p. 64. Also in "A Critique of the Ruling Elite Model," *American Political Science Review*, LII (1958), 463–470, the political system is related to political decisions, which in turn means government decisions; see especially p. 469.

28. *A Framework for Political Analysis* (Englewood Cliffs, 1965), p. 55.

29. The company's Tennessee Coal and Iron Division is Birmingham's largest employer. In his statement at a news conference on the company's policy, Mr. Blough said: "[F]or a corporation to attempt to exert any kind of economic compulsion to achieve a particular end in the social area seems to be quite beyond what a corporation should do . . ." and, as one would expect, he added that it was "quite beyond what a corporation can do." He continued by again emphasizing that for a company to "attempt to have its ideas of what is right for the community enforced upon that community, by some sort of economic means" was "repugnant" to him and

other company officers. *U.S. News and World Report* (November 11, 1963), p. 24.

30. To prevent, on the one hand, stalemate among the diverse groups and, on the other, collusion among production groups, it is crucial that the consumer group have considerable influence with the corporate councils. At minimum its members should have at their disposal extensive research facilities—including field investigators—from a Department of Consumers (the late Senator Kefauver suggested its establishment) as well as the assistance and support of the department in formulating their general policy.

Trade unions should remain, in my view, outside of the corporate constituency. For if they are to effectively represent the interest of the workers, they must remain uncompromised by identification with corporate policy. As workers gain greater rights in determining policy, they will probably, as a general rule, be less in need of the protection of the union. However, unions would still perform the essential task of defending the rights of individuals and groups who are believed to have been arbitrarily or unfairly treated by the corporate authorities. Within the corporate sector of the political community, the union must perform the important task of the opposition party, but unlike the usual political party, it must remain in perpetual opposition. On this point, see H. A. Clegg, *Industrial Democracy and Nationalization* (London, 1951), p. 145; and Adolf Sturmthal, *Workers Councils* (Cambridge, Mass., 1964), pp. 190–191.

It might be argued that there is little difference between the interest of the union and the interest of workers who would be actively engaged as members of management. Thus, workers' interests would be represented twice, both within and outside the corporate constituency. The argument wrongly assumes that workers, unlike other people, do not have conflicts of interests as citizens, consumers, wage earners, and producers of services and goods. If doctors, lawyers, and professors have a need for outside representation (American Medical Association, American Bar Association, and American Association of University Professors), despite their engagement in managerial affairs, then it would not appear paradoxical that workers have a different interest as members of corporate boards, departmental division committees, etc. (as producers) from their membership in the union (as wage earners).

31. Contrary to the view of some students, the British experience in nationalization of industry is not indicative that the democratization of large-scale industries is impossible. From the outset of the postwar experience, the Labour Party opted for centralization of control with no attempt to inaugurate a system of workers' participation beyond a warmed-over Whitney scheme of "joint consultation" on a strictly advisory basis between trade union officials and management. It is true that despite vigorous and prolonged discussion during the interwar years between Fabians and Guild Socialists, the Labour Party was unable to resolve the contradiction between the principles of political accountability and workers' participation in decision-making. But this is not surprising, since neither side in the discussions ever succeeded in coming to the heart of the issue. The scheme of workers' control advocated by G. D. H. Cole and his school excluded governmental and consumer representation in the control of industry on the erroneous belief that workers represented the interests of the entire society. Thus they never came to grips with the problem of integrating political accountability and industrial democracy. The Fabians, whose view

eventually prevailed, naïvely assumed that, since the essence of democracy is parliamentary representation of majority will, the legal transformation of a factory from private to public would somehow gratify the men who worked in it and further the cause of democracy. In effect, they held that the problem of worker participation in the management of industry could be dispensed with since the workers, as other groups in society, are effectively represented by their party in parliament. The validity of this contention aside, which is similar to the position taken by Grant McConnell, they were, in my view, basically in error in their presupposition that man's political interests are one-dimensional—all that is required is that his interests as results be adequately represented. The widespread disillusionment with the Labour Party's program of nationalization among workers in existing nationalized industries stems largely from this error. On the latter point, see Richard Crossman, *Socialist Values in a Changing Civilization* (London, 1955), Fabian Tract 286; Denis Butt, "Worker's Control," *New Left Review* (August, 1961); and Ken Coates, "Democracy and Workers' Control," in *Towards Socialism*, Perry Anderson and Robin Blackburn, eds. (London, 1965).

The Yugoslavian experience in workers' control—which has apparently been quite successful—throws considerable light on the feasibility of decentralizing decision-making in industry. However, the lessons that can be derived from the devolution of decision-making in the comparatively small, multifirm industries of Yugoslavia are not necessarily applicable to a highly complex, large-scale enterprise characteristic of giant American corporations. For a perceptive account of the Yugoslavian experience, see Frederick Singleton and Anthony Topham, *Workers' Control in Jugoslavia* (London, 1959), Fabian Research Series 233.

[12] FACING UP TO INTELLECTUAL

PLURALISM

A few years ago, at one of those international and interdisciplinary conferences called to consider nothing less than the fate of mankind, a famous physicist eloquently expressed his exasperation with the intellectual scene around him. In the past, he claimed, there had been "public discourse" which was universal in the sense that it spoke "in terms intelligible to all, of things accessible to all, of meanings relevant to all." Today the specialized sciences not only do not contribute to such discourse, but have "emasculated, impoverished [and] intimidated" all those who would continue it, by imputing an "arbitrary unrooted [and] unfounded quality" to their efforts. The realm of social philosophy has become an emptiness. The artists, no less than the microbiologists and pure mathematicians, are devoted to "preserving the vigor and integrity and life of their own skills, but are not, in the first instance, addressing themselves to man at large." Indeed, the various natural sciences do not even share a common foundation. Each one "deals with different kinds of harmony. And none of them can be completely reduced to others. They are in themselves a plural and multiple reflection of reality."[1] This condition of intellectual specialization is the pluralism to which the title of this chapter refers. It is not concerned with the structure of society, but with the disintegration of social theory. For the social, quite like the natural sciences, are fast becoming irreducible to each other, separate and self-enclosed worlds.

Facing up to the world of mutually divorced sciences does not mean that one must deplore the growth or character of scientific knowledge. The harangues against science that are so regularly and ritualistically delivered by literary men are but a form of self-pity. They are only self-expressions of those who feel isolated and ignored by a world they refuse to understand.[2] Self-expression for its own sake, however, is designed only to ensure such isolation. Certainly it contributes nothing to the possibilities of "public discourse." Should one really lament the "fate" of "public discourse," which is just another name for political theory? Might it not be better just to inquire how and why it did disappear? To be sure, the great tradition that began with Plato is extinct, and political theory no longer evokes the inventiveness and vigor that the specialized sciences can stimulate. There is, however, no reason to believe that this was caused by some external agency or "fate." It is rather a question of the inner history of political theory. What were the assumptions of the political theories of the past that rendered them so vulnerable? When and how did they grow and decline? And just what was it that changed the structure of political theory so radically? Above all, one must be reasonably precise about just what it was that has declined.

The great tradition of political theory consisted of a limited number of individual works of encompassing scope and imaginative and revealing insight into what seemed to be, and perhaps was, the totality of organized moral experience. They were not addressed to "all," but they certainly referred to "all." It is the absence of such works, not the absence of all sorts of political opinions and discussions, that marks not only the present, but also the years since the death of John Stuart Mill and Karl Marx. An examination of the inner structure of the most significant works of this tradition can show us how it deteriorated. Originally political theory was contemplative and critical and proposed to remain aloof from the political opinions of the day that it judged and condemned in the name of more rational ways of thought.[3] Toward the end of the eighteenth century, in the course of one of its most intense efforts at dethroning a reigning mythology, political theory gradually assumed the new task of actively molding opinion as a practical enterprise designed to reorder society. This entry into history was intellectually less radical than had been the severity with which classical theory had judged the world. It was, however, far more specific in its aims. The dynamic of this new way of thinking was obviously tactical, rather than contemplative. It thus became exposed both to practical and to scientific specialization.

There are some serious writers who once recognized this state of affairs who now claim that political theory is far from dead and that it is actually in a flourishing condition.[4] While it is conceded that no commanding individual work has appeared, this is said to be a matter of no importance. It is, however, a point of great significance, since the tradition of political theory *did* consist eminently of just such creations. The *Republic, Leviathan,* and the *Social Contract are* political theory. The diverse lesser writings that cluster around the established canon are just, as one always says, "merely of historical interest." They contribute to our understanding of their "age" or of their great contemporaries, but they are not read for their own sake. The prevalence of political preferences, beliefs, analyses, models, however numerous, however rational or irrational, and however diverse, does not add up to anything resembling any of the constituent parts of the great tradition. No Rousseau, no *Social Contract,* no political theory. Another specious argument is that since no science has found any answers to the great questions of political theory, such as "what is justice," it cannot be said to have replaced political theory in the way that modern chemistry replaced alchemy. The analogy is revealing. For chemistry did not replace alchemy. It did not find the elixir of life. Astronomy does not answer the questions astrology claimed to answer. However, chemistry and astronomy did destroy the credibility of the entire enterprises in which alchemy and astrology were engaged. They rendered the latter ridiculous in the eyes of all rational men. The sciences, natural and social, do not provide answers to the questions "what is just" or "who should govern," but they have discredited many of the answers traditionally given to these questions, because very often the latter were based upon psychological, economic, and historical speculations. These speculations may, and often were, inspired guesses and we probably are no wiser in these matters than were some of our illustrious ancestors. However, the credibility of speculative thought has been destroyed by science, even if it has not been replaced. Moreover, the inhibiting effect of science has been devastating. To pretend that nothing has happened is, therefore, comforting at best. Certainly it is not true. One cannot be impressed by imaginative flights of fancy upon matters which, in theory at least, are subject to exact analysis and investigation. It was possible once, but it is so no longer. The great works of the tradition were a mixture of moral reason and sociological intuition. The function of intuition has been replaced by uncoordinated special sciences, and the ethical and polemical treatises that now live apart from them simply lack the scope of the old combination. They are formal and hypothetical models, using history only to illustrate possibilities. Nor should they do more. But their very existence in no way proves the viability of the great tradition. Science may have no answers to moral questions, but it has obviously made it impossible to deal with them in the traditional way. That is what our introductory quotation means by "the emasculating" effect of the specialized sciences upon public discourse. That, to be sure, is not the whole story.

Among those who do recognize the impact, especially of sociology, upon political theory, there are some who have suggested possibilities for a revival of the great tradition on the basis of what H. L. A. Hart in his admirable *The Concept of Law* has called "the minimum content of Natural Law."[5] This consists solely of the universal human desire to survive. Professor Hart does not, of course, use this notion to build a political theory, but among his readers at least one has suggested that it might provide the first step for such an enterprise.[6] The appeal of this idea is easily understood, because it would re-create that element of universality, that capacity to speak "of meanings relevant to all" which "public discourse" now so evidently lacks. The wish to survive, however, does not really constitute a very promising base for *any* political theory. Even if it were universally shared, it is difficult to see its political relevance. The obvious fact of historical life is that men are both willing to die and to kill for political ends. To be sure, one must live in order to live well, but the mere wish to live cannot in itself lead to any theory about how we should live. In fact, the very idea that this should be possible points to a diagnosis of, rather than a cure for, the present difficulties of finding universal "meanings." To a large extent it was European ethnocentrism and indifference to historical variety and change that made discourse "relevant to all" seem so plausible. Once, however, the full range of psychological and social phenomena encompassed by "all" is really grasped, nothing seems to be commonly shared except, perhaps, the wish to survive. If that be the sum total of what concerns "all," then there is no possibility of building a political theory with "a cosmopolitan intent" similar to those of the past.

The Structure of Classical Political Theory

In speaking of the great tradition, it is of great importance not to forget the immense variety that it encompassed. The unity of its many aspects is only a formal one. Not the content of the classics of political thought, but the succession of individual works, each of which was complete in itself and unique, creates a sense of there having been *a* tradition, above all, because for so long nothing comparable has appeared. By examining the character of these writings and especially the great changes in political thought that began during the latter part of the eighteenth century, it may become more evident why intellectual pluralism has been disintegrative. That does not in itself imply that there was any degree of uniformity in the thought of the past, or even during the modern age. On the contrary, the all but jungle-like variety of ideas is what renders the study of intellectual history ever fascinating. No amount of retrospective analysis should, therefore, diminish one's awareness that it is a tradition of many incompatibles, not of unilinear growth and decline. The recognition that there were more differences than uniformities in the "public discourse" of the past must, finally, cast doubt upon all those efforts which propose to resuscitate the great tradition by reviving some single belief, attitude, or set of intellectual preconditions that, supposedly, engendered the glories of the past.

In trying to trace this extremely complex history of ideas one need not resort to sociological simplifications or speculations. It is far from self-evident that it was "social changes" as such which directly undermined the great tradition. We know very little about the psychological processes by which personal experiences are translated into intellectual systems. We know even less of the relations, if any, between such reified abstractions as "industrialization," or "revolution," or the very term "social change" and the creative impulses of individuals. It may well be doubted whether such highly generalized concepts, developed entirely for purposes of retrospection, can be sensibly said to "cause" or "explain" individual thought directly. What do we know of the events that really stir the mind to specific activity? We assume much, but in fact we know almost nothing. What we do have is the evidence of what was written. Without referring to any hidden "causes" or unconscious material forces or general social conditions, we may see what classical political theory and its successors, the ideological systems, were integrally. This may at least show just what it is that has for so long disappeared from the intellectual scene, and what has remained today. It says nothing, of course, about the social function of political theory at this or any other time.

Among the many explanations for the simultaneous rise of science and philosophy in ancient Greece, one seems of particular relevance to political theory. It is Sir Karl Popper's suggestion that the new theories were a species of myth, but myths of an entirely new character in that they did not invite mere credence, but open, critical discussion.[7] Now the intellectual function of myth (which says nothing about such much-disputed matters as their origin, *social* function, development, or implications) is to "furnish a 'logical' model by means of which the human mind can evade unwelcome contradictions." Foremost among these is, of course, the realization that living means dying. "The function of myths is to 'mediate' such contradictions, to make them appear less final than they really are and thus more acceptable."[8] The peculiar character of scientific and political theories in classical Greece was, however, their entirely new double thrust. On one hand they were devastating critical discussions of the inherited myths and various popular beliefs. On the other hand they offered new visions to repair the damage thus created and to establish moral discourse on a new, rational level. The latter was to be capable of withstanding rational criticism such as the older myths had not been able to survive. The *Republic* is thus, among other things, a veritable graveyard of venerable myths and conventional adages. In this respect it is a work of chilling skepticism. And this interrogation of beliefs that cannot endure scrutiny was at all times an integral part of classical political theory. The spectacle of disintegrated opinions, no less than the unsatisfactory, often asocial, character of the older opinions, invited new myths. The *Republic* as a whole is also a myth in that it creates a vision of order out of a pervasive sense of discontinuity and disharmony. Evading the incoherent evidence of direct experience and the irreducible conflicts of social opinion, it presents an account of the necessary order that is fully accessible only to reason and that, as a cosmic model, embraces the smallest individual, the entire world of nature, past and present. As such it is a work of art, an object of contemplation and a judgment upon actuality. It invites one to rigorous reasoning, however, not to passive credulity. And this is true even of the various myths proposed in the *Republic*. They do not suffer from this weakness of popular myths. They are frankly presented as educative instruments or as declared allegories designed to awaken consciousness of possibilities that cannot be directly expressed.[9] At all times the new myths of order are means of coming to an understanding of order in the face of irrationality and disorder that are at variance with the aspirations not only of the philosopher, but, as he demonstrates, even of those who appear to cling to their delusions with such tenacity. In this respect Aristotle does not differ from Plato. Though his myth of harmony is constructed out of the disparate materials of the natural and historical world, the end served is the same. In both each step of the argument is defended and debated and open to further discussion in a way that is designed to shut out mere credulity. It is just this feature of public discussion, as opposed to passive acceptance, that marks rational and objective thought. It is the integration of public argument into the structure of theory itself that marks it as rational, not any personal attitude of neutrality or indifference to the matters at hand.

When one looks at the long periods of European history, and at non-European societies, in which no comparable scientific or political theory flourished, it is not the absence of imaginative, inventive, or mythical thinking that is striking. The period from Aristotle or, at best, from the Roman Stoics to the Renaissance is obviously not marked by a general incapacity for belief, for visionary enterprise, or for ingenious speculation. What is wanting is the critical spirit, that astringent capacity to play the double game of analyzing and destroying existing myths and rising above them by proposing new, less fragile models, which are, therefore, a judgment and an enlightenment simultaneously. Machiavelli, so completely un-Platonic in all other respects, did have that capacity, as did those among the early modern theorists who, like Sir Thomas More, did find their inspiration in Plato. Machiavelli's assault upon Christian political passivity and reclamation of pagan civic energy was two-sided in this way. So also was *Utopia* as a non-Christian order, where natural sin was forgotten to reveal the natural possibilities of a calm rationality that cast a devastating light upon all historical conditions and probabilities.[10] In offering a contrast between the humanly possible, that is, a myth of a society of men realizing every capacity for reason, and all actuality, *Utopia* is self-evidently radical, as were Plato and Aristotle. It is, however, in no sense activist. It is not a "crib," to use Professor Oakeshott's word.[11] It is not a recipe for any present or future political system. In the place of a politically unacceptable Christianity, it sets a myth that judges the latter in terms of a picture of what men on earth *might* be. That was also Machiavelli's task. He did not really offer advice to self-made men in need of orientation because they had been deprived of the intimations offered by tradition.[12] Machiavelli's anti-Paradise is structured around a picture of Republican Rome whose destruction and memory had already inspired myths of "mediation" in those Roman historians whom he knew so well. The myth of Republican virtue and the recognition that it had declined, had indeed *necessarily* died, provide the setting for a vision of a world order in which nothing really changes. The basic elements of life, human and non-human, are uniformly the same, and as such capable of being known and managed. To do this effectively is the end of civic virtue, a virtue not of an extraterrestrial kind, such as urged by Christianity, but one typified by men such as Romulus and Numa. In this there was ground for hope; for great as these heroes had been, they had only possessed to a very high degree abilities available to many men. However, even at its height, fate, fortune, or just a combination of perfectly natural circumstances can overwhelm virtue. Both civic virtue and its death are thus absorbed in a single mythical vision that permits hope because virtue can be created, but also invites resignation because in the long historical run it must decline, as everything does, only to re-emerge at some other time and place.[13] For Machiavelli this myth, however, had a purpose beyond that of consoling him for the death of Roman virtue and its failure to revive in Italy. It inspired him with a sense of the ever possible, and also gave him a stick with which to beat Christianity—less for its lack of credibility than for its political vices. In this last respect he was not different from all the others who looked to Greece or Rome, whether to their philosophers, to their historians, or to their statesmen and soldiers. All found in antiquity in general, and in paganism in particular, myths designed to incriminate by unfavorable comparison the moral and political teachings and beliefs of Christian Europe.

The classicism of the earlier period of modern political thought was wholly retrospective, an effort to recapture the sense of civic ethos and to return to civic life a dignity that Christianity had denied it. It was, more directly, aimed at undermining the notion of original sin by creating myths of human possibilities. This, however, was not a form of prophecy or an effort to return to antiquity as a practical proposition. It meant to restore classical values as a way of judging the political and moral world around one. History was for this sort of theory, as it remained for its last great exponent, Rousseau, "a tissue of fables whose morals are well adapted to the human heart."[14] Antiquity was a storehouse of such "fables" that did not parade around as historical facts, but was a reminder of how men might live if they but would. In the face of a religion that preached humility and historical actualities that displayed nothing but aggression, classical antiquity could be used to evoke images of a religion that sustained a cooperative social order and so shame both the traditional Church and State. From this vantage point princes, lords, peasants, and clergy, all excluded from the high culture of classical learning and sensibility, could all be found morally wanting. For the classically inspired, moreover, this exercise in condemnation was a way of regaining the lost world of the polis. It ceased to be an object of mere longing and was recaptured through contemplation and mythical re-creation. It gave the man of letters a sense of identity and a spiritual home more genuinely his own than any available to him among his contemporaries.

Classicism was slow to die. It just petered out gradually under the impact of new impulses. The hyper-rationalism that emerged in reaction against the fanaticism of the wars of religion was not inherently incompatible with it, but it moved in other directions. In England, where classical political ideas had become direct participants in the struggles of ideas during the Civil War, they lost much of their luster. As Hobbes noted, their dangers became apparent when they ceased to be philosophical myths and became programs of action.[15] The intellectual horror created by the spectacle of fanaticism could find neither consolation nor principles of rational criticism in this myth now. The rose of reason on the cross of irrational actuality would have to be found in something more universal, more comprehensive, and historically more invulnerable than republican virtue. That was the function of the new myth of human nature. Psychology was to replace the "fables" of history. For Hobbes and Locke the roots of common sense, civilian, peace-oriented nonfanatical reason had to be discovered in the realm of totally nonhistorical possibilities. History, especially ancient history, had revealed its rational feebleness as a guide to direct action. In its place a nature hidden and remote was conjured up to reconcile philosophy to mankind. Where the naked eye saw only fanaticism and dogmatism, "science" might yet uncover hidden springs of natural, human reason sufficient to provide at least the basis for a stable, inglorious, but comfortable social order. Antiquity, as Hume observed, had, after all, been "violent" and so "unnatural."[16] Human nature, more accessible and universal than principles of civic virtue, might yet yield standards for an easier, less orderly, but far more wealthy and tolerating and accepting society. Profoundly attractive as this myth has remained, it had within it the seeds of its own destruction. Psychology was not to remain a subject for mere speculation. It was not meant to be. The results of its investigation have, however, destroyed the myths it was meant to sustain. The end of its efforts is nowhere in sight, but the possibility of easy myth-creating generalizations is gone. The rational pattern of natural politics, of nature's self-evident laws and of nature's rights, if it has survived the assaults of scientific scrutiny at all, lives on as an analytic and hypothetic category, not as a myth. And liberalism built on a philosophy of "as if" and "let us assume for the sake of argument" is a memory of its former self, not a living theory of politics or the shattering assault upon all myths of violence and oppression that it once was.

English ideas were soon to be felt on the Continent, where the struggle of the ancients and moderns was, especially in political theory, a long, drawn-out affair. Some, to be sure, shared Hume's confident opinion that "Europe is at present a copy at large, of what Greece was formerly, a pattern in miniature."[17] For the more radical this was not an acceptable picture of actuality, and classicism continued to serve them well. Others were, however, impressed, if not by Hume, certainly by Montesquieu. In a reassertion of Aristotelian thought, Montesquieu found both exemplary and critical patterns of harmony emanating in the direct past of modern Europe. Deeply attractive as classical virtue was to him, he rejected it as remote and irrelevant to an order that could be made to reveal moral and political possibilities of its own. Europe could yield its own myths. Above all, however, classicism ceased to be philosophical in the myths that were being created in the course of those changes in opinion by which "the Church of the *philosophes* . . . developed from being an opinion into being a sect."[18] As Rousseau observed, there was no longer much of a difference between the Jesuits and their sworn enemies. Both sides intended to rule by controlling the opinions of the general public.[19] The philosophers whom he feared and disliked were not prepared, as he was, to describe and denounce the ways of the world; they proposed to reorder the lives of their contemporaries. In this change of attitude classicism often provided a program of patriotic action, and the ancient city became a model for the future. It was not, however, an intellectual guide any longer. Condorcet saw Socrates not as a philosopher, but as an early fighter against and victim of priestcraft.[20] When in the course of the French Revolution classicism provided the operative rhetoric for radicals, if not their actual programs, its days were numbered.[21] As an inspiration to philosophy classical thought was exhausted. As a practical party program it proved ephemeral. Hegel was as perceptive as usual when he made his *Phenomenology* an extended elegy upon the spirit of Hellenism. Graecophilia lived on in aesthetics and in general culture-criticism until Nietzsche. As a politically relevant program or as a philosophic orientation it was dead. When Benjamin Constant relegated classical political values to the dust heap of morally and politically oppressive myths he was hitting a straw man.[22] All eyes were now fixed upon the future, even those that claimed they contemplated history.

The Structure of Ideology

There are today among those who deplore the decline of political theory some who urge us to return to the Enlightenment.[23] There they see a model of theory designed to give moral guidance and orientation to political activity. That a demand for just such a supply of political purposes exists no one can deny. Political theory as a guide to political action has, however, a history that should be carefully reviewed before one calls for its revival. Is it really so altogether desirable that political philosophy provide marketable ideologies for political movements and their leaders? Does the degeneration of myth into strategy, which is the sum of the history of political thought since the Enlightenment, suggest nothing but the necessity of starting this process all over again? Was it really the quest for analytic objectivity, the quest for social sciences rather than the absorption of philosophy by ideology, that fatally weakened the thought of the last century? If, in the long run, nineteenth-century political ideas have provided the groundwork for dissolution-by-specialization, their more immediate decline was due to their own inner structure as myths of action. Without imputing any moral weakness or hidden tendencies of "totalitarianism" to the liberating and brilliant thought of the Enlightenment era, one can still question its impact upon philosophy—for better or worse.

However much the various political theories of the nineteenth century differed from each other, and overtly they were created in utter hostility to each other, they now seem to share some very considerable likenesses. All were engaged in building myths to cope with the failure of the French Revolution, or rather to undermine the myths that had flourished when it began. The Enlightenment was in for a deadly reappraisal. Its hopes had to be revealed as somehow unreal. The Revolution itself, moreover, had to be made to disappear, since it had not brought about either a rational society or government by the men of reason. The most fundamental aspiration of the older "lumières," however, was not abandoned, indeed it became dominant: The intellectuals must change the world by directly molding the consciousness of their contemporaries. In an inverted way even Burkean conservatives admitted as much when they saw the Revolution as a conspiracy of the *philosophes*. The Revolution itself as a proof of the failure of these efforts had to be embalmed in myths, most usually in myths that assuaged disappointment by minimizing the importance of the events of 1789. A whole new conception of history was devised to muffle the actual. The future as History promised a second round to the radicals who simply projected the Revolution into the years to come. History as an organic growth from past to present was allowed to integrate it so as to render it less significant for the many to whom the Revolution had been a total mistake from the first. For both, however, it was a myth-generating occurrence that could be endured only by being transformed into an historical pattern.

History became the cosmological myth of the century and it was the French Revolution writ large. Action and reaction, analysis and creativity, liberty and order, critical and organic ages, exploiting and aspiring classes, old states and young nations made history into a drama in which impersonal entities re-enacted the pattern of the Revolution. It was a spectacle that rendered tolerable the memory of the actual Revolutionary years and the present impotence of the men of letters. Not the violence of revolution, but the complex confusion that it had left behind demanded an ordering and reducing myth. The Enlightenment, above all, had to be exposed and its myths destroyed if more successful political enterprises were to flourish in the new, future-directed world of ideas-turned-into-programs. Seen in their own circumstances, the ideologies, whether conservative, liberal, socialist, nationalist, or anarchist, were in no intelligible sense "secularized" Christianity or "messianic" prophecies. They were political responses to political needs, the intellectual successors to an expired classicism and fulfilling comparable theoretical tasks.

The overwhelming influence of conservative theory, even over the minds of the most radical, can be readily understood as part of a common need to overcome the immediate revolutionary past. The conservatives had naturally been the first to feel it and to cope with the painful fact that the Revolution had occurred at all. Somehow they had to make it disappear or lose its full importance. De Maistre enveloped it in providential history, as but one horrible punishment among many that the divine order inflicts upon sinful mankind. Alternatively he might see it as only the latest and far from unique act in a series that began with the Protestant Reformation.[24] For less mystically inclined conservatives, such as de Tocqueville, the Revolution could be reduced to no more than the logical completion of the administrative policies of the *ancien régime*. As for the *philosophes*, it was agreed that they were capable only of destruction. This, somehow, permitted treating them as men of no importance, of no future influence. Such very different men as Saint-Simon and Mazzini were quite at one in this opinion. The analytic spirit of the Enlightenment, the latter proclaimed, had done its good and necessary work, but it had no future value in an organic, creative age that would build the harmonious society.[25] Saint-Simon would not even patronize the *philosophes*. The Revolution was a small, but extremely hateful, miscalculation on the part of the "uninventive." It had interrupted the *real* revolution, which had begun in the Renaissance and would soon be completed by the industrial elite and the new creative intellectuals.[26] Only those who understood history could lead man, as John Stuart Mill saw him, as a "progressive being." If the past was the unbroken series of conflicts between the conventional many and the venturesome few that he painted in *On Liberty*, it was clear that the constructive intellectual must enter the political arena and make the future what it must be. Marx was scarcely alone in calling for an end to merely contemplative philosophy. Nor was he alone in devising a philosophy of history in which the dead revolution would yet be reclaimed.

These changes in political theory amount to the transformation of political theory into ideology. It was not an accident but a purposeful change. The myth of the historical importance of the man of letters as the ruler of public opinion or the awakener of public- or class-consciousness was inherent in all these theories. In a way it was the counterpart of the romantic notion of the poet as a bard, as the prophet who gives voice to the inarticulate collective consciousness of a people. Condorcet had still seen the role of the enlightened man as that of a rational schoolteacher. His system of universal public education was only partly designed to dispel superstition and to teach useful arts and sciences. Its final aim was self-liquidation at a time when all men had become capable of self-education.[27] The more "creative" visionaries of later years saw their task in less rationalist terms. They were political leaders and seers who gave expression to the sub-rational needs of the groups whom they represented either by birth or choice, because they, and they alone, knew what must come. The final ludicrous caricature of this myth can be found in the writings of Karl Mannheim, both in his view of the intellectual as the articulator of group consciousness and as the only class-free man who alone can and must dominate those whose thinking cannot rise above the limits of collective experience and interests.

The belief that political theory is a part of, and should participate in, the organization of public opinion for purposes of supporting specific political movements and policies had the natural consequence of reducing theory to mere strategy. The inherited intellectual capital of those popular movements that built their slogans on these all-explaining, all-predicting theories soon became very small indeed. When one speaks today of the end of ideology one thinks mostly of the end of the political vigor inspired by catchwords and of movements whose intellectual content had always been negligible.[28] The theories that were meant to become strategies (though not debased ones, perhaps), however, had been exhausted long before the Second World War. Karl Marx built the very last of the myths to destroy and replace the Enlightenment by fulfilling its practical aims. Those who are astonished by the elitist character of twentieth-century thought might well consider whether this is not the result of the pre-eminently tactical nature of nineteenth-century philosophies. Tactical politics is not a game for amateurs—not even democracy, as a set of strategies, is that. The mythological task of mediating between the actualities of the French Revolution and the aspirations of reason had been fulfilled in direct action, in political participation, and program-making. This intellectual dissipation was no less inherent in the grandiose ideological systems than in the more modest and pragmatic schemes. The manufacturing of political purposes, so often demanded today as a practical political necessity, is a relic of ideological political activity, but it does not respond to any direct intellectual need.

At the very moment of its birth, ideology was already faced by at least one theorist who attempted to disinfect its language by analysis. It was one of Jeremy Bentham's many merits that he saw at once that the purposeful misuse of language was inseparable from the aims of the new heirs of Gorgias. Like his followers today, Bentham was too confident that this exposing of "fallacies" would improve the linguistic habits of those whose purposes were so well served by distortion. Perhaps this is one of the remaining myths to protect reason against the spectacle of triumphant irrationality. The intensity of analytical rationalism today cannot be understood except as an effort to expose the myths of ideology. Sickened and exhausted by propaganda and the general debasement of language and ideas as weapons in ideological warfare, it aims at disinfecting theoretical language. It does not propose to move men to action, but to reflection. The premium put upon detachment is designed to save the remnants of political theory from its self-created illusions and pretensions to power.[29] It is difficult to see why this should arouse so much distrust and hostility, considering the follies of the political preachers who offered political "guidance" to its all-too-eager consumers. Philosophy as a theory of knowledge may, as Nietzsche said, be "a doctrine of forbearance" that does not try to "rule."[30] Indeed it does not propose to "rule" as its predecessors did. It does, however, try to preserve one of the functions of classical philosophy: its critical myth- and convention-doubting work. Ideology and strategy were the real deviations from philosophy. The analysis of language maintains the distinction between the mere expression of personal opinions and rational discourse, whereas ideology deliberately confused the two in its active intention to become accepted and dominant public opinion. It is only those who cannot forego intellectual brandy, who cannot endure cool analysis. To be sure it is limited to those objects of concern with which it can cope: a specific political vocabulary, a single legal system, a small number of political arrangements. It tends toward provincialism and lacks the scope of the works of the great tradition. It is, moreover, a technical enterprise that does not claim to be public discourse "relevant to all." Above all, it follows the specialized sciences rather than organizing them. The rise of these special sciences, in fact, occurred apart from analytical theory. It was part of the inner dissolution of the ideological systems. For strategy was not their only weakness. Their ultimately democratic character was also a cause of intellectual instability.

Condorcet had already foretold that democratic man would need a new history, the history of man. How was the history of the small men and women who never had done or said anything notable to be written? Who would want to write such dull works, given the fascinating character of the history of great men and events? Condorcet's solution already gave a hint of things to come. As has been well noted, his theory of history has two themes, "intensive" and "extensive" progress.[31] The momentous advances of the past were all the work of a few men of genius; the rest of mankind scarcely participated in them, except as passive beneficiaries. The future might find ordinary men able to join progress more actively as they grew more enlightened, but their past was one that could be treated only as a collective background for the great men who had made things happen. In Kant's treatment of the same issue, one can find an even more prophetic suggestion. The history of the bulk of mankind could be treated scientifically, as it were, in terms of statistical regularities.[32] As such they were the "matter" of history. The great actors, presumably, were to go on being treated in the manner of Plutarch. The necessity of writing the "history of man," combined with its difficulty and the lure of so easy and apparently "scientific" a solution, which promised at once certainty and predictability, proved irresistible. That society, the collective life of all men, was the concern of history was taken for granted by all, even by those far from democratic theorists who hoped only to prove the impossibility of democratic forms of government or who studied primitive men and "inferior" races only to demonstrate the superiority of their own groups. The social Darwinist intent upon showing the difference between the fit and the unfit was no less concerned with the "history of man" than was Marx, who wanted to find proof of certain future liberation in "laws" of gross change that revealed the necessary and creative power of oppressed collectivities coming, one after the other, into their own. The impersonal character of history seen as a drama of collectivities, of races, nations, classes, and the like, was, however, a purely programmatic enterprise. Its real concern was not actual man, but an abstraction and an imaginative myth of collective life and thought that fitted into the spiritual unease created by the French Revolution and its aftermath. It contributed little to historical accuracy, though it provided a tremendous and eventually fruitful impetus for such work. In the end it was the genuine democratization of scholarship, as well as the inherent demands of a science of *men* that dissolved these purely programmatic solutions to the difficulty of writing the history of *man.*

There are, however, remnants, by no means uninfluential, of the habit of dealing with ordinary men as a material entity and with extraordinary men as psychological phenomena. Even more prevalent is the bitter withdrawal of those whose hopes of dominating the classes ended in despair. As long as "they" were an "object" to be looked at, "they" could be treated as "they" now often are, as "the masses," as an undifferentiated human block, whose characteristics are the sum of what separates "them" from the creative few. When "the masses" ceases to be a term applied to those who are wanting in high culture, it often becomes a sociological metaphor. It is as the non-classes or non-elites that the masses can be described in a vocabulary fit only to describe simple material objects. The masses, we are told, are "atomized," they do not come in "layers," they are "amorphous," "compact," and their relations to the elite are not "filtered'" through "intervening" relationships. Their social life is marked by "discontinuities" and "rootlessness."[33] Such is the language of the historian of man who has learned to look at men as "massed objects" out there for him to measure. Moreover, even those who are not given to this crude materialism and are eager to discuss the history of man in psychological terms have been forced by the illusions of patterned history to deal with groups as having a reactive life dominated by external circumstances, while great creative men are analyzed biographically to show how they developed ideas which then become a part of a collective consciousness that has been created by impersonal forces and by such purely abstract categories as "economic" and "technological" conditions. The result of not going beyond Condorcet is to have two completely different psychologies, one centered on the individual, which is usually more or less Freudian, and one which deals with collective states of consciousness derived from Marx's philosophy of history. They are graded as "true" or "false" according to their place in the pattern of historical necessity.[34]

When the history of men is taken seriously, as it often is today, then its democratic impulse becomes evident. It concerns itself with the minutiae of the life of ordinary persons, their opinions, diet, life cycle, means of subsistence, and skills. Such inquiries, however, not only do not yield world-shaking generalizations, they necessarily demand specialization. To the extent that this is what social science aims at—the faithful recording of the social experiences of every sort of human being—it becomes a series of often unrelated sciences. Psychological inquiries into individual minds do not help us with the history of "great movements" and the demographic study of villages does not contribute to the understanding of the psychological growth of individuals, to mention only two examples. There is no *prima facie* reason to believe that there are all-inclusive patterns or that the investigation of diverse aspects of human experience and conduct will yield any encompassing designs. Above all, there is not the slightest support for the fond illusion of nineteenth-century positivism, and its survivors, that a complete social science capable of answering every social question will put an end to all our quandaries and disagreements.[35] Far more likely is the emergence of disparate harmonies and regularities within restricted fields of scientific inquiry, and with it the need for mutual toleration. The sort of discourse "relevant to all" and the unitary vision of society that the ideological systems provided is incapable of sustaining genuine scientific history or "field" work. That hardly justifies one's lamenting the end of nineteenth-century political theory. Nevertheless, those who regard an interest in what "is" as an abandonment of the duty to promote what "ought" to be and see nothing but a manifestation of "false consciousness" in the efforts of social science are indeed mourning the passing of the age of ideology. And it is pure nostalgia, since not even the most radical critics of this order have much to say about the future which, presumably, is to summon us from the past and present.[36]

Instead of regretting the end of the great tradition or pretending that it is still alive or that something like it is just around the corner, one might just as well face up to the pluralism of political ideas that do not individually or together constitute a political philosophy. To be sure, one might wish to return to classical philosophy with the same joy of discovery and the same sense of mission that Plato inspired in the humanists of the early modern era. It does not seem possible; for its history is not new to us. Theory today can only keep alive memories of the great tradition. This is by no means a contemptible task. In reinterpreting and reliving the intellectual past, one fulfills at least one of the functions of political mythology: to remain in touch with the past and to experience the present as part of a continuity. The very prevalence and variety of political notions, moreover, makes the need for critically judging unreasoned and uninformed opinion all the more pressing. And this is something that the skeptical intelligence is eminently well qualified to do. Lastly, the far from satisfactory performances of the specialized sciences cry out for scrutiny by the theoretically trained mind. Beyond that, facing up to pluralism suggests an attitude of resignation and tolerance. One cannot be a philosopher without a philosophy, but surely one can be a critic without a cause.

[NOTES]

1. Robert Oppenheimer, "Specialization and Common Discourse," in *World Technology and Human Destiny*, Raymond Aron, ed. (Ann Arbor, 1963), pp. 203–206.
2. The ultimate example of this sort of self-pity can be found in Erich Kahler, *The Tower and the Abyss* (New York, 1957).
3. This cardinal difference between political philosophy and political opinions and the relationship of the two is brought out with great force in Leo Strauss, *What Is Political Philosophy?* (Glencoe, 1959), pp. 10–18. The present essay does not, however, follow the rest of the argument developed there.

4. E.g., Isaiah Berlin, "Does Political Theory Still Exist?" in *Philosophy, Politics and Society*, Peter Laslett and W. G. Runciman, eds., Second Series (Oxford, 1962), pp. 1–33.
5. H. L. A. Hart, *The Concept of Law* (Oxford, 1961), p. 189.
6. W. G. Runciman, *Social Science and Political Theory* (Cambridge, 1963), pp. 168–170.
7. Karl R. Popper, *Conjectures and Refutations* (New York, 1962), pp. 120–135.
8. Edmund Leach, "Lévi-Strauss in the Garden of Eden: An Examinatiton of Some Recent Developments in the Analysis of Myth," in *Reader in Comparative Religion*, W. A. Lessa and E. Z. Vogt, eds. (New York, 1965), pp. 576–577.
9. These remarks owe much to Paul Friedländer, *Plato*, trans. by Hans Meyerhoff (New York, 1958), I, 171–210.
10. A more detailed discussion of these themes is to be found in J. H. Hexter, "The Loom of Language and the Fabric of Imperatives: the Case of *Il Principe* and *Utopia*," *American Historical Review*, LXIV (1964), 945–968.
11. Michael Oakeshott, *Rationalism in Politics* (New York, 1962), pp. 24–26.
12. For a discussion of Machiavelli's lack of "realism," see Federico Chabod, *Machiavelli and the Renaissance*, trans. by David Moore (London, 1958).
13. Niccolò Machiavelli, *The Discourses on the First Ten Books of Titus Livius;* I, Introduction, Chaps. IX, XI, XXXIX; II, Introduction, Chaps. II, V, XXIX, XXX, XLIII.
14. *Emile*, trans. by Barbara Foxley (London, 1948), pp. 120–121.
15. *Behemoth, The English Works of Thomas Hobbes*, VI, 218, 233, 262.
16. "Of Commerce," *Essays Moral, Political and Literary*, T. H. Green and T. H. Grose, eds. (London, 1898), I, 291.
17. "Of the Rise and Progress of the Arts and Sciences," in *ibid.*, p. 183.
18. Mario Roustan, *The Pioneers of the French Revolution*, trans. by Frederic Whyte (Boston, 1926), p. 263.
19. *Rousseau Juge de Jean-Jacques, Oeuvres* (Paris, 1959), I, 890, 967–968.
20. *Tableau des Progrès de l'Esprit Humain, Oeuvres de Condorcet* (Paris, 1847), VI, 66–67.
21. Opinions differ as to the importance of classical myths in structuring revolutionary politics. However, even those who minimize their impact recognize that revolutionary rhetoric, whatever its weight may have been, was dominatd by classical images; Peter Gay, *The Party of Humanity* (New York, 1964), pp. 162–181. The point to be stressed is that the "cult of antiquity" did provide, to the exclusion of other myths, the verbal weapons of the militants. One may doubt the importance of political language in the Revolution, but its classicism was overwhelming.
22. Benjamin Constant, *Oeuvres Politiques* (Paris, 1874), pp. 258–285.
23. Alfred Cobban, *In Search of Humanity* (London, 1960), pp. 11–28, 223–245.
24. *The Works of Joseph de Maistre*, ed. and trans. by Jack Lively (New York, 1965), pp. 50, 61, 132–133.
25. Joseph Mazzini, "Faith and the Future," *Essays* (London, 1887), pp. 7–58.
26. Frank E. Manuel, *The New World of Henri de Saint-Simon* (Cambridge, Mass., 1956), pp. 262–271.

27. *Sur l'Instruction Publique, Oeuvres,* VII, 378, 528-529.

28. Jean Meynaud, *Le Destin des Idéologies* (Lausanne, 1961).

29. E.g., S. I. Benn and R. S. Peters, *Social Principles and the Democratic State* (London, 1959); H. L. A. Hart, *op. cit.;* Brian Barry, *Political Argument* (London, 1965).

30. *Beyond Good and Evil, The Philosophy of Nietzsche* (New York, n.d.), Modern Library ed., pp. 500-501.

31 Frank E. Manuel, *The Prophets of Paris* (Cambridge, Mass., 1962), pp. 75-77.

32. *Idea for a Universal History with Cosmopolitan Intent, The Philosophy of Kant,* trans. and ed. by Carl J. Friedrich (New York, 1949), pp. 116-117.

33. William Kornhauser, *The Politics of Mass Society* (Glencoe, 1959), pp. 42, 44, 47, 73, 75, 76, 94, 150, 157, 210.

34. The most influential work of this order is still Erich Fromm's *Escape from Freedom* (New York, 1941).

35. E.g., Barrington Moore, Jr., "Tolerance and the Scientific Outlook," R. P. Wolff *et al., A Critique of Pure Tolerance* (Boston, 1965), pp. 53-79.

36. Herbert Marcuse, *One Dimensional Man* (Boston, 1964), pp. 170-199.

INDEX OF NAMES